# LOOK UP,
## *My Soul*

# LOOK UP,
## *My Soul*

# THE DIVINE
# PROMISE OF
# HOPE

❦

## GERALD N. LUND

DESERET
BOOK

**Library of Congress Cataloging-in-Publication Data**

Lund, Gerald N., author.
   Look up, my soul : the divine promise of hope / Gerald N. Lund.
      pages cm.
   Includes bibliographical references and index.
   ISBN 978-1-60907-004-5 (hardbound : alk. paper)
   1.  Hope—Religious aspects—The Church of Jesus Christ of Latter-day Saints.  I. Title.
   BX8643.H67L86 2012
   234'.25—dc23                                                                    2011050447

Printed in the United States of America
Publishers Printing, Salt Lake City, UT

10   9   8   7   6   5   4   3   2   1

To all those individuals—
in the scriptures, in Church history,
and in today's challenging world—whose
remarkable examples of faith, courage,
patience, and endurance strengthen and
rekindle our own hope

I KNOW IN whom I have trusted.

My God hath been my support; he hath led me through mine afflictions . . . ; and he hath preserved me. . . .

He hath filled me with his love. . . .

Behold, he hath heard my cry by day, and he hath given me knowledge. . . .

O then, if I have seen so great things, if the Lord in his condescension unto the children of men hath visited men in so much mercy, why should my heart weep and my soul linger in the valley of sorrow? . . .

Awake, my soul! No longer droop in sin. Rejoice, O my heart. . . .

. . . Do not slacken my strength because of mine afflictions.

Rejoice, O my heart, and cry unto the Lord, and say: O Lord, I will praise thee forever; yea, my soul will rejoice in thee, my God, and the rock of my salvation.

—2 Nephi 4:19–21, 23, 26, 28, 29–30

# Contents

## II. The Need for Alignment

## III. The Value of Perspective

## IV. Fulfillment

# "It Is Better to Look Up"

I N THE OCTOBER 2011 general conference, Elder Carl B. Cook, of the Seventy, told of an experience he had during his first week as a General Authority. It had been a particularly tiring week, and his briefcase was overloaded and his mind preoccupied with this question: "How can I possibly do this?" As he stepped onto the elevator, his head was down and he stared at the floor.

The elevator stopped on another floor and someone else got on. Elder Cook didn't look up to see who it was. As the door closed, the person asked, "What are you looking at down there?"

Elder Cook instantly recognized President Thomas S. Monson's voice. He looked up and responded, "Oh, nothing."

President Monson smiled, pointed heavenward and lovingly suggested, "It is better to look up!" As the elevator continued downward, President Monson explained that he was on his way to the temple.

They both got off the elevator and parted ways. Elder Cook said this, "When he bid me farewell, his parting glance spoke again to my heart, 'Now, remember, it is better to look up.'"[1]

## Surprised by Hope

People often ask me if I'm working on a new book. If I say yes, they invariably ask me what it is about. When I told them I was working on a book on hope, I typically got one of three reactions:

- A generic "Oh," which I interpreted to mean, "Nice, but not too exciting."
- A surprised "Really?" followed by, "That's good. There isn't much written on hope out there."
- A fervent "When will it be out? It's a really hard time for me (or my son, my daughter, a neighbor, my best friend, etc.) right now. I really need something like that."

The genesis of this book was a class I taught in our ward. I was sensing that there seemed to be a lot of people out there struggling with life. They were pressed down by it and trying to cope with chronic discouragement. So I decided to devote a class to the topic of hope. I was a little taken aback by the response. An unusual number of people came up afterward to express how much they needed that topic right now and how relevant it was to what they (or people close to them) were going through. I decided to look into it further to see if there was enough to sustain a book.

Many years ago, C. S. Lewis, the famous Christian writer from England, wrote a book called *Surprised by Joy,* which included the story of his conversion to Christianity. I must admit, as I started to explore the topic, I was "surprised by hope." One thing became immediately evident. It seemed as though I wasn't the only one sensing this pervasive gloom and dejection. In addition, the Brethren were speaking frequently on the subject in conference. So much for there not being much material out there.

Another thing that surprised me was just how central hope is to the gospel of Jesus Christ. How had I missed that all these years? I knew it was one of the "big three" Christian attributes—faith, hope, and charity—but I had always secretly wondered why hope took precedence over other things like repentance or personal revelation. I don't wonder about that anymore. Instead, I am filled with a sense of wonder—along with some embarrassment that it took me so long to get here—at what I have come to understand about hope. It has expanded my understanding of the entire gospel plan and deepened my appreciation for the love and wisdom of our Heavenly Father.

I would like to express my sincere appreciation to those whose stories are included either in a chapter or in an additional section between chapters. Good teaching always involves two major objectives: We teach for *understanding* and we teach for *application*. The chapters in the book try to teach the principles and doctrines related to hope. Without that understanding, we cannot fully appreciate hope. But the stories and examples used herein are meant to illustrate *how* those principles are actually applied in our lives. They make the doctrine of hope more tangible and alive.

Many of those who shared their stories chose to remain anonymous, but that does not lessen the value of their contributions. I thank them for their willingness to share what, in many cases, are painful and tender things.

One small housekeeping matter: I often emphasize key words or phrases in scriptural passages or quotations with italics. Rather than tediously indicating each time that the emphasis is mine, I have only specified when the emphasis was in the original.

This has been a difficult book for me to write, and my first attempts fell far short of where I wanted the book to be. I wish to express my thanks to those who read the manuscript early on and gave me input. Their honesty, forthrightness (always served up with a generous dose of tactful kindness), and considerable wisdom and insights have had an enormous impact on the end product. My deepest thanks to each of you.

As usual, I owe much to the consistent support, encouragement, and solid efforts of the Deseret Book staff. It takes a tremendous amount of diligence and care to edit, design, publish, and market a book such as this. Once again, they have done so with their usual commitment to excellence.

Though I never saw this coming, as it turns out, this book completes what could be considered a somewhat loosely linked gospel trilogy. *Hearing the Voice of the Lord* (2007) focused on personal revelation. *Divine Signatures* (2010) showed how personal revelation—especially those events we called "divine signatures"—can expand our understanding of God's nature and deepen our faith and trust in Him. *Look Up, My Soul* (2012) takes that concept one step further.

In this book, hope is defined as not just trust in God, but trust in His promises. We learn of those promises through revelation, and it is through revelation that the promises are confirmed. Thus, the three books stand together as a witness of the reality, majesty, perfections, power, and glory of our Heavenly Father and His Beloved Son.

To Them, I owe the greatest debt of all.

## "Look Up, My Soul"

Early in my life, I learned to love the hymns we sing. As I moved into adulthood, I came to realize that they are like the scriptures in some ways. The lyrics are filled with eternal truths, contain concepts that inspire, and have the power to heal the wounded soul (see Jacob 2:8). I can remember one of those moments many years ago when I was weighed down by a particular difficulty. Then in sacrament meeting, we sang a hymn that I wasn't familiar with: "Before Thee,

Lord, I Bow My Head." I immediately fell in love with the words, but it was the third verse that hit me with particular force.

*Look up, my soul; be not cast down.*
*Keep not thine eyes upon the ground.*
*Break off the shackles of the earth.*
*Receive, my soul, the spirit's birth.*[2]

That is my hope for this book. May it help us all to remember President Monson's counsel, "It is better to look up."

---

Notes

1. Carl B. Cook, "It Is Better to Look Up," *Ensign,* November 2011, 33.
2. "Before Thee, Lord, I Bow My Head," in *Hymns of The Church of Jesus Christ of Latter-day Saints* (Salt Lake City: The Church of Jesus Christ of Latter-day Saints, 1985), no. 158.

I

# The Importance of Hope

*Hope is not knowledge, but rather the abiding
trust that the Lord will fulfill His promises to us.
It is confidence that if we live according to
God's laws and the words of His prophets now,
we will receive desired blessings in the future.*

Dieter F. Uchtdorf

*Humble yourselves in the sight of the Lord, and he shall lift you up.*

JAMES 4:10

# CHAPTER ONE

# "LOOK UP, MY SOUL"

——— ❧❖❧ ———

## Elizabeth Horrocks Jackson

ELIZABETH HORROCKS WAS born in Cheshire, England, the oldest of eleven children. At fifteen, she was baptized into The Church of Jesus Christ of Latter-day Saints. Seven years later, she married Aaron Jackson. Over the next six years they had three children. On May 22, 1856, the Jackson family joined other Latter-day Saints at Liverpool, England, and embarked on the *Horizon* as members of the Edward Martin Handcart Company going to Utah.

Due to their late departure and numerous delays, they did not leave Iowa City until July 15, long past the recommended time for starting a journey across the plains. Three months later, on October 19, the company reached the last crossing of the Platte River (present-day Casper, Wyoming). By then, the company was on reduced rations, and Aaron had contracted mountain fever and was very weak. The weather had turned bitterly cold, and a major winter storm was threatening. The river was wide, the current strong, the water cold and nearly chest-deep in some places.

As the family came up to the river, Elizabeth tied up her skirts and started across with the children. Aaron followed, but made it only a short distance before he collapsed on a sandbar, too exhausted to go farther. Finally a man on horseback helped him get across. As the family reached the far side, the blasts of the first winter storm of the season burst upon them. The next day they walked for ten miles in deepening snow before stopping at a place called Red Buttes. There they camped for several days, so utterly exhausted they could go no farther. Elizabeth describes what happened while they were there:

> My husband had for several days previous been much worse. He was still sinking, and his condition now became more serious. As soon as possible after reaching camp I prepared a little of such scant articles of food as we then had. He tried to eat but failed. He had not the strength to swallow. I put him to bed as quickly as I could. He seemed to rest easy and fell asleep. About nine o'clock I retired. Bedding had become very scarce, so I did not disrobe. I slept until, as it appeared to me, about midnight. I was extremely cold. The weather was bitter. I listened to hear if my husband breathed—he lay so still. I could not hear. I became alarmed. I put my hand on his body, when to my horror I discovered that my worst fears were confirmed. My husband was *dead.* He was cold and stiff—rigid in the arms of death. . . . I called for help to the other inmates of the tent. They could render me no aid; and there was no alternative but to remain alone by the side of the corpse till morning.

One can hardly imagine the horror and sorrow and anxiety that came upon her in those long hours of the night. Terrible enough that he should die, but to have to lie there beside his corpse for the rest of the night? Who can fathom such mental anguish?

She continues:

> When daylight came, some of the male part of the company prepared the body for burial. And oh, such a burial and funeral service. They did not remove his clothing—he had but little. They wrapped him in a blanket and placed him in a pile with thirteen others who had died, and then covered him up in snow. The ground was frozen so hard that they could not dig a grave.[1]

## Ellen (Nellie) Pucell Unthank

Ellen Pucell, who everyone called Nellie, was the youngest of thirteen children. Her family was among the first group of converts when Heber C. Kimball came to England in 1837. Nineteen years later, Nellie's father and mother and her older sister, Maggie, traveled to Liverpool. There, along with many others, including the Aaron Jackson family, the Pucells joined the Edward Martin Handcart Company and came to America.

What must have seemed like a grand adventure turned tragic when the terrible winter storm caught the company at the last crossing of the Platte. Many people perished, including Nellie and Maggie's parents, who died within five days of each other. The newly orphaned Nellie celebrated her tenth birthday near Red Buttes. Maggie was fourteen. Too weary to go any farther, the company stayed at Red Buttes until the rescue party from Salt Lake found them. With bitter cold still dogging them, the company moved farther west to what became known as Martin's Cove, and waited for the weather to break. By this time, several more people had died, and many others—including Maggie and Nellie—had severe frostbite on their hands, feet, and ears. Nellie's feet were especially bad.

By the time the rescue wagons brought Nellie and Maggie back to Salt Lake City a few weeks later, it was too late to do anything for Nellie's feet. She had been rescued from death, but not from suffering. In a brief biography of Nellie's life, we read the following:

> When they took off her shoes and stockings the skin with pieces of flesh came off too. The doctor said her feet must be taken off to save her life. They strapped her to a board and without an anesthetic the surgery was performed. With a butcher knife and a carpenter's saw they sawed the blackened limbs off. It was poor surgery, too, for the flesh was not brought over to cushion the ends. The bones stuck out through the ends of her stumps.[2]

The two Pucell sisters traveled with other handcart families to live in Cedar City in Southern Utah. There both sisters eventually married. Nellie became a plural wife of William Unthank, being sealed to him for time and eternity.

The story continues:

> Those stumps were festering running sores as long as she lived. She never knew a moment of freedom from pain. To her, pain and suffering was the normal condition and freedom from it was the rare moments of forgetfulness. Dr. Geo. W. Widdleton offered to trim her legs up by cutting the bones off farther up and bringing the flesh down over the ends so they would heal and enable her to wear artificial limbs, but the horrors of that first amputation were so vivid in her memory that she could never consent to another operation.[3]

Instead, William Unthank hollowed out two pieces of aspen logs and filled them with wool for his wife. This helped dull the pain and gave her a little more mobility as she plodded about in doing her duties.[4]

And so Nellie Unthank waddled through life on her knees. In poverty and pain she reared a family of six children nor [ever] asked for favors of pity or charity because of her tragic handicap. William was a poor man and unable to provide fully for his family; so Nellie did all she could for herself. She took in washing. Kneeling by a tub on the floor she scrubbed the clothes to whiteness on the washboard. She knit stockings to sell, carded wool and crocheted table pieces. She seldom accepted gifts or charity from friends or neighbors.[5]

## A Legacy of Sacrifice and Suffering

It became a tradition in the Church for a time that the last verse of "Come, Come, Ye Saints" was sung with lowered voices and hushed reverence:

> *And should we die before our journey's through,*
> *Happy day! All is well!*

We know from some of the pioneer journals that such emotion was not the case for the pioneers. They sang that verse full throated and with heads high. And why not? There were times on the trek when it seemed like those who passed away were the lucky ones. They were in a state of peace and rest. They were "free from toil and sorrow too."

That last verse is a wonderful expression of faith and courage, but to me, the second verse is equally impressive.

*Why should we mourn or think our lot is hard?*
*'Tis not so; all is right.*
*Why should we think to earn a great reward*
*If we now shun the fight?*[6]

Why should they think their lot was hard? Because it was! Incredibly so! All those who came across the plains to Utah had to sacrifice and endure much. Many suffered almost beyond our comprehension.

President Gordon B. Hinckley once said of the pioneers:

It is good to look to the past *to gain appreciation for the present* and *perspective for the future.* It is good to look upon the virtues of those who have gone before, *to gain strength for whatever lies ahead.* It is good to reflect upon the work of those who labored so hard and gained so little in this world, but out of whose dreams and early plans, so well nurtured, has come a great harvest of which we are the beneficiaries. *Their tremendous example can become a compelling motivation for us all.*[7]

I have spent a good deal of time studying the lives of the pioneers. I have read their journals, studied their history, walked a good portion of the trails they traversed. The inspiration of their example has always been strong for me personally. I can testify of President Hinckley's promise. The lives of those pioneers have become a compelling motivation for me, especially when times have gotten a little rough in my life or the lives of my family.

But recently I have begun to notice something I had overlooked before. There is something more going on with these people besides faith and testimony and courage. They don't emphasize it much, but if you look for it, it's all through their histories. In addition to faith and testimony and courage, there was hope. And that hope became a motivating and sustaining power as they endured the trials of coming to Utah. Let me illustrate.

We read of the shock, horror, grief, and despair that Elizabeth Horrocks Jackson experienced that night when her husband died just a foot or two away from her. Shock, horror, grief, and despair—yes. But hopelessness? No. Here are her next words:

> [Aaron] was left there to sleep in peace until the trump of the Lord shall sound, and the dead in Christ shall awake and come forth in the morning of the first resurrection. *We shall then again unite our hearts and lives, and eternity will furnish us with life forever more.*
>
> I will not attempt to describe my feelings at finding myself thus left a widow with three children, under such excruciating circumstances. I cannot do it. But I believe the Recording Angel has inscribed in the archives above, and that my sufferings for the Gospel's sake will be sanctified unto me for my good.[8]

Considering her circumstances, that is astonishing.

When I read the account of Nellie Pucell Unthank, I found myself filled with awe at what this remarkable woman did, even after losing both legs to frostbite. Did you notice that something was missing from her story, though? Where is her bitterness toward the unfairness of her life? Where is her resentment against God? Where is her despair at how difficult her daily life was?

The person who wrote her story didn't say anything about hope or faith—at least not specifically—but here is what he did write about Nellie's life and how she felt about being a faithful Latter-day Saint.

The Bishop and the Relief Society sometimes gave a little assistance which Nellie gratefully accepted, but once a year, to even the score, she took her children and cleaned the meeting house. The boy carried water, the girls washed the windows and Nellie, on her knees, scrubbed the floor. . . .

In memory I recall her wrinkled forehead, her soft dark eyes that told of toil and pain and suffering, and the deep grooves that encircled the corners of her strong mouth. But in that face there was no trace of bitterness or railing at her fate. There was patience and serenity for in spite of her handicap she had earned her keep and justified her existence. She had given more to family, friends and to the world than she had received.[9]

Again, in my mind, the word that best describes her is *astonishing!*

### Hope Is to Trust in the Promises of the Lord

In a dozen different places, the scriptures link together three great Christian attributes—*faith, hope,* and *charity* (e.g., see 1 Corinthians 13:13; Ether 12:28; Moroni 7:1; D&C 6:19). The frequency of this linkage suggests that these three attributes have great importance to us. In fact, in one place we are told, "If you have not faith, hope, and charity, *you can do nothing*" (D&C 18:19).

Earlier in my life, it seemed odd to me that hope would be one of the "big three." The other two are clearly of great significance. Faith in Jesus Christ is the foundational doctrine, the absolute prerequisite to making the plan of salvation a reality in our lives. And charity is the great outcome of faith and belief. When we are truly converted and striving to be a disciple of Christ, we try to love God and our fellow men as Christ does. His pure love is the model for all of our relationships.

But hope?

Well, of course hope is important, I thought to myself. But is it really up there in importance with faith and charity? What about all the other important doctrines and principles?

Why not faith, *obedience,* and charity?

Why not faith, *repentance,* and charity?

Why not faith, *service,* and charity?

Why not faith, *revelation,* and charity?

In the past few years, I am finally coming to understand why hope takes precedence over those other doctrines and principles in that triad of virtues. In the October 2008 general conference, President Dieter F. Uchtdorf spoke on the power that can be found in hope. He compared faith, hope, and charity to a three-legged stool, which can "stabilize our lives regardless of the rough or uneven surfaces we might encounter at the time." He then gave this powerful definition of hope: "Hope is not knowledge, but rather *the abiding trust that the Lord will fulfill His promises to us.* It is confidence that if we live according to God's laws and the words of His prophets now, we will receive desired blessings in the future."[10]

President James E. Faust put it in nearly identical terms: "Hope is trust in God's promises, faith that if we act now, the desired blessings will be fulfilled in the future."[11]

## The Need for Hope in Our Time

Most members of the Church today are not faced with the same kinds of challenges, trials, and sacrifices that the pioneers experienced. We are not facing ice-clogged rivers or blizzards raging around our tents. We are not asked to subsist on four ounces of flour per day, to press on pulling our handcart without a husband, or to leave a child buried in a shallow grave along the trail.

But we are facing some pretty serious challenges of our own.

Today, many families are caught in difficult financial circumstances. They are unemployed. They've seen serious reductions in their retirement funds and life savings. They are losing their homes through foreclosure. A growing number of natural disasters destroy homes, property, and livelihoods and leave loved ones dead or seriously injured. Pornography, selfishness, and infidelity destroy numerous marriages and families. People addicted to alcohol or drugs bring years of sorrow and heartbreak to their family members. And knowing that things in the world are going to get worse before they get better only adds to our sense of hopelessness.

Some people are dealing with these trials well, but many others—even including those in the Church—are losing hope. Frustrated that God is not hearing and answering their desperate cries for help, they bitterly turn away from Him and reject the Church with all of its requirements and demands.

Here are some comments and questions I have heard over the past few years:

- A returned missionary in his late twenties: "The Brethren keep encouraging us older men to marry, but why should I date and get serious with a girl? All around me, including in my own family, I see failing marriages. The future is so uncertain. What if I can't love and care for a family and make them happy?"
- A seminary student after a fireside talk on the Second Coming: "I hope I die. I don't want to be on the earth if things are going to be so horrible."
- A recent college graduate: "Why even try to plan for the future, let alone retirement? The world is facing economic collapse and it will all be for nothing."

- A man in his mid-forties, a fifth-generation Latter-day Saint: "I've tried to be faithful my whole life. I served a mission. Married in the temple. Now, my life is a wreck. I've prayed. I've fasted. I've begged the Lord to help me. And nothing has changed. So I'm done with it."

- A woman to the teacher just before a gospel instruction class was to begin: "Just thought I'd warn you. If you tell me one more thing I'm supposed to be doing to be a better person, I'm going to stand up in the middle of your lecture and scream."

- A young single adult to her institute instructor after class: "Thank you so much for that lesson, Brother Jones. It was so inspiring, and I'm so depressed."

- A father who lost his home, his wife, and several children in a devastating earthquake: "Why, God? Why?"

- A single woman in her thirties: "I have decided that God isn't going to answer my prayers. I have to face the fact that I am going to be alone the rest of my life. And that reality is so depressing and so discouraging that I often cry myself to sleep at night."

- A stake president: "In addition to the usual concerns about transgression and apathy, I worry about some of our stalwarts. They know the gospel is true. They serve faithfully. But the joy is gone."

- An elderly couple: "We had always heard people joke about old age not being for sissies, but we never understood it until now. Life grows increasingly difficult as our pains increase and our capacities diminish."

- The parents of a wayward child: "He's lied to us, stolen our credit cards, forged checks, cost us tens of thousands of dollars. We've spent thousands more on his legal defense, been to jails to bail him out, nursed him through several attempted suicides. He's been breaking our hearts for nearly twenty years now. But the hardest thing of all is that we can see no end to it, no solutions, no way out."

- A highly successful entrepreneur in fast and testimony meeting, with tears: "We are moving out of the ward this week. Our house is in foreclosure. I'm looking for a job. The hardest thing I've ever had to do in my life is try to explain to my sixteen-year-old son why we are moving in with Grandma."

## When Life Weighs Us Down

More and more people describe themselves as being dissatisfied, frustrated, discouraged, desperate, stressed out, dejected, melancholy, gloomy, weary, helpless, and hopeless. They feel disconnected, doubtful, disengaged, disheartened, disillusioned, distressed, and despairing.* My goodness, the list alone is enough to leave anyone feeling overwhelmed and downhearted. But there is some light out there in what seems to be a growing darkness. First of all, this isn't the way things should be. Nor is it a natural state of affairs. President George Q. Cannon made this observation:

Whenever darkness fills our minds, we may know that we are not possessed of the Spirit of God, and we must get rid

---

* We should note here that sometimes depression and despair stem from physiological causes or mental illness. These manifestations require professional help, including constant monitoring, prescription medicines, and professional counseling. While I hope this book might provide all readers with hope, this discussion about overcoming depression and despair should not be seen as a substitute for professional help where needed.

of it. When we are filled with the Spirit of God, we are filled with joy, with peace and with happiness no matter what our circumstances may be; for it is a spirit of cheerfulness and of happiness.[12]

Elder Jeffrey R. Holland quoted a famous American novelist to make another important point:

> I wish to . . . fortify you, if I am able, against doubt—especially self-doubt—and discouragement and despair. . . .
>
> I wish at the outset to make a distinction F. Scott Fitzgerald once made, that *"trouble has no necessary connection with discouragement—discouragement has a germ of its own, as different from trouble as arthritis is from a stiff joint"* (*The Crack-Up,* 1945). Troubles we all have, but the "germ" of discouragement, to use Fitzgerald's word, is not in the trouble, *it is in us.* . . .
>
> It's frequently a small germ, hardly worth going to the Health Center for, but it will work and it will grow and it will spread. In fact it can become almost a habit, a way of living and thinking, and there the greatest damage is done. *Then it takes an increasingly severe toll on our spirit, for it erodes the deepest religious commitments we can make—those of faith, and hope, and charity.*[13]

I love that concept. Discouragement, depression, and despair may be *common* companions of adversity and tribulation, but they are *not inherent* within the nature of life's challenges.

## "Lift Up Your Heads"

Many years ago, while traveling for the Church Educational System (CES), I had an interesting experience in the highlands of

Guatemala. We stopped at a turnout at the top of one of the mountain passes to take photos of the spectacular scenery. As we were doing so, we saw a father and a young boy approaching. The father carried a huge load of firewood, using a leather headband instead of ropes. Called a *mecapal* (meh-CAW-pal) in Spanish, this headband had two woven cords extending back past his ears that were fastened to ropes that held the sack in place. He was bent forward so that the weight of the wood was distributed across his shoulders and back.

It was such a wonderful example of the native culture that we offered to pay him if he would allow us to photograph him. He was quite pleased to be so honored by these *gringos* and their cameras. He moved over to where the mountain dropped off, and posed with his son. It was a delightful shot, and we all started snapping away. Then one of my colleagues said something about the light not being quite right on his face. He spoke Spanish, so he called out, "Señor, can you please lift your head a little higher?" The man complied immediately, then gave a low cry and stumbled backward, nearly falling before he caught himself. Down came his head again, and the load was stabilized.

"He can't lift his head," said our local CES coordinator. "He has to keep his head down to keep the load balanced."

We apologized for nearly sending the poor man tumbling down the mountain, took some more pictures, and paid him generously.

About a month later, I was reading in the book of Mosiah about the accounts of Limhi and his people and of Alma and his people. Both groups had been captured and put into terrible bondage by the Lamanites, who "put heavy burdens upon their backs, and did drive them as they would a dumb ass" (Mosiah 21:3). That reminded me of the father and son in Guatemala. Did the *mecapal* or some similar device go that far back in time, I wondered.

As I read on, something else struck me with great force.

And it came to pass that so great were their afflictions that they began to cry mightily to God. . . .

And it came to pass that the voice of the Lord came to them in their afflictions, saying: *Lift up your heads* and be of good comfort, for I know of the covenant which ye have made unto me; and I will covenant with my people and deliver them out of bondage.

And I will also ease the burdens which are put upon your shoulders, that even you cannot feel them upon your backs. (Mosiah 24:10, 13–14)

Instantly, the image of that father raising his head and nearly stumbling backward off the mountain came to my mind. When someone is carrying a burden like that, you don't ask them to lift up their head. It will throw them off balance, perhaps even make them fall down. I saw a great lesson in that. To look up to God when life presses in with crushing, relentless pressure may seem counter-intuitive—especially if one feels abandoned by God in the first place—but that is exactly what hope asks of us. And the promise is, if we do, our burdens can be removed or lightened, or we can be strengthened so we can bear them successfully.

Hope is the antidote for despair. It may not solve the problem, or immediately remove the burden, but it can buoy us up and give us the strength and courage we need to go on. It was hope that overcame despair in the lives of Elizabeth Horrocks Jackson and Nellie Pucell and so many others who have faced tremendous burdens. They lifted up their heads and looked to God, and in doing so found greater strength, greater help, greater endurance.

In this book we are going to talk about hope. We are going to try to answer some basic questions:

- What is hope?
- How does it work with faith and charity?
- Why is hope so important to our spiritual progress?
- How do we gain, strengthen, and maintain hope, especially in times of despair?
- What are the promises in which we can trust in order to foster hope?

Considering the times in which we now live, finding answers to these questions seems especially relevant.

---

## Notes

*Part I Epigraph.* Dieter F. Uchtdorf, "The Infinite Power of Hope," *Ensign,* November 2008, 22.

1. *Leaves from the Life of Elizabeth Horrocks Jackson Kingsford* (Ogden, Utah, December 1908), 5–6; emphasis in original.

2. William R. Palmer, "Pioneers of Southern Utah," *The Instructor,* April 1944, 154.

3. Ibid., 154–55.

4. See Andrew D. Olsen, *The Price We Paid: The Extraordinary Story of the Willie and Martin Handcart Pioneers* (Salt Lake City: Deseret Book, 2006), 426.

5. Palmer, "Pioneers of Southern Utah," 155.

6. "Come, Come, Ye Saints," in *Hymns of The Church of Jesus Christ of Latter-day Saints* (Salt Lake City: The Church of Jesus Christ of Latter-day Saints, 1985), no. 30.

7. Gordon B. Hinckley, *Faith: The Essence of True Religion* (Salt Lake City: Deseret Book, 1989), 102.

8. *Leaves from the Life of Elizabeth Horrocks Jackson Kingsford,* 7.

9. Palmer, "Pioneers of Southern Utah," 155. On August 3, 1991, President Gordon B. Hinckley of the First Presidency dedicated a statue of Nellie Unthank on the campus of Southern Utah University (see "Handcart pioneer memorialized," *Church News,* 10 August 1991, 3–4).

10. Uchtdorf, "The Infinite Power of Hope," 21, 22.

11. James E. Faust, "Hope, an Anchor of the Soul," *Ensign,* November 1999, 60.

12. George Q. Cannon, *Gospel Truth,* edited by Jerreld L. Newquist (Salt Lake City: Deseret Book, 1974), 17.

13. Jeffrey R. Holland, "For Times of Trouble," in *1980 Devotional Speeches of the Year* (Provo, Utah: Brigham Young University Press, 1980), 39. Brother Holland was the Commissioner of the Church Educational System at the time he gave this talk.

# When Tragedy Strikes

❧

W E OFTEN READ or hear about the dramatic sacrifices and sufferings of the early pioneers. They have become an important
part of our heritage. President Gordon B. Hinckley said that their
stories can help us "to gain strength for whatever lies ahead" and
"become a compelling motivation for us all."[1] I have found that to be
true many times in my own life.

But suffering, loss, and grinding adversity were not reserved for
those crossing the plains or colonizing the West. We find examples all
around us of individuals who face tremendous and often prolonged
tribulation, and yet who meet it with the same courage and fortitude
as Elizabeth Horrocks Jackson or Nellie Pucell Unthank. Here is one
example.

### Stephanie Nielson

In the summer of 2008, Stephanie Nielson, a member of The
Church of Jesus Christ of Latter-day Saints, was living in Mesa,
Arizona, with her husband, Christian, and their four children, the
oldest of whom was not yet seven. Stephanie, who was twenty-seven
at the time, was a beautiful woman with dark black hair, green eyes,

and a sprinkling of freckles across her cheeks and forehead. She loved being a mom and called it her "divine purpose in life."

On August 16, 2008, the Nielsons left their children with Christian's parents and took off with Doug Kinneard, a close friend, in a private airplane. They flew to New Mexico and spent the day relaxing and sightseeing. After refueling in New Mexico, they took off again, heading for home. The plane had barely lifted off the runway when it stalled and smashed into the ground, bursting into flames. Fire totally engulfed the aircraft and the people inside. All three were rushed to a burn center in Phoenix, where Kinneard died a short time later. Both of the Nielsons were put into medically induced comas, and the doctor said their chances for survival were not good. Stephanie's body was so badly burned that the only thing family members recognized were her feet because her toenails were painted red.

After five weeks in a coma, Christian awoke and started on the road to recovery. But Stephanie was kept unconscious for three months while doctors performed numerous procedures. Finally, in early November, the doctors determined it was time for her to wake up. A short time later, while the nurses were changing Stephanie's dressings, Stephanie saw her body for the first time. "It was burned, and it was black and swirly with pinks and purples," she recalled later. "I couldn't even comprehend what my face looked like."

It was five more weeks before she had the courage to take a hand mirror and look at her face. "I did it slowly. I started with my lips, and went up to my head, and just sort of kind of took it all in, piece by piece by piece," she said. "It was hard, it was so hard . . . but I saw my eyes, and I had eyes, and my eyelashes were there. And so I, I still felt like, you know, I . . . I was there."

The skin on her face was so badly burned the doctors had to cut it all away, leaving only raw muscle and tissue. Then, using skin from deceased persons, grafts from the few parts of Stephanie's body that were not burned, and cultured skin tissue from a lab in Boston, the doctors painstakingly began the process of rebuilding her face. This left a patchwork of skin joined together with thick, but very tender scars that made any movement excruciatingly painful.

Before the accident, Stephanie had shared her love for life and family on a blog she called "NieNie Dialogues." When her blog fans learned what had happened, they spread the word across the Internet. There was a huge outpouring of shock and grief and support. Donations poured in to help cover the enormous medical expenses. Eventually the family received about $250,000.

The hardest part for Stephanie was not the physical pain. During her more than four months in the hospital, her children stayed with other family members. She had missed many significant events—a birthday, Halloween, Thanksgiving. Now, at last, the time for re-union had come. The reunion was bittersweet. The first to walk into the hospital room was Jane, her younger daughter. The girl was speechless when she saw her mother. "I was like, 'Hi, Jane,'" Stephanie said. "And then I will never forget her look that she gave me . . . she put her head down. She wouldn't look at me for the rest of the time. I wanted to die." Stephanie's older daughter, Claire, would only talk to her mother through a curtain.

There was more heartbreak to come; while Stephanie's older son, Oliver, greeted her calmly, her youngest child—Nicholas, who was just eighteen months old at the time of the crash—didn't know her. Stephanie's sister, Lucy Beesley, had been caring for Nicholas and he now called her "Mom." Nicholas, Stephanie said, would cry for his mom. . . . "It was awful."

She couldn't do even simple things like comb her daughters' hair or build blocks with her son. She said, "Once those little things were taken away, it felt like my life was gone."

Her family and friends—and thousands of bloggers—encouraged her to keep fighting, just as she had for her life. Stephanie said it was her father who finally helped her turn a corner. "This is just your recovery," he said. "You won't be walking like this forever. And your face is going to get better. And look at this beautiful family you have created. You can't just give up on them. You're a mother, that's your job, that's what you want to do. So do it."

And she did. Soon things began to improve. On her third visit to the hospital, the daughter who couldn't bear to look at her told her mother she had lost a tooth. Stephanie said, "Come show it to me." Stephanie remembered what followed: "So she finally came in with the tooth in her hand, and you know, looked at me, and we smiled, and we laughed like we used to."[2]

It has now been nearly three years since the accident. Stephanie continues to write her blog, which is now more popular than ever. Her story has been told numerous times in the media, including on ABC television's *20/20* and on *Oprah*. Her courage and example have touched many lives and inspired others who have also endured great pain and suffering. One of the reasons Stephanie inspires people is that she exudes hope and joy, in spite of the pain. Another is that, through it all, she never lost her faith in God. Here is one sampling from her blog that illustrates that point:

> I asked Mr. Nielson* with tears in my eyes if he could still see me.
>
> He was shocked at the question and slightly confused. But he answered anyway; he said he didn't compare me to anything, especially my appearance before the accident.
>
> Maybe he doesn't, but I do.

---

* Mr. Nielson is how Stephanie always refers to her husband on her blog.

Sometimes I actually scare myself.

Yesterday at the grocery store a woman turned around to me in the line and with an exhausted look she blurted out: "Oh, I feel just the way you look!!"

I wanted to curl up and cry in the fetal position right there in aisle three. I looked away and tears stung my eyes. I wasn't prepared to have confirmed to me what I had felt earlier that morning after I had scrubbed my fragile body in the shower until it bled.

Part of the deal I chose, I guess.

I guess I should just suck it up and remember my blessings.

But part of me hurts for outward beauty.

When I lie in my bed as still as can be, I feel like the Stephanie before. Out of my eyes I feel just the same. I feel perfect. My skin isn't strained and my joints don't rip my thin skin over and over with each movement.

That's why getting up is hard to do.

I had another perfect moment today as I lay on my couch. The sky was a lovely shade of blue. My weeping willow's leaves glowed bright yellow and it moved so slowly and gracefully in the autumn wind.

I was so quiet.

I was so still.

And the Lord was talking to me. He was whispering to me his love for me. He was proud of me and I felt my blessings restored to me. He is so real. He is there. He sees so much more than we do. He is the light and truth and anything that is good that I have, is of Him.

And then, I felt beautiful.[3]

---

## Notes

1. Gordon B. Hinckley, *Faith: The Essence of True Religion* (Salt Lake City: Deseret Book, 1989), 102.

2. Excerpts and summary are based on Alice Gomstyn and Shana Druckerman, "Stephanie Nielson's Story: After Tragic Crash, Mom of Four Nearly Lost It All," from *ABC 20/20,* 12 May 2011; http://abcnews.go.com/2020/stephanie-nielsons-tragic-crash-mom-lost/story?id=13574901.

3. *NieNie Dialogues,* "Do you still see me?" 5 November 2009; nieniedialogues.blogspot.com/2009/11/do-you-still-see-me.html.

*If you have not faith, hope, and charity,
you can do nothing.*

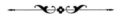

DOCTRINE AND COVENANTS 18:19

# Chapter Two

# Faith, Hope, and Charity

## A Synergistic Relationship

IN THE PREVIOUS chapter, we spoke briefly of what Elder Jeffrey R. Holland called *"the deepest religious commitments we can make,"*[1] namely, faith, hope, and charity. These three attributes—all of which are gifts of the Spirit—are discussed separately numerous times in the scriptures, but they are so often linked together that we can conclude that they are interrelated, interdependent, and interactive.

Speaking about faith, hope, and charity, Elder Russell M. Nelson said, "These three attributes are intertwined *like strands in a cable* and may not always be precisely distinguished."[2] Elder Neal A. Maxwell said, "The triad of faith, hope, and charity . . . *has strong and converging linkage. Faith and hope are constantly interactive, and may not always be precisely distinguished or sequenced."*[3] The Lord Himself said that without faith, hope, and charity we can do nothing. That speaks volumes about how important they are—not just independently, but as an interdependent triad of spiritual gifts and virtues. To put it another way, there seems to be a *synergistic* relationship between the three.

"Synergy" occurs when you have two (or more) things functioning together in a way that creates something new, something greater than the sum of the individual parts. One of the best examples of a synergistic system is found in a successful marriage. Let's take the example of a man and woman—both single—who work together for the same company. They are bright, effective, and productive employees. Assuming they are nearly equal in their abilities, together they produce more than double what either one can separately. In their private lives they also contribute value to their families and society.

Then they fall in love and marry. This doesn't diminish their productivity or value, but something new is created. Now we have an interactive, covenant partnership—a synergy—and something greater than what they could produce by themselves is created. They join their unique talents, abilities, and spiritual gifts and create something new and profoundly different from what they could ever do individually. I believe this is why God said to Adam that it "was not good that the man should be alone," and then said, "Therefore shall a man leave his father and his mother, and shall cleave unto his wife; and they shall be one flesh" (Moses 3:18, 24). Obviously "one flesh" cannot be taken literally. He was talking about them becoming one unit, one functioning system with two separate parts, like a lock and key, or a car's transmission and its wheels.

So it is with hope. It too is a gift of the Spirit as well as an attribute of our character. It forms a synergistic relationship with faith and charity, two other spiritual gifts. The three together form something which they cannot do without the interdependent action with each other. Therefore, let us begin our study of hope by putting it into its context with the other two gifts and attributes.

## Attributes of the Soul

It is interesting to me that faith, hope, and charity have two important things in common. First, each is an *attribute*—a condition of the mind, heart, and spirit rather than a performance or set of physical skills. Strength, stamina, and endurance are terms we use to describe the physical body's ability to perform. But faith, hope, and charity are qualities that define what we *are* more than what we *do.* They represent our feelings, desires, values, and motivations. These inner qualities have a great influence on how we act and what we do, but in and of themselves they are not actions in the same way that prayer, forgiveness, service, scripture study, fasting, and so on are actions.

The other important thing they have in common is these attributes are all gifts of the Spirit. They are given to us when we put our hearts and our actions in alignment with God's will. Without that spiritual endowment, our efforts and actions would not be sufficient to save us.

Part of the synergistic power of faith, hope, and charity is that they are bound together by the permeating power of Jesus Christ and His Atonement.

- We have faith *in* Christ.
- We have hope *through* Christ.
- We love *as* Christ.

When faith, hope, and charity center on Jesus Christ, and the gifts of the Spirit are given, then a powerful synergy is created that opens up incredible possibilities, including drawing upon the powers of heaven. With the three elements working together, we say, as Paul did, "I can do all things through Christ which strengtheneth me" (Philippians 4:13).

## The Relationship of Faith and Hope

Consider these statements about faith as they will provide an important foundation for our review:

- Faith in Jesus Christ is the first principle of the gospel.
- "*Faith is to hope* for things which are not seen, but which are true."
- "Faith in Jesus Christ is kindled by hearing the testimony of those who have faith."
- "Strong faith is developed by obedience to the gospel of Jesus Christ."
- "Faith is a principle of *action and power.*"[4]
- Faith is a gift from God but must be cultivated and exercised to become a principle of power.

Moroni adds another key concept. We should not refuse to believe something is true because we don't have evidence or proof that it is true. This witness (or confirmation) comes only "after *the trial of your faith*" (Ether 12:6).

These statements about faith help define the process by which faith is acquired. The process involves two required conditions (preconditions, if you will) and three simple steps. These could be diagramed as follows:

### The Trial of Faith

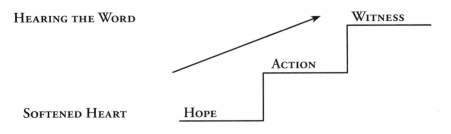

HEARING THE WORD            WITNESS

ACTION

SOFTENED HEART        HOPE

Here briefly is how it works:[5]

## The First Requirement: Hearing the Word

Before the process of faith in Jesus Christ can even begin, there is something that must happen first. We must hear some portion of the word of God, also commonly called the gospel. Joseph Smith said, "Faith comes by hearing the word of God, through the testimony of the servants of God"[6] (see also Romans 10:17). This is what is meant when we say that faith is kindled (ignited, or started) by hearing the testimony of one who has faith.

Hearing the word usually comes by literally hearing someone of faith bear his or her testimony about a principle or truth of the gospel, or of the living reality of Jesus Christ. This can happen as full-time missionaries fulfill their callings. It can come in a sacrament meeting, a general conference, a seminary classroom, or even in a casual conversation. We also "hear" the word when it comes to us in written form, such as the scriptures, reports from general conference, or an inspiring article in other sources.

Here is a key point to remember about hearing the word. In the previous chapter, we cited President Dieter F. Uchtdorf's definition of hope as "the abiding trust that the Lord will fulfill His promises to us."[7] When you think about it, the word of God is filled with promises—promises of knowledge, happiness, joy, forgiveness, redemption, fulfillment, sanctification, empowerment, comfort, eternal life, eternal family, the resurrection, and hundreds of other promises. That's why it's called the gospel, which means "good news" or "glad tidings." Therefore, hearing the word means we are being taught the promises God has extended to us.

## The Second Requirement: A Softened Heart

The second requirement is that one's heart must be softened enough that he or she is willing to listen to what is taught and to at least consider the relevance of what he or she has heard. Nephi taught that the Holy Ghost carries the word *unto* the heart (see 2 Nephi 33:1). Not *into* the heart—*unto* the heart.

The word *heart* in the scriptures is most often used symbolically to represent the inner person, the "real me," or in other words, the seat of our will, our moral agency, our personality, character, and in-dividuality. It is where we determine what we are and what we will do. We choose to open our hearts to some people and to close them off to others. No one can force their way into our hearts. It is one of our most sacred of freedoms. The Holy Ghost can enter *into* the heart of an individual only if that person opens his or her heart. Thus, our agency is always protected.

If we are open to the Spirit, then He can extend His gifts to us in abundance.

But if our hearts are skeptical or insensitive, if we are doubtful or apathetic to the point that we dismiss out of hand the word which is shared with us, then the process of faith is left dormant. It can go no further. This is what Alma meant when he said, "Give place, that a seed [the word] may be planted in your heart" (Alma 32:28. See also the parable of the soils in Matthew 13 where the image of planting a seed is also used). From this we learn that the condition of our heart *is a choice we make.* It is not a condition imposed upon us, *not even by suffering and adversity.*

Once these two preconditions are in place, we are ready to begin the process known as exercising and learning by faith.

## Step 1: Hope, Desire, Trust

Different prophets have defined faith in Jesus Christ as hope (or assurance) of things which *are not seen* but which are true (see Hebrews 11:1; Alma 32:21). That's important. *Faith is hope.* Remember Elder Neal A. Maxwell's words: "Faith and hope are constantly interactive, and *may not always be precisely distinguished or sequenced.*"[8] One could almost say that faith is hope, and hope is faith.

But this hope is in things "not seen." To better understand that, let's go back to the promises. We said that God's promises are an integral part of the word. Most of these promises, however, cannot be "seen"—i.e., experienced with the normal senses. We can't touch forgiveness and redemption. We cannot look ahead and see our eternal family in the celestial kingdom. We can't hold the power of the priesthood in our hands and examine it. Thus, when the scripture says that faith is to hope for things which are not seen, but which are true, the idea of "seeing" has a broader meaning and includes understanding, comprehending, proving, confirming, or having tangible evidence of the reality of something.

Let's use an example to illustrate how this first step actually works. Suppose the missionaries meet a wonderful young family. The father and mother love and honor each other and have a deep and tender love for their three children. They are good and decent people and their hearts are open to spiritual things. When the missionaries teach them that their family relationships do not have to end with death (one of the promises of the word), the father may think to himself, "Oh, I *hope* that is true." And almost instantly, that hope turns into desire. "And if it is true, I *want* that for my family." Because his heart is open, the Spirit can enter and stir these desires and create hope that the promises are true.

This is an important point. The gifts of faith, hope, and desire are closely linked and operate together. They are interactive and interdependent. These desires (or hopes) do not have to be powerful, clearly defined feelings at first. They may be hard to describe in words, but they can be deeply felt. Almost always these are manifestations of the Spirit, and therefore come as thoughts and feelings (see D&C 8:2–30) rather than in more direct forms.

Rarely will the father leap to his feet as soon as he hears the concept of eternal families taught and cry out, "Oh, thank you, elders. When can we be baptized?" Why not? Because all he has at this point is their "opinion." Just because the missionaries said something doesn't automatically make it true. A natural response (which is often nudged along by Satan) would be for the father to say, "Prove it to me. Show me that it's true. Then I'll listen to your message."

And there's the rub. The missionaries cannot prove it to him. All they can do is teach the word clearly and then testify with power of its truthfulness in hopes he will open his heart to the Spirit. That's the bad news. The good news is, that doesn't mean there is no proof available. There is a way the father can come to *know* for himself. And fortunately, it doesn't require a huge leap of faith on his part. All he has to do is be willing to test it, to "experiment" on the word as Alma said (Alma 32:27). Then, as Alma says, "If ye will awake and arouse your faculties, even to an experiment upon my words, and exercise *a particle of faith,* yea, even if ye can *no more than desire to believe,* let this desire work in you, even until ye believe in a manner that ye can give place for a portion of my words" (Alma 32:27). How interesting. Even a glimmer of hope, even the tiniest spark of desire is sufficient to kindle, or ignite, the spark of faith and invite the Spirit in.

## Step 3: Witness or Confirmation

We're going to skip the second step—action—for a moment so as to better illustrate how the overall process works. Again, let's look at what Moroni said about this process of faith: "I would show unto the world that faith is things which are hoped for and not seen; wherefore, *dispute not because ye see not,* for ye receive *no witness* until after the trial of your faith" (Ether 12:6).

Moroni uses the word "witness" here, but we could use several synonyms that are implied by the word. In a courtroom, a "witness" gives *evidence,* or *testimony,* to *prove* or *confirm* something to the jury. So we might paraphrase his statement to read, "You receive no proof, no evidence, no confirmation, no validation, no testimony that the promises are true until after the trial of your faith."

Please note that Moroni is not suggesting that you have to accept the word (and the promises) without confirmation, only that the confirmation (the proof) comes *after* our faith is tried. So the question is, What exactly does Moroni mean by "the trial of your faith"?

## Step 2: Action and the Trial of Faith

The Bible Dictionary teaches that faith is a principle of action: "True faith always moves its possessor to some kind of *physical and mental action.*"[9] Thus, the second step in the process of faith can be summed up in one word—*action.* Once we have hope that the word we have heard is true and our hearts desire to win the promises for ourselves (step 1), then we have to take action. We must *do something.* Remember what James said? "Even so faith, *if it hath not works,* is dead, being alone" (James 2:17).

Note the action verbs Alma used when he was teaching this process to the Zoramites: *awake, arouse, experiment, exercise, desire, believe, work, give place.* Those are the kinds of things an investigator is asked to do, though not usually in those words. If they refuse to act on what they have heard until they have convincing evidence, then they are not exercising their faith and the process will not go forward, because the Spirit will be kept out of their hearts.

Which brings us to Moroni's concept of the "trial of our faith." Typically, when we hear that phrase, we think of someone going through a particularly difficult time in life. "Her mother has cancer," we say. "That's a real trial of her faith." Or "He lost his job, then his home. They're going through a trial of faith." This view is not incorrect, but I believe that Moroni meant so much more than that. I think the "trial of our faith" refers to the test inherent in the very nature of the process.

The real test of faith is that we are willing to act on the hope and desires we have, *rather than waiting for a witness or confirmation before we move forward.* It is such a simple process, but with such enormous consequences. The process starts with hearing the word (and the accompanying promises). If our hearts are open, we will be touched by the Spirit, who then begins to extend His gifts to us. We feel a sense of hope (a gift) that the promises are true, and we desire (a gift) those promises for ourselves. If we then act on that hope and desire, a confirming witness will follow (yet another gift).

## The Windows of Heaven

Some unbelievers mockingly refer to those who have "blind faith." God wants our faith to be founded on knowledge and evidence, but He says that we must act first in order to obtain that evidence. How ironic. Those who demand confirmation first miss the opportunity to get the witness. And those who are willing to act without confirmation end up *getting the witness.*

Here is an actual example of how this process works in real life. When I was the bishop of our ward, I met a father who made his living as a sales representative for a large manufacturer. Over the previous few months, the company had cut back the number of product lines this man managed, and they kept reducing his territory. He was still employed, but his income had been reduced significantly.

One night he came to my office. "I have a dilemma," he said. He explained how tight things had been financially for his family and then concluded with this: "We haven't paid our power bill for two months now, and they are threatening to shut it off if I don't pay them eight hundred dollars by tomorrow."

I thought he was going to ask for welfare assistance, so I said, "And you don't have it?"

His response surprised me. "Actually, I do have just about that exact amount in the bank, but it's money we set aside for tithing, and my wife wants to pay that first."

Then I understood. He had come for counsel on his dilemma. So we talked for a few minutes about the *promises* related to tithing. I testified that I knew from my own personal experiences that the Lord blesses us when we pay an honest tithe. (Here is the first condition: Hearing the word.)

His head came up. "Are you saying that if I pay my tithing, the Lord will send me enough money to pay the power bill?"

I had to shake my head. "I can't tell you how the Lord will bless you, because I can't see the future." (Faith is to hope for things not seen.) "But I promise that He *will* bless you."

"By tomorrow?" he shot right back.

I started again. "I can't tell you—"

"I know, I know," he said in great dejection. The anguish I saw in his eyes was a reflection of the struggle going on in his heart. (The "trial of our faith" is a not a metaphor. It is a real test.) After a long silence, he said in a low voice, "But, Bishop, what if they turn off my power tomorrow?"

I didn't know what to say for a moment; then a thought came, and I replied, "If they cut off your power, that would be a shame. But if you don't pay your tithing, I can promise you that you will lose another kind of power. Is that what you want?" (Remember, faith is a principle of power. I was invoking another promise—that of divine help.)

He looked at me for several seconds, sighed painfully, and then got slowly to his feet. "I'll bring my tithing to you first thing in the morning," he said. (The Spirit was present, and because this man was willing to respond to it, the gifts of faith and hope became operative in his life.)

I had his tithing the next morning. He then immediately went to the power company and worked out a way to pay them a little each month until he was back to full employment again. "I never thought they'd do it," he said to me in wonder. (Confirmation 1.)

The following week he called me to report that earlier that day he had received a call from his sales manager. Another salesman was seriously ill and would be out of commission for several weeks. The manager had asked if he could cover that salesman's commitments, and offered to pay him in advance if he did so. The next day, this brother went back down to the power company and paid his bill in full. (Confirmation 2.)

About a month later, the man's company came out with a new line of products and asked him to take it out across the entire region. He was back to full employment. (Confirmation 3.) Note that the blessings in all three confirmations were part of the grace and power extended to him from the Lord and through the Spirit.

### Exercising and Learning by Faith

There are two commandments in the scriptures relating to faith in Jesus Christ. We are told to *exercise* our faith (see 1 Nephi 7:12; D&C 44:2). We are also commanded to *learn* "by faith" (D&C 88:118). In the example of the man paying his tithing before paying his power bill, we see both commandments being fulfilled. This struggling brother *exercised* his faith by acting on the thin hope that the Lord would bless him if he paid his tithing—a promise that he could not "see" being fulfilled. He thought there was no way out of his predicament and was therefore wavering in his hope. When God sent not one, but three separate confirmations, the man *learned* that the promises were true. First, he exercised faith, and then he learned by faith.

To put it another way: Exercising faith is the *process.* Learning by faith is the *outcome.* Both require the grace of God—expressed in the spiritual gifts we are given, *and* our own free-will actions and choices.

In his talk on learning by faith, Elder David A. Bednar described this process and its outcome as an upward-spiraling "helix."[10] A helix is similar in shape to a funnel tornado—narrow at the bottom, wide at the top. So it is with faith. It may be very small and hard to define at first, but, if exercised, it brings its own witness or confirmation. This confirmation then strengthens our faith and expands it further. When the next trial of our faith comes, our faith will be stronger because we have learned for ourselves through the Spirit to trust in God's promises. (Remember, hope is to "trust in the promises.") Now we will be exercising much more than just a particle of faith. We have evidence that the process worked before, and this strengthens our hope that it will work again. We will have greater trust in the promises.

Thus, like a helix, our spiritual power rises higher and higher at the same time it expands outward, as exercising and learning by faith follow one after the other. And thus, step by step, through the grace of Christ and with the help of the Spirit, we move onward and upward, more and more able to call down the powers of heaven in our behalf.

## The Relationship of Hope and Charity

Up until this point we have been discussing the interrelationship of faith and hope. What about charity? Where does it fit into our quest for hope? Where do we find it in this model of exercising and learning by faith? Our purpose is not to fully explore the doctrinal aspects of charity. What we want to do is answer three basic questions:

- What is charity?
- Why is charity important to us?
- How do we obtain charity?

## What Is Charity?

The answer to that is simple. Moroni defined it for us: "Charity is the pure love of Christ, and it endureth forever; and whoso is found possessed of it at the last day, it shall be well with him" (Moroni 7:47).

In today's world, *charity* typically refers to giving of one's means and/or time to help others. We talk about charitable organizations, or giving to our favorite charity. But Elder Marvin J. Ashton, of the Quorum of the Twelve, noted that it is more than that:

> Charity is, perhaps, in many ways a misunderstood word. We often equate charity with visiting the sick, taking in casseroles to those in need, or sharing our excess with those who are less fortunate. But really, true charity is much, much more.
>
> Real charity is not something you give away; *it is something that you acquire* and *make a part of yourself.* And when the virtue of charity becomes implanted in your heart, you are never the same again.[11]

So while it is not incorrect to speak of charity in this more limited sense of helping others, it only begins to describe what charity really is. In its fullest sense, charity is love. But not just any love. It is the perfect, holy, infinite love of the Savior. He is the model, the ultimate example of what pure love means and how it acts. We all know that we should love God and love our neighbor as our self, but what does that mean in real-life situations? In the day-to-day press of life—some would say "the daily grind"—we may wonder what charity requires of us in specific situations.

Here is just one example of some very difficult, real-life questions.

Your oldest child is violating the standards of the Church, which you hold to firmly in your family. You're afraid that his or her example will influence the younger children negatively. What is the loving thing to do? For him? For the other children? For yourselves? Should you give your child the "You can live our standards or you can find another place to live" ultimatum? That makes sense in some ways. But what if there's a pretty good chance that by doing so you will put him or her into physical and moral danger? What if this only drives the child farther away from God? What if the child is not yet eighteen and a legal adult? Does that change how we should act?

Trying to implement Christ's perfect model of love can be perplexing at times. How do we know what He would do in such circumstances? There are two answers to that, as I see it. First, we can study His life—and that includes more than just His mortal life—to learn how and when to show love, or if there are conditions or limitations which legitimately restrict the expression of love. Second, we can go to the Father and ask what it means for us to respond in pure love to any given situation. But in both of these cases, before we take action, the Spirit will be required to help us know what to do and how to do it. Remember, charity is a gift of the Spirit.

One other thought before we leave this question. When we say that charity is the pure love of Christ, most of us immediately think of His love for others. But let us not forget that He also loved God. And didn't He also love truth? Justice? Purity? Service? Should we not seek to follow His example in those things as well?

## Why Is Charity Important to Us?

There are many ways to answer this question, but since our focus is on the relationship of charity to hope, let me again suggest two answers. Remember, charity plays a key role in the process of exercising faith. We noted earlier that we have faith *in* Christ, and hope *through* Christ, and we love *as* Christ. Note that striving to love as Christ loves is an attribute of our character and requires us to make choices and to act in certain ways. But again we must remember that we cannot do this on our own; we must actively seek for this gift of the Spirit.

Think about an investigator of the Church for a moment. If he really wishes to be Christlike, and has studied Christ's life to better understand what that means, how would these injunctions from the Savior affect his response to the missionaries' message?

- "Ask, and it shall be given you; seek, and ye shall find; knock, and it shall be opened unto you" (Matthew 7:7).
- "Doubt not, but be believing" (Mormon 9:27).
- "Search diligently, pray always" (D&C 90:24).
- "If ye continue in my word, then are ye my disciples indeed; and ye shall know the truth, and the truth shall make you free" (John 8:31–32).

Charity's role in the process of faith is that it often *defines* how we are to act; and then, with inspiration, we put those actions into play in our lives.

Here is a second reason why charity is so important. In *Lectures on Faith,* we learn that one of the requirements for people to have the faith necessary to achieve salvation is that they have "an actual knowledge" that their life is pleasing to God.[12] Assuming that our hope is to one day hear these words for ourselves, "Well done, thou good and faithful servant" (Matthew 25:21), then we must act in ways that are pleasing to God. Here again, charity becomes the *defining standard* for how to act.

Let's put it into a simple chain of reasoning. When the pure love of Christ becomes our model for action, those actions will please God. Knowing that our lives are pleasing to Him strengthens our faith. When our faith is stronger, then hope is brighter. Therefore, charity directly contributes to our hope.

## How Do We Obtain Charity?

We are indebted to Moroni for the answer to this question: "Wherefore, my beloved brethren, pray unto the Father *with all the energy of heart,* that ye may be filled with this love, which he hath *bestowed* upon all who are true followers of his Son, Jesus Christ" (Moroni 7:48).

It's that simple. Charity is not something we can work ourselves into mentally. We don't get up one morning and say to ourselves, "I think I will get charity today." It is "bestowed" upon us; it is a gift of the Spirit. Without the Spirit, we cannot feel a fulness of Christ's love, understand what that love requires of us in specific situations, or find the spiritual willpower to do what charity requires. Fortunately, because it is a gift of the Spirit, we can seek after charity earnestly (see D&C 46:8).

## Dave

Here is an example from my own experience of how this process works. This story is a little painful for me to relate because it was not one of my finer moments.

When I was teaching institute in Southern California many years ago, I had a student who was the most obnoxious and irritating person I have ever personally known. I shall call him Dave. Dave was loud, pushy, rude, insensitive, and very annoying—no, extremely annoying. The other students fled when they saw him coming. He worked afternoons and evenings, so his mornings were spent at the institute building. He was always around. Since most of our classes were held in the morning, Dave was available to attend many of them. And here he really "shined." He had a knack for waiting until that moment when the Spirit was strongest, then saying some off-the-wall comment like, "Hey, Brother Lund, you're wrong about that," or "How come we never get to have a party in class?"

One day, he was really on a roll, and it was just one thing after another until even the students were glaring at him and telling him to be quiet. This attention only spurred him on. Just as we were nearing the end of the lesson and I started to bear my testimony, up came his hand again. I ignored it, so he blurted out another comment that was completely out of line. I was so frustrated, I lost it. I actually swore at him and told him to leave class. It was one of the milder swear words, but nevertheless, I did swear at him.

I was utterly humiliated. What a great example—an institute teacher swearing at one of his students in class! That night I vowed that something had to change. I decided it had to be me. I had to be more patient, more tolerant. I had to remember that Dave was a child of God. Either that or I would just have to grit my teeth and endure him as best I could. I tried. I tried being nice to him. I tried talking to him about his behavior. Nothing much changed.

It was a short time later that I was reading in the Book of Mormon and came across Moroni's counsel to pray for the gift of charity "with all the energy of heart" so we can be "filled with this love" (Moroni 7:48). Instantly I knew that the Lord was speaking to me. That very night, I added Dave to my prayers. Only I didn't pray that he would change, or that I would know what to do with him.

I simply began to plead with the Lord to fill my heart with the pure love of Christ for that boy.

It didn't happen overnight. It took weeks, actually, and at first I didn't really connect what was happening with my daily prayers. The first thing I noticed was that I began to get insights into why Dave was the way he was. He came from a totally dysfunctional home. I don't think he had ever been taught about personal hygiene. He was significantly overweight. The institute was the only place where he had any social interaction with others, but his atrocious social skills pretty well eliminated any hope he had for dating and courtship or even basic, casual friendships.

With those insights, I began to be more patient with him. I tried to take time and really listen to what he had to say. I looked hard for something to compliment him on and then tried to mean it when I said it. Gradually, I found my feelings toward him changing. To my amazement, I found that I was coming to love Dave, in spite of what he was. Or maybe, because of it.

I still remember the day one of the girls came up to me after class. "Brother Lund, what's the matter with Dave?" she asked.

I groaned. "What's he done now?"

"That's just it," she said. "Nothing. He's been so nice lately. Haven't you noticed?"

She was right. Dave was still coming to class, and he was still raising his hand, but when he did, it was to ask a sincere question or make an appropriate comment. He was actually contributing to the discussion.

Over the next few months, Dave and I became good friends, and he became more integrated with the other students. And I realized something. I thought all along that Dave was the problem. But the Lord had shown me that I was the problem. I wanted him to change, and he wouldn't. Then I changed, and so did he.

Here, then, is the complete chain of reasoning: When the pure love of Christ becomes our model for action, those actions will please God. *When we pray earnestly for the gift of charity, we can know what we need to do to please God.* Knowing that our lives are pleasing to Him strengthens our faith. When faith is stronger, then hope is brighter. Therefore, charity directly contributes to our hope. This is how charity works in the process of exercising and learning by faith.

### Triangulation and Spiritual Positioning

In mathematics there is a principle called "triangulation." This principle uses geometry and trigonometry to calculate the precise location of any given point by measuring the angles from that point to at least three other known points—thus *tri-* (three) *angulation* (angles). The marvels of our current global positioning system use this principle. A GPS receiver uses signals from a series of satellites in the sky to calculate where we are with great precision. This system has dramatically changed how we locate where we are on Earth. It can also tell us what direction we are moving, determine how fast we are traveling, and calculate how much time it will take for us to reach a specified destination. It can even calculate our elevation in relationship to sea level.

I believe that the gifts of faith, hope, and charity provide us with "spiritual triangulation," an SPS, or spiritual positioning system, if you will. Working like satellites in the sky, faith, hope, and charity help us chart our spiritual position, determine our speed and direction, and indicate how much distance there is between us and our final destination. We might even say we can use faith, hope, and charity to measure our "elevation"—i.e., our position on the upward path to exaltation.

Which brings us back to our original question. Why talk about faith and charity in a book on hope? Because when adversity and tribulation and tragedy come into our lives, they may shake our faith to the core. Our hope may fade away, and we may fall into despair. We may lose our spiritual bearings and drift off in the wrong direction. We may even turn bitter against God because we have no compass to guide us through the wilderness.

In this time in the history of the world, we need those spiritual gifts; we need that kind of spiritual direction finder. We need the kind of hope that is generated and supported by faith and charity. Together, they can bring us safely home. Therefore, seeking the gifts and inspiration of the Spirit, both through humbly pleading for them and by striving to live so our hearts will be open to the promised blessings, is a primary key in gaining hope.

---

## Notes

1. Jeffrey R. Holland, "For Times of Trouble," in *1980 Devotional Speeches of the Year* (Provo, Utah: Brigham Young University Press, 1980), 39.

2. Russell M. Nelson, *Perfection Pending and Other Favorite Discourses* (Salt Lake City: Deseret Book, 1998), 116.

3. Neal A. Maxwell, "'Brightness of Hope,'" *Ensign,* November 1994, 35.

4. LDS Bible Dictionary, s.v. "Faith," 670–71.

5. For those interested in learning more about faith and how we learn by faith, I recommend a careful study of David A. Bednar, "Seek Learning by Faith," *Ensign,* September 2007, 60–68.

6. Joseph Smith, *Teachings of Presidents of the Church: Joseph Smith* (Salt Lake City: The Church of Jesus Christ of Latter-day Saints, 2007), 385.

7. Dieter F. Uchtdorf, "The Infinite Power of Hope," *Ensign,* November 2008, 22.

8. Maxwell, "'Brightness of Hope,'" 35.

9. LDS Bible Dictionary, s.v. "Faith," 670.

10. Bednar, "Seek Learning by Faith," 63.

11. Marvin J. Ashton, "The Tongue Can Be a Sharp Sword," *Ensign,* May 1992, 18–19.

12. *Lectures on Faith* (Salt Lake City: Deseret Book 1985), 38.

# A HYMN TO CHARITY

———◦◦◦———

WE HAVE SEEN that charity is a gift of the Spirit. We have also seen that charity is a key action in strengthening and fortifying hope in these latter days. But it is not always easy to determine exactly what that means for us in specific situations or circumstances.

Two prophets have written about the qualities of charity and given us further information on what they mean for us. Moroni's explanation is found in the Book of Mormon (Moroni 7:44–48). The Apostle Paul's explanation of charity to the Corinthians is considered to be one of the most sublime pieces of world literature (see 1 Corinthians 13). Since Paul's account is the fuller one, we shall include selections of it here with some commentary on its implications for us.

## 1 Corinthians 13

"Though I speak with the tongues of men and of angels, and have not charity, I am become as sounding brass, or a tinkling cymbal.

"And though I have the gift of prophecy, and understand all mysteries, and all knowledge; and though I have all faith, so that I could remove mountains, and have not charity, I am nothing.

"And though I bestow all my goods to feed the poor, and though I give my body to be burned, and have not charity, it profiteth me nothing." (1 Corinthians 13:1–3)

There is no principle or practice in the gospel as transcendent as that of charity. It is the attribute which sanctifies all others and makes them acceptable to God. Charity should define *us*. It not only tells us *what to do,* but *why* we should do it. Even though we may be outwardly religious, brilliant, eloquent, or capable, without charity, we become as hollow and meaningless as the sound of blaring trumpets and crashing cymbals. Even impressive outward acts of sacrifice, service, and kindness bring no spiritual profit if they are done without charity.

"Charity suffereth long," (1 Corinthians 13:4)

In Greek, the word *long* means "long of spirit," and implies patient endurance and holding out, even under great stress. Suffering, trials, tests, adversities, and persecutions do not threaten the enduring patience of charity, as Christ Himself demonstrated. Charity outlasts all of these challenges.

"and is kind;" (1 Corinthians 13:4)

Charity is tender and compassionate. It is deeply concerned for the needs and sufferings of others. It is filled with sensitivity, concern, and empathy. Kindness is what charity *is;* being kind is what we *do* when we have charity.

"charity envieth not;" (1 Corinthians 13:4)

When we have this highest form of love, we are not grieved or jealous when another possesses gifts or blessings we do not. We feel no obligation to make others like ourselves, nor to make ourselves over in the image of others.

"charity vaunteth not itself;" (1 Corinthians 13:4)

*Vaunt* is related to the Greek word for a braggart, or someone who feels compelled to constantly sing his or her own praises. Charity does not glory in its own achievements or try to put itself ahead of others by boasting of its own goodness.

"is not puffed up," (1 Corinthians 13:4)

Nor does charity have an inflated opinion of its own importance. It is not anxious to impress others nor is it concerned with outward show in order to validate its own importance.

"Doth not behave itself unseemly," (1 Corinthians 13:5)

Pure love never acts out of place in a rude or crude manner. It is full of proper decorum and appropriate behavior. It does not belittle others or act in a loud and raucous manner.

"seeketh not her own," (1 Corinthians 13:5)

This purest of Christian attributes does not pursue its own ends alone, but is deeply concerned with the spiritual and temporal welfare of others. It does not pursue selfish advantage to the detriment of others. It is unthinkable that charity would care only about itself.

"is not easily provoked," (1 Corinthians 13:5)

Charity is not touchy or easily exasperated. To be provoked to anger or retaliation is foreign to the nature of Christ's love. By virtue of its longsuffering patience and perfect kindness, charity never loses control.

"thinketh no evil;" (1 Corinthians 13:5)

The Greek word *thinketh* here means "to reckon or keep an account of." Charity does not keep a tally of the wrongs committed against it, holding them in store so they can be used later to "get even." Nor does charity impute evil motives where there are none. It does not automatically assume the worst about people and react accordingly.

"Rejoiceth not in iniquity, but rejoiceth in truth;" (1 Corinthians 13:6)

Charity doesn't find pleasure in any kind of iniquity, either in oneself or in others. When evil befalls another, perhaps even an enemy, charity does not gloat over his or her misfortune, thinking that somehow it was deserved. It is saddened by evil in any form and is gladdened whenever truth and righteousness prevail.

"Beareth all things, believeth all things, hopeth all things, endureth all things.
"Charity never faileth." (1 Corinthians 13:7–8)

The enduring quality of charity is almost beyond comprehension. Its staying power has no limits. It can endure calumny, abuse, persecution, adversity, betrayal, injustice, and suffering. It can outlast anything. The hope that comes from charity is one of never-fading brightness. Its belief and trust know no end. There is nothing that can cause the pure love of Christ to falter, cease, or fall from its place.

Charity cannot be swayed from its perfection. Without charity, all other things must fall.

> "And now abideth faith, hope, charity, these three; but the greatest of these is charity." (1 Corinthians 13:13)

Each of these Christian virtues are of eternal value, but charity is the gift of the Spirit that follows faith and hope. It not only gives expression to our faith but drives it toward the highest of actions. It not only enriches our hope but it enlivens our lives.

# Faith, Hope, and Charity in Real Life

———— ❧✦❧ ————

THIS IS AN account from a woman who often questions whether her faith is as strong as it needs to be. She often feels as though hope slips away from her too easily.

I know this woman well and admire her greatly for what she is and the struggles she has overcome. I use her story (but not her name) with her permission because it is such a wonderful example of the interrelationship of faith, hope, and charity. It illustrates that even as we may question our spiritual positioning with the Lord, we can move ahead—exercising faith, gaining a growing trust in His promises, and seeing our hope grow slowly but steadily. I love the sense of wonder she expresses when the confirmation and blessings come. It almost seems to surprise her that the Lord would reach out and bless someone such as herself. But to my way of thinking, the tender mercies are a clear and powerful witness of just how much the Lord loves this daughter of His.

My husband runs a construction company and, with the economy being hit as hard as it has been, we've struggled financially when we didn't get the jobs we bid on. During the cold winter months, we bid on numerous jobs, only to come in second or third in the bidding each time. We were getting

53

frustrated and wondering how we could come so close and yet lose the bids, some by just hundreds of dollars. We were questioning why our prayers weren't being answered.

We had a friend of ours who was going through a tough time and needed a place to stay. My husband felt that we should invite him to stay with us. That came as a bit of a shock to me because we had our children to care for, and things were pretty tough financially. However, I agreed, and we opened up our home and moved our kids around to make room for him to stay. Then there came a new surprise. Because of their situation at home, the father invited his six children to come and stay with us. We thought it was just for the weekend; they ended up living with us for another month and a half! Suddenly our house was overflowing. Several children had to sleep on cots or on the floor.

I grew close to these children, and we developed a very strong bond with one another. You might think the burden of having seven extra people to feed and care for would be overwhelming, but the hardest part for me was the emotional aspect of not being able to fix what was broken in the lives of these kids and their parents.

Faith is probably the biggest thing I have trouble with. I go to church every Sunday. I hold a calling. I have been taught the gospel, and I graduated from seminary. So one would think that I should have all the basics down, but I still struggle with faith. I am someone who needs to see to believe. I continue to do what I do because the Church teaches great values and I want my kids to live those values. I strive each week to listen to the lessons and be open-minded, but at times I ask myself—Why can't I just have faith and believe? Why?

I don't feel like I get answers to my prayers like other

people do, but I do believe that my prayers are answered through tender mercies. Not anything big and fabulous, just something that lets me know that what I am doing is okay and that Heavenly Father knows my struggles and is aware of me. Often these tender mercies come through friends, or from being at a certain place at a certain time so I can receive needed blessings or hear something that I need to hear.

During this emotionally exhausting/overwhelming/draining time, my husband and I started to get jobs we had bid on. One of the jobs we had previously lost was granted to us when the client found out the first bidder was not qualified. We bid another job, and we were fortunate to be the low bidder. Then we bid a job that was the biggest job our company had ever done, and we were awarded that job as well! One night, my husband and I were talking about the work that now lay ahead of us. We had work for many months; so much work, in fact, that we were able to pass on to others some of the smaller jobs. As we were talking about this, my husband said, "Have you noticed that since we took in this family we have been blessed to get every job we have bid on?"

With a humble heart, I said, "Yes."

I know this was a tender mercy from my Father in Heaven to let us know that He had heard and answered our prayers. I felt it was His way of letting us know that He knew how difficult this time was for us, and for me in particular, and He blessed us for opening our home and serving others. This tender mercy blessed my life in a way that keeps me, despite my doubts, doing what I am doing. I think faith is something I will always struggle with, but it is these small tender mercies that give me the hope to keep going and the strength to want to believe.

*Wherefore, whoso believeth in God might
with surety hope for a better world, yea,
even a place at the right hand of God, which
hope cometh of faith, maketh an anchor
to the souls of men, which would make them
sure and steadfast, always abounding in
good works, being led to glorify God.*

ETHER 12:4

CHAPTER THREE

# THE DOCTRINE OF HOPE

———— ～◦～ ————

### Strengthening the Bridges

A CHRISTIAN MISSIONARY to Africa shared the following challenge she and her husband faced when they were called to serve in Zaire, now known as the Democratic Republic of the Congo. In an effort to help the local people become more self-sufficient, their church had purchased the equipment necessary to make a sawmill and to drill wells. Burleigh and Virginia Law Shell were asked to truck that equipment from Lusambo, where the river barges docked, deep into the interior to a place called Wembo Nyama, a distance of about two hundred fifty miles. Never before had such machinery been taken to that area, and this created an unexpected problem.

Mrs. Shell, who tells the story, explains:

> Between Wembo Nyama and Lusambo there were many bridges. Some crossed small streams but many spanned deep, swirling rivers. All were constructed from the most fragile-looking materials. Poles and logs, cut and sawed from the forest trees, had been joined together by vines. Across the top, more poles formed the bed of the bridge. Sometimes a

few boards on the top of the poles formed a track for the wheels, but often there was nothing. . . . Below, in the swirling streams, snakes hid among logs and rocks. In some there were even crocodiles.

At many of these bridges, there were signs posting the weight limit for the bridge. Most of the signs said 3-T, meaning three tons. A few said 5-T, but none of them said 8-T. The missionaries had been furnished with a large truck to carry the machinery. Even after leaving behind every nonessential piece of equipment or crate of supplies, each load, along with the truck, weighed about sixteen thousand pounds, or eight tons.

Greatly alarmed, Virginia asked her husband what he was going to do. His response was classic. "There isn't anything I can do to lighten the load. I'll just have to reinforce the bridge." And that's what he did. He cut extra poles and carried them with him. He would place them beneath the bridge, shoring it up just long enough to cross, then take them out again and move to the next bridge. In that way they eventually carried more than sixty tons of heavy machinery to the region the mission served.

Virginia concludes her story with this: "In any heartbreak there is just so much hurt, so much pain, so much loneliness. Those are part of human experience and God does not always deaden them or take them away. But though He does not always lighten the load, He does reinforce the bridge."[1]

## The Doctrine of Hope

In the previous chapter, we saw how faith, hope, and charity—those gifts of the Spirit, and those three attributes which Elder Jeffrey R. Holland called "the deepest religious commitments we can make"[2]—are linked together and are interactive and interdependent.

The Lord has said that "if you have not faith, hope, and charity, *you can do nothing*" (D&C 18:19). Could the importance of hope be emphasized any more clearly than that? So let us now examine hope as one of the spiritual gifts, as a doctrine, as a principle, and as an attribute of the heart, mind, and spirit.

We know that God's overall purpose—His work and His glory—is to bring His children "immortality and eternal life" (Moses 1:39). Eternal life means to both *live with* and *be like* God. To achieve that, four conditions are required—or as Lehi put it, "must needs be" (2 Nephi 2:11):

1. We had to leave God's presence and become mortal so that we could prove ourselves (see Abraham 3:25; Exodus 16:4). This proving had to happen where we were required to walk by faith and not by sight.

2. Proving ourselves required agency and a world where we were free to choose between opposing ideas, opportunities, and experiences (see 2 Nephi 2:11–16).

3. Our spirits had to receive a physical body, because "spirit and element, inseparably connected, receive a fulness of joy" (D&C 93:33).

4. We had to learn how to live in our physical body and experience dwelling in a physical world.

When Father Lehi said that there "must needs be . . . an opposition in all things" (2 Nephi 2:11), he wasn't just talking about opposition in the sense of someone or something that is trying to block our way. He was also speaking of opposites—good and evil, pain and pleasure, life and death, spirit and body, virtue and vice. We find these opposites permeating the whole of our mortal existence.

Without this opposition, we could not have moved forward toward the goal of returning to live with God and becoming like Him.

To further His plan for us, God created a world where we could live away from His presence. It was a perfect world, because God's perfect nature would not allow Him to create anything less than perfection. In the beginning, there was no death in the world, no suffering, no pain. This was the world that Adam and Eve inhabited. It was a wonderful place—a paradise—but it did not fulfill all of the necessary conditions.

This is important for us to understand. Our first parents were placed in a world without opposition. They dwelt in the presence of God. Fruits and flowers grew spontaneously. All was peaceful and beautiful. Eden was a perfect paradise. But it wouldn't do as a permanent home. There were no opposites to choose between; therefore their agency was severely limited. There were no challenges, no required effort, no threats.

It was a paradise, but it was *not* a proving ground. As long as Adam and Eve stayed in Eden, the plan for mankind's growth and development could not move forward. That is why the Creation and the Fall of Adam are linked together in the plan. When Adam and Eve transgressed God's commandment, paradise was no more.

Here's another thing to consider. As long as Adam and Eve stayed in the garden, *there was no pressing need for hope either.* Why? Because there was nothing in Eden to discourage them. There was no suffering, no evil, no disease, accidents, war, terrorism, crime, death, injury, pain, suffering, handicaps, weakness, failure, or a thousand other challenges. There was no pain, no adversity, no failure. (There were also no children to keep them up at night, or be sick, or drain their financial resources, or talk back to them, or break their hearts when they came of age.)

So there was no discouragement, no depression, no despair. It may sound wonderful (at least for a month or two), but that kind of life could never move us forward toward God's ultimate goal for us, which is a fulness of joy.

It is precisely because we live in what John Milton called "paradise lost" that it becomes critical for us to understand what hope is and how we get it. If we lose hope, we stop the process of gaining faith. Our progression stops. The power withdraws. In a fallen world, hope is absolutely essential if we are to come through this life with any degree of joy and happiness.

The author Samuel Smiles described the benefits of hope in a difficult world:

"Hope is like the sun, which, as we journey towards it, casts the shadow of our burden behind us. . . .

"Hope sweetens the memory of experiences well loved. It tempers our troubles to our growth and our strength. It befriends us in dark hours, excites us in bright ones. It lends promise to the future and purpose to the past. It turns discouragement to determination."[3]

## What Is Hope?

The Apostle Paul used an interesting metaphor to describe hope when he said: "Which hope we have as an *anchor of the soul,* both sure and stedfast" (Hebrews 6:19). This anchor depends in part on our understanding the doctrine of hope.

A doctrine is a truth about God, His plan, His teachings, and His purposes for us. Knowing and understanding the doctrines of the kingdom are critical to our spiritual well-being. President Boyd K. Packer once said: "True doctrine, understood, changes attitudes and behaviors. The study of the doctrines of the gospel will improve behavior quicker than a study of behavior will improve behavior."[4] And Elder Neal A. Maxwell summarized the importance of doctrine in three words: "Doctrines drive discipleship."[5] Therefore, hope is much more than just a nice concept to discuss in gospel doctrine class. It becomes a key to dealing with life successfully.

The word *hope* is found nearly two hundred times in the four standard works. In a large majority of cases, it is used as a noun (e.g., "have hope"), but it is often used as a verb (e.g., "Hope for a better world"). It is never used as an adjective or adverb in the scriptures (i.e., "hopeless" or "hopeful"). When used in the doctrinal sense (i.e., not as we use it in normal conversation, such as, "I hope I passed that test"), it rarely stands alone. It is frequently linked together with what we hope for—hope of His glory; hope for salvation or eternal life; hope in the glorious resurrection; hope for deliverance; hope for a better world; hope and perfect love. Also, it is often paired with some kind of a modifier—a perfect brightness of hope; a firm hope; a more excellent hope; sufficient hope; confirming hope; lively hope; continual hope.

A study of the Hebrew words which are translated as hope in the Old Testament is instructive. Their meaning is "confidence"; "to trust in for safety and protection"; "expecting and earnestly desiring"; and "to hope that a thing will be effected, and to wait steadily and patiently till it is effected."[6]

There it is again—the idea of hope being tied to future promises. This is exactly how President James E. Faust and President Dieter F. Uchtdorf defined hope. Hope is based on and derived from a knowledge of and trust in the promises of God. It is this trust in the promises that becomes an anchor to our souls. That can be true even in the most difficult of circumstances, such as when your husband freezes to death beside you; when you lose both feet and have to walk on stumps for the rest of your life; or when you are terribly burned but still survive and live with pain thereafter.

The following scriptures on hope can further enrich our understanding of what hope is and how it works.

- "The hope of the righteous shall be gladness" (Proverbs 10:28).
- "Hope deferred maketh the heart sick" (Proverbs 13:12).
- "Now the God of hope fill you with all joy and peace in believing, that ye may abound in hope, through the power of the Holy Ghost" (Romans 15:13).
- "Look unto God with firmness of mind, and pray unto him with exceeding faith, and he will console you in your afflictions, and he will plead your cause, and send down justice upon those who seek your destruction" (Jacob 3:1).
- "Bear with those afflictions, with a firm hope that ye shall one day rest from all your afflictions" (Alma 34:41).

## Hope—A Choice

We discussed earlier how faith, hope, and charity are attributes, or character traits. They represent what we *are,* which then determines what we *do.* And since these are acquired attributes and not inherent natural traits, we must choose to cultivate them and make them part of our lives. But it would be a serious mistake if we think these attributes or traits are developed solely through our own efforts and actions. We must always remember these are gifts of the Spirit. Our actions only meet the conditions that then bring the grace and gifts into our lives.

As Elder Jeffrey R. Holland said, discouragement and despair are not an inherent part of adversity and tribulation either.[7] They may be a natural reaction when we are in difficulty, but we can choose whether or not we give in to those negative emotions.

In the early years of psychology, some psychologists tried to explain behavior as a simple stimulus/response pattern of action. For example, we see a spider (the stimulus) and recoil in disgust (the response). But soon the psychologists realized that while this simple formula may explain some things, most other behaviors are far more complex than that. Some people, for example, spend their lives studying spiders and will let them crawl over their hands, an idea which makes some of us shudder even reading about it. So their explanation was modified to include *perception* along with stimulus and response. How we perceive the stimulus (that is, whether or not we believe spiders are fascinating) will greatly affect our response to that stimulus.

STIMULUS ⟶ PERCEPTION ⟶ CHOICE ⟶ RESPONSE

But I believe something more than that is needed to explain our behavior. I would add a fourth element and that is *choice.* We could diagram it this way.

Here's an actual experience from a wise young husband. What were the stimuli? The perceptions? The choices? The responses?

When we had been married a few years, I came home from work one day and found my wife in a frazzle. The house was in a mess, the children were racing around, yelling and fighting, and she was at her wit's end. When I asked her how she was, she burst into tears. Trying to be helpful, I took her in my arms and said, "Honey, everything's all right. I love you, dear. There's no need to get uptight about it. Really, it's all right."

I was totally taken aback by her reaction. "Don't you tell me everything's all right," she snapped. "You come home after a quiet day at work, where you get to talk to adults, where people listen to you and do what you ask. How many dirty diapers did you change today? How many fights did you break up?" And she spun away and ran into the bedroom. I was stunned. I was trying to be helpful, and she reacted like I had insulted her. Now, I can see I was not being helpful at all.

After two or three similar experiences, I finally got a little smarter. If I came home and found my wife in that state of affairs, I did one of two things. I either called a babysitter and got my wife out of the house, or I took all the children and got them out of the house so she could have some time alone. Then, later, when the children were in bed and all was quiet, I would take her in my arms and say, "I love you, dear."

And she would say, "I know."

Stimulus, perception, *choice,* response. And choice makes all the difference.

## We Can Choose Hope

So it is with hope. Part of the doctrine of hope is that it is a choice we make. We can choose to fight against those mental tendencies to look for someone to blame, to feel sorry for ourselves, or to give in to hopelessness. Agency is one of the great gifts of God. So why would we think that we have no choice in how we respond to various aspects of life? Why would we assume that adversity or tragedy somehow robs us of agency?

Neal A. Maxwell explained it in this way:

Real hope . . . keeps us "anxiously engaged" in good causes even when these appear to be losing causes on the mortal scoreboard (see D&C 58:27). Likewise, real hope is much more than wishful musing. It stiffens, not slackens, the spiritual spine. Hope is serene, not giddy, eager without being naive, and pleasantly steady without being smug. Hope is realistic anticipation that takes the form of a determination—not only to survive adversity but, moreover, to "endure . . . well" to the end (D&C 121:8).[8]

Understanding the doctrine of hope is a source of strength for me. I have learned that

- Hope is reminding myself that despair is not an inherent part of the challenge.
- Hope is counting blessings rather than cursing circumstances.
- Hope is saying, "I do not ask to see The distant scene— one step enough for me."[9]
- Hope is a beckoning light when "despair distills upon us as the dews from heaven."[10]
- Hope can "stabilize our lives regardless of the rough or uneven surfaces we might encounter at the time."[11]
- At times, hope can lighten the load; other times, it strengthens the bridges.

Notes

1. Virginia Law Shell, "The Bridge," *Guideposts* (January 1975): 10–11.

2. Jeffrey R. Holland, "For Times of Trouble," in *1980 Devotional Speeches of the Year* (Provo, Utah: Brigham Young University Press, 1980), 39.

3. Samuel Smiles, quoted in James E. Faust, "Hope, an Anchor of the Soul," *Ensign,* November 1999, 60.

4. Boyd K. Packer, "Little Children," *Ensign,* November 1986, 17.

5. Neal A. Maxwell, "The Holy Ghost: Glorifying Christ," *Ensign,* July 2002, 61.

6. William Wilson, *Old Testament Word Studies* (Grand Rapids, MI: Kregel Publications, 1978), 221–22.

7. See Holland, "For Times of Trouble," 39.

8. Neal A. Maxwell, *One More Strain of Praise* (Salt Lake City: Bookcraft, 1999), 74.

9. "Lead, Kindly Light," in *Hymns of The Church of Jesus Christ of Latter-day Saints* (Salt Lake City: The Church of Jesus Christ of Latter-day Saints, 1985), no. 97.

10. Holland, "For Times of Trouble," 40.

11. Dieter F. Uchtdorf, "The Infinite Power of Hope," *Ensign,* November 2008, 21.

# "I Choose Hope"

## By Tammy Sanderson

WE OFTEN THINK of hope as wanting a certain result when the outcome is not yet known. But hope can also be something we need if we are to rise above the challenges and despair from outcomes that have already occurred and cannot be changed. This deeper hope also allows us to find joy in the promises of a future outcome we know can be ours. Both aspects of hope came into play in my life a few years ago.

One afternoon, I heard a report on the radio of a terrible accident on the freeway near our home. Our daughters were supposed to be home, and they were not answering their cell phones. Oh, how I hoped they were not involved in the accident, especially after hearing that there had been a fatality. Then a highway patrolman and our bishop delivered us the terrible news. Our daughters *had* been in that accident. Lindsay, our sixteen-year-old daughter, had been killed instantly. Kaylee, our eighteen-year-old daughter, had been taken to the hospital. Even as the tears came, I *hoped* Kaylee was all right.

I couldn't believe Lindsay was gone. I couldn't understand it. I couldn't wrap my head and heart around it. How could it be? Just a few hours earlier, when Kaylee had returned for her first weekend home from college, the three of us had walked together around our neighborhood.

My husband and I were taken to the hospital to see Lindsay's body. As we drove, I hoped she hadn't suffered. I hoped she was at peace, and I knew deep inside that she was at peace. My heart—my whole being—was broken, but I knew our Heavenly Father's plan. I knew her spirit was safe. The Comforter enveloped me and reassured me of our Father's love.

Afterward, we drove for an hour to another hospital to see Kaylee. I found myself hoping some more. I hoped she was okay—physically, emotionally, and mentally. When we arrived, we learned that she didn't yet know what had happened to Lindsay. She was frustrated that no one would answer her questions. Then we had to answer the hardest question we had ever been asked, "Is Lindsay all right?"

Again I found myself hoping. I hoped that Kaylee would understand this part of our mortal journey. Physically, Kaylee was okay—a separated shoulder and some other minor physical injuries that would heal. But how would she take the news of Lindsay's death?

That night in the hospital, with one daughter gone and another physically wounded and emotionally broken, I spent the longest night of my life. How I hoped and prayed the Lord would carry Kaylee and all of us through this awful ordeal. I hoped Kaylee would understand that, although she had been driving the car that spun out of control and went under a semitruck, it was not her fault. I hoped that she would believe what the highway patrolman had told her—that the car had malfunctioned and caused the accident, not her. She did believe it. She was blessed with peace. And she has shown a great hope and trust in Heavenly Father's plan for Lindsay and for herself.

During that long, dark night in the hospital, hope took on a different meaning for me. Yes, I still desired certain outcomes in this life. But I knew the Father's plan was real, and, although I didn't know what the outcomes in this life would be, I knew what the potential outcomes were for the next life. I knew hope would get me though the unknowns here on earth and bring me peace until our reunion. I knew that Lindsay's spirit lived on and that I would be able to see her again.

Hope is trusting in God's promises. I had to fully put my trust in the Lord and His promise of the eternal nature of our family based on our temple covenants and the sealing power of the priesthood. I understood hope on a new level.

I have never known such pain and heartache. I have also never known such a sweetness and outpouring of love and comfort. There are still so many times that my heart aches and my tears flow. Oh, how I miss my Lindsay! There are also many times that my heart aches and my tears pour out for the grief felt by my husband, Kaylee, and our two younger sons. I watch their heartache and tears. I also watch them *hope*—they *hope* that they will be with Lindsay again; they *hope* that they will live lives worthy of being where she is; they *hope* for strength and comfort—the comfort that comes only through the Holy Ghost.

I listen to my family bear testimony of the reality of eternal families and of how the Lord has carried them through the pain. I watch them find joy in the gospel and in life, and I know they have come to understand hope on a different level. I am so grateful for that understanding, and I rejoice in their hope and their strength.

Lindsay's death has been hard—the hardest thing I have known in my life. But for me, hope has become more than a want, a belief, or an emotion—it has become an action, a choice. I know each and every day I can choose how to live. I can choose to live in hope, or I can be swallowed up in despair. I have watched people choose hope, and I've watched people succumb to despair. It breaks my heart when they choose the latter.

*I choose hope.* I choose to hope that others mean well even when they make insensitive remarks. I choose to hope that what I have learned can strengthen others. It is not a one-time choice. I have to choose it over and over again. I choose hope when I feel the simple pain of walking past Lindsay's picture, of singing her favorite hymn, or of having an empty seat in the car or at the table.

I choose hope when her friends pass milestones like prom, graduation, and marriage. I choose hope when she is not there for her brother's baptism, or to see her sister open her mission call, or when I recap to old friends what our family has been up to.

I choose to believe the words of the Lord through His prophets: "I can do all things through Christ which strengtheneth me" (Philippians 4:13). I choose to find joy in life, joy in the promises of eternity. I also know that I must continually choose to "press forward with a steadfastness in Christ, having a perfect brightness of hope, and a love of God and of all men," so that I may be worthy of the promise that "[I] shall have eternal life" (2 Nephi 31:20).[1]

---

Note

1. Tammy Sanderson is from Highland, Utah. Used by permission. Emphasis in original.

*There is no physical pain, no anguish of soul,
no suffering of spirit, no infirmity or weakness that
you or I ever experience during our mortal journey
that the Savior did not experience first.*

DAVID A. BEDNAR

# CHAPTER FOUR

# A HOPE IN CHRIST

A S WE BEGIN speaking of hope and its relationship to the Savior, let me share two quick accounts of two very different circumstances.

### "Your People Are So Happy"

Some years ago, an acquaintance of mine, whom I'll call Barbara, shared this story. She said that a close neighbor of hers was a "born again" Christian. They became good friends and spent a lot of time together. When Barbara's ward held a ward dinner, she invited her friend. The friend and her husband came to the dinner, and they seemed to have a good time.

A few weeks later, the friend invited Barbara and her husband to a social activity her church was sponsoring. Barbara felt a little nervous, not knowing what to expect, but since her friend had accepted her invitation, she felt she needed to reciprocate. She and her husband went and had a wonderful time. They were warmly welcomed and readily accepted by the group.

On the way home, Barbara thanked her friend for the invitation, and then made this observation: "Your people are so happy. How come?" Then came this classic answer: "Because we believe we have been saved by Jesus. Don't you?"

It had been more than a year after that experience when Barbara shared the experience with me. But even after so long, I could tell she was still pondering on it. After a moment of silence, she said to me, "Since that night, I am trying to have more joy in my life by remembering what Christ has done for me."

## Hope in the Plan of Salvation and the Atonement of Jesus Christ

The following story was shared with me by a woman who chooses to remain anonymous.

About two and a half years ago, while on a business trip, my husband told me over the phone that he had been unfaithful and was coming home to divorce me and marry the woman with whom he had been having an affair. And he did.

When I learned that my husband had betrayed me and our marriage covenants, I felt pain so great that I could not even stand up. There are no words in the English language capable of describing this kind of agony. I curled up in the fetal position, wondering how I could still be alive when I was in so much pain. How could my human body withstand it? How could a broken heart keep on beating? I prayed to die—cowardly, I know, but I simply couldn't handle the pain.

And it was then, at that very moment in the depth of my agony, that I realized how much the Savior loved me—as an individual, as a daughter of God. I didn't feel this in any selfish way because I think I'm the greatest. I felt it because I knew He had suffered exactly what I was suffering. Here I was, overcome by pain so great that I wanted to die, and yet,

He went through it willingly—for me. He loved me enough to go through that pain so He would know how to help me heal. I knew then that He had felt what I was feeling, that He had walked that exact path before I did. I knew at that moment I was not alone.

What contrasting stories—one spoken from pure joy, the other from the deepest agony. I think we would all agree that the plan the Father put in place for us, and the Savior's role in making that plan work, should fill us with joy. That is why we call it the *gospel*—"the good news." Even as we struggle with adversity and tribulation, we should find joy in the gospel plan and the principles set forth to make it work.

And yet, life is still out there, bearing down on us like a high-speed freight train.

In the first chapter of this book, we quoted a stake president who made this observation about some of the members of his stake: "In addition to the usual concerns about transgression and apathy, I worry about some of our stalwarts. They know the gospel is true. They serve faithfully. But the joy is gone."

Is it possible that we can get so caught up with our obligations and service in the Church that we lose sight of what it is all about, viz., that "men are, that they might have joy" (2 Nephi 2:25)? Can being a person of covenant become a burden to be endured? Can discipleship drive us to discouragement and despair? Have we become so intent on keeping the ball in the air that we have forgotten what the game is all about? Can we experience "spiritual burnout"?

Sadly, it seems to be so for some people—not bad people, but good people who are striving to do what is right and please God. Therefore, in our discussion on hope, let us not forget its foundation, which is simply this: *All hope in this life and the next centers in Jesus Christ, and what He did under the direction of our Heavenly Father.*

Elder Joseph B. Wirthlin succinctly summarized it: "Seeing life from an eternal perspective helps us focus our limited mortal energies on the things that matter most."[1]

Thus do the scriptures testify. They testify that Christ is not only the basis for our hope, but the center of it as well:

- "Wherefore, ye must press forward with a steadfastness in Christ, having a perfect brightness of hope, and a love of God and of all men" (2 Nephi 31:20).
- "And they never did look upon death with any degree of terror, for their hope and views of Christ and the resurrection" (Alma 27:28).
- "While many thousands of others truly mourn for the loss of their kindred, yet they rejoice and exult in the hope, and even know, according to the promises of the Lord, that they are raised [through Christ] to dwell at the right hand of God, in a state of never-ending happiness" (Alma 28:12).
- "Look unto me in every thought; doubt not, fear not. Behold the wounds which pierced my side, and also the prints of the nails in my hands and feet" (D&C 6:36–37).

President Gordon B. Hinckley said:

The crowning element of our faith is our conviction of our living God, the Father of us all, and of His Beloved Son, the Redeemer of the world. It is because of our Redeemer's life and sacrifice that we are here. . . .

. . . He becomes our rescuer, saving us from damnation and bringing us to eternal life.

In times of despair, in seasons of loneliness and fear, He is there on the horizon to bring succor and comfort and assurance and faith. He is our King, our Savior, our Deliverer, our Lord and our God.[2]

### The Enabling Power of the Atonement

Part of what the Atonement of Christ has made possible is explained by the concept of grace. The Bible Dictionary has this to say about grace:

The main idea of the word is *divine means of help or strength,* given through the bounteous mercy and love of Jesus Christ. . . .

. . . It is likewise through the grace of the Lord that individuals . . . *receive strength and assistance* to do good works that they otherwise would not be able to maintain if left to their own means. This grace is *an enabling power.*[3]

The scriptures teach clearly and plainly that "no flesh . . . can dwell in the presence of God, save it be through *the merits, and mercy, and grace* of the Holy Messiah" (2 Nephi 2:8), and that "it is by grace that we are saved, after all we can do" (2 Nephi 25:23). Throughout the scriptures, we are commanded to engage in good works, and to emulate Christ's perfect example in how we live. But these "works" of ours only open up our hearts so we can receive the fulness of His grace. It is His grace and mercy which pays the price of our sins and redeems us so that we can return to live with God and become like Him.

That is the redemptive power of the Atonement. But there is another aspect of the Atonement which has immediate applicability to us. Elder David A. Bednar, who was then president of BYU–Idaho, further explored the idea that grace is "an enabling power" in a talk he gave at the Provo campus of Brigham Young University. His address is so clear and so relevant to our discussion, I shall draw heavily on his words to explain what is meant by this phrase.

My objective . . . is to describe and discuss both the *redeeming* and *enabling* powers of the Atonement of Jesus Christ. . . .

If I were to emphasize one overarching point this morning, it would be this: I suspect that you and I are much more familiar with the nature of the redeeming power of the Atonement than we are with the enabling power of the Atonement. It is one thing to know that Jesus Christ came to earth to *die* for us. That is fundamental and foundational to the doctrine of Christ. But we also need to appreciate that the Lord desires, through His Atonement and by the power of the Holy Ghost, to *live* in us—not only to direct us but also to empower us. I think most of us know that when we do things wrong, when we need help to overcome the effects of sin in our lives, the Savior has paid the price and made it possible for us to be made clean through His redeeming power. Most of us clearly understand that the Atonement is for sinners. I am not so sure, however, that we know and understand that the Atonement is also for saints—for good men and women who are obedient and worthy and conscientious and who are striving to become better and serve more faithfully. I frankly do not think many of us "get it" concerning this enabling and strengthening aspect of the Atonement, and I wonder if we mistakenly believe we must make the journey from good to better and become a saint all by ourselves through sheer grit, willpower, and discipline, and with our obviously limited capacities.[4]

This concept of an enabling power that can strengthen us and fortify us is taught throughout the scriptures. I cite only a few:

- "My grace is sufficient for all men that humble themselves before me; for if they humble themselves before me, and have faith in me, then will I make weak things become strong unto them" (Ether 12:27).
- "They that wait upon the Lord shall renew their strength; they shall mount up with wings as eagles; they shall run, and not be weary; and they shall walk, and not faint" (Isaiah 40:31).
- "The Lord God showeth us our weakness that we may know that it is by his grace, and his great condescensions unto the children of men, that we have power to do these things" (Jacob 4:7).
- "I know that I am nothing; as to my strength I am weak; therefore I will . . . boast of my God, for in his strength I can do all things" (Alma 26:12).
- "I can do all things through Christ which strengtheneth me" (Philippians 4:13).

Those are wonderful promises, enough to give even the weakest of us a greater hope that we can succeed and overcome.

## "He Will Take upon Him Their Infirmities"

As part of our discussion on hope and the Atonement of Christ, there is another significant point about the grace and mercy of Christ that is important for us to understand.

In the great Messianic prophecy of what is called "The Suffering Servant" description of the Messiah, Isaiah talks about Christ being a man of sorrows, being despised and rejected. He said that He would be wounded for our transgressions, bruised for our iniquities, and that with His stripes (i.e., the welts and lacerations caused by the scourge), we would be healed (see Isaiah 53:3, 5). But in the midst of that scriptural passage, there are two odd phrases—odd in that it doesn't speak of His suffering, but of *ours*: "Surely he hath borne *our* griefs, and carried *our* sorrows" (Isaiah 53:4). Not our sins or our transgressions. Our griefs; our sorrows.

In the book of Hebrews, we find another insight into the Atonement. Paul wrote that "in all things *it behoved him to be made like unto his brethren,* that he might be a merciful and faithful high priest. . . . For in that he himself hath suffered being tempted [tried, or tested], he is able to succour them that are tempted [or tried and tested]" (Hebrews 2:17–18).

Jacob, in his great chapter on the Atonement, makes a specific point we might not have expected: "And he cometh into the world that he may save all men if they will hearken unto his voice; for behold, he suffereth the pains of all men, yea, the pains of every living creature, both men, women, and children, who belong to the family of Adam" (2 Nephi 9:21; see also D&C 18:11). Note that Jacob doesn't say that Christ suffered personal pain *for* the sins of every living creature. That may be implied, but what it says is that He suffered "the pains of all"—*our* pains.

One last reference before we turn to the most explicit passage of them all. After talking about the Lord's loving kindness and His goodness unto us, we read, "In all their afflictions he was afflicted" (D&C 133:53; see also vv. 42–53). Think about that. Through our sins and transgressions, our rebelliousness and our folly, we often bring afflictions upon ourselves—the devastating effects of drug addiction are good examples of that. But many of our afflictions are not of our own making. They are caused by others—sometimes deliberately and maliciously, other times through carelessness or selfishness. We don't cause natural disasters, or force a drunk driver to hit our car, or order a suicide bomber to explode a bomb in our midst, or choose a debilitating birth defect. Afflictions are part of living in a fallen world. That doesn't make them any less devastating.

In other cases, our afflictions are caused by our mistakes—not our sins, but our *errors*. A lapse of judgment at work may cause us to make a mistake that terminates our employment. A momentary distraction while driving—such as trying to break up two squabbling kids—can lead to a fatal accident and a load of guilt for the driver. Or, we often start something with the best of intentions, only to watch it unravel because our abilities and skills don't match our desires. These are very real afflictions too, but they don't come from doing something morally wrong. I believe Christ takes these kinds of affliction upon Himself as well.

Now to Alma's most detailed explanation of this aspect of the Atonement:

> And he shall go forth, suffering pains and afflictions and temptations of every kind; and this that the word might be fulfilled which saith *he will take upon him the pains and the sicknesses of his people.*
>
> And he will take upon him death, that he may loose the bands of death which bind his people; and *he will take upon him their infirmities,* that his bowels may be filled with mercy, *according to the flesh,* that he may know according to the flesh how to succor his people according to their infirmities. (Alma 7:11–12)

Because of the sacredness of that concept, I should like to let those who have been sustained and set apart as prophets, seers, and revelators explain in more detail what this means for us.

*President James E. Faust.* The injured should do what they can to work through their trials, and the Savior will "succor his people according to their infirmities." He will help us carry our burdens. Some injuries are so hurtful and deep that they cannot be healed without help from a higher power *and hope for perfect justice and restitution in the next life.* Since the Savior has suffered anything and everything that we could ever feel or experience, He can help the weak to become stronger. He has personally experienced all of it. He understands our pain and will walk with us even in our darkest hours.[5]

*Elder Neal A. Maxwell.* Jesus' daily mortal experiences and His ministry, to be sure, acquainted Him by observation with a sample of human sicknesses, grief, pains, sorrows, and infirmities which are "common to man" (1 Corinthians 10:13). But the agonies of the Atonement were infinite and first-hand! Since *not all human sorrow and pain is connected to sin,* the full intensiveness of the Atonement involved *bearing our pains, infirmities, and sicknesses,* as well as our sins. Whatever our sufferings, we can safely cast our "care upon him; for he careth for [us]" (1 Peter 5:7).[6]

*Elder Neal A. Maxwell.* Can we, even in the depths of disease, tell Him anything at all about suffering? In ways we cannot comprehend, *our sicknesses and infirmities were borne by Him* even before they were borne by us. The very weight of our combined sins caused Him to descend below all. We have never been, nor will we be, in depths such as He has known. Thus *His atonement made perfect His empathy and His mercy and His capacity to succor us,* for which we can be everlastingly grateful as He tutors us in our trials.[7]

*Elder David A. Bednar.* The Savior has suffered not just for our iniquities but also for the inequality, the unfairness, the pain, the anguish, and the emotional distress that so frequently beset us. . . .

There is no physical pain, no anguish of soul, no suffering of spirit, no infirmity or weakness that you or I ever experience during our mortal journey that the Savior did not experience first. You and I in a moment of weakness may cry out, "No one understands. No one knows." No human being, perhaps, knows. But the Son of God perfectly knows and understands, for He felt and bore our burdens before we ever did. And because He paid the ultimate price and bore that burden, He has perfect empathy and can extend to us His arm of mercy in so many phases of our life. He can reach out, touch, and succor—literally run to us—and strengthen us to be more than we could ever be and help us to do that which we could never do through relying only upon our own power.[8]

### "Come unto Me"

Let us return to our two opening stories. Yes, we should be filled with joy to know that we are saved by the grace of Jesus Christ, to know that our sins can be forgiven and that we can be made clean again. Many Christians call themselves "born again" Christians. Well, so do we. Perhaps our definition of what it means to be saved is different from other Christians, but we believe we are born again through baptism and receiving the Holy Ghost and having our hearts changed so that we desire the good. And I love that answer to the question about why they are so happy: "Because we think we're saved. Don't you?" Let us answer that question with a strong affirmation of our faith.

The anguish in the account of the woman whose husband called her on the phone and announced he was leaving her for another woman is another matter. Even here, though, there is cause for hope. Jesus knows our pain, our suffering, our devastation at such a betrayal. And through the Atonement, He can make that right too.

Here is how the woman concludes her story:

> I have to put myself in the Savior's hands every day. It is a constant battle for me. I think the adversary hits us where we are the weakest. I'm not going to give in. I want to make it to the celestial kingdom. If I have to go through this trial, I'm going to learn and, hopefully, become a better person. Even though this trial of mine is so miserable, I know that eternal life is so many more times wonderful.
>
> I always keep Elder Joseph B. Wirthlin's quotation about the principle of compensation handy: "The Lord compensates the faithful for every loss. That which is taken away from those who love the Lord will be added unto them in His own way. While it may not come at the time we desire, the faithful will know that every tear today will eventually be returned a hundredfold with tears of rejoicing and gratitude" (Joseph B. Wirthlin, "Come What May, and Love It," *Ensign,* November 2008, 28).

Remember:

- We have faith *in* Christ.
- We have hope *through* Christ.

- We love *as* Christ.
- And it is the permeating power and grace of Jesus Christ and His Atonement that brings the spiritual gifts which enable our best efforts and bring us to new levels of gospel living.

The Father and the Son, working together in perfect harmony, are the basis of all our hope for a better world—here, and in the life to come. Thus it could be said that we have hope in Christ because

- He provided the way and the means for us to overcome death.
- He provided redemption for our sins so we can return to live with Him and the Father.
- He has perfect knowledge and understanding of our thoughts, actions, longings, sorrows, desires, hopes, and dreams.
- We are "encircled about eternally in the arms of his love" (2 Nephi 1:15).
- He suffered for our sins, mistakes, sicknesses, inequalities, handicaps, anguish, losses, and infirmities so that He could bear us up with perfect empathy in our afflictions and somehow make all things right.
- His grace is an enabling power that blesses and strengthens us so we can progress, overcome, and triumph in this life, and thus become encircled "in the robe of [His] righteousness" (2 Nephi 4:33).
- He makes "weak things become strong" (Ether 12:27), and thus becomes "my strength and my song" (Isaiah 12:2).
- He "healeth the wounded soul" (Jacob 2:8).

- He is our Shepherd, our Redeemer, our Savior, our Deliverer, our King, the Light of the World, the Bread of Life, the Living Water, the Way, the Truth, and the Life, the Rock of our Salvation, the sacrificial Lamb, our Advocate with the Father, the Prince of Peace.

I believe the full acceptance of each of these aspects of the Savior's life is what constitutes "a perfect brightness of hope" (2 Nephi 31:20). That is why He can extend this everlasting invitation to all:

Come unto me, all ye that labour and are heavy laden, and I will give you rest.

Take my yoke upon you, and learn of me; for I am meek and lowly in heart: and ye shall find rest unto your souls.

For my yoke is easy, and my burden is light. (Matthew 11:28–30)

---

## Notes

*Epigraph.* David A. Bednar, "In the Strength of the Lord," BYU Speeches, 23 October 2001; http://speeches.byu.edu/reader/reader.php?id=789.

1. Joseph B. Wirthlin, "The Time to Prepare," *Ensign*, May 1998, 14.

2. Gordon B. Hinckley, "Our Mission of Saving," *Ensign*, November 1991, 54.

3. LDS Bible Dictionary, s.v. "Grace," 697.

4. David A. Bednar, "In the Strength of the Lord," BYU Speeches, 23 October 2001; emphasis in original; http://speeches.byu.edu/reader/reader.php?id=789.

5. James E. Faust, "The Atonement: Our Greatest Hope," *Ensign*, November 2001, 20.

6. Neal A. Maxwell, *"Not My Will, But Thine"* (Salt Lake City: Bookcraft, 1998), 51.

7. Neal A. Maxwell, *Even As I Am* (Salt Lake City: Bookcraft, 1982), 116–17.

8. Bednar, "In the Strength of the Lord."

# Hope from Hopelessness

—◆—

Some of the most difficult challenges in life come through the evil and wickedness of others—including some who are closest to us and in whom we trust the most. Sexual abuse is one of those evils. It can profoundly affect people's perception of themselves. It often affects their perception of and feelings toward God. It can leave deep emotional and spiritual scars that remain throughout life. It often has a devastating effect on one's hope.

I am grateful for Melissa's willingness to share her struggle with abuse and how she found hope and healing through the Atonement of Christ. I pray her story will inspire and rekindle hope in others who have suffered as she has.

## Hope

Hopeless. That's how I continually felt despite the fact that I grew up in a righteous home where the gospel was taught. Hopeless—despite the fact that I accompanied my parents while my dad served as a mission president, and I served as a missionary in his mission. Hopeless—despite the fact that I was married in the temple to a wonderful man and had wonderful children and a great life. Hopeless—despite the fact that I was active in the Church and had served in the presidencies for both the Young Women and Relief Society auxiliaries.

My hopelessness came from the years of sexual abuse I experienced as a child. The memories had been suppressed, but the effects of that abuse were still a very real part of my life. Those dark moments left me feeling unworthy and out of control. Those moments had redefined who I was and how I lived my life, and I believed that could never change.

I believed in my Heavenly Father; I knew the Church was true. I had stood as a stake Young Women president and testified powerfully to the young women of the truthfulness of the Church and of living prophets and that Heavenly Father loved us and heard and answered prayers. I testified of the times I'd seen His hand in my life and the miracles I'd known had come by His power.

But my testimony of God's love was like rain hitting the pavement. Looking back, I see that God's love was there—and I knew it was there—but it couldn't penetrate my wounded heart. My testimony was real, I believed those things without a doubt, but when it came to Him loving me, I believed I was not worthy of that love. I was not good enough, and so I worked hard to prove I *was* worthy.

Because I had lost so much control during my abuse, I coped by trying to control every part of my life, including my eternal salvation. I felt I had to be perfect. My house had to be perfect—perfectly clean, perfectly organized, perfectly run. I struggled when my children made mistakes. I felt I had to be the perfect mother, the perfect daughter, the perfect friend, and the perfect neighbor. And, of course, I had to serve perfectly in my callings. I wrote to the missionaries, I watched people's children, I brought in meals, I offered emotional support and served my extended family. I attended what felt like every church meeting, every community, school, and church event, every ward activity, every ward temple session. I served with full effort in my callings and helped others with theirs.

I felt blessed and uplifted from my service, but though I worked myself to exhaustion, I still could never feel my Heavenly Father's love, or that I was good enough for Him. So much of my life was spent trying to connect to my Heavenly Father, but I felt unworthy and unclean and too impure to access Him.

In my early thirties, I started having seizures. After extensive testing, the doctors couldn't find anything neurologically wrong with me. Looking back, I believe the seizures came because I needed to face the trauma of my past. What had been shut out so many years before was finally coming to the surface. My body was telling me I needed to conquer this obstacle. It was time.

My past was affecting myself and my family. I knew my family needed the real me; they needed my whole heart. Although I was married to a wonderful man, I couldn't let myself trust him or completely open my heart to him. I had learned to keep my husband and kids at a distance most of the time. I felt physically and emotionally overwhelmed. I was struggling to function. I could no longer push my abuse aside and pretend it hadn't happen or that it was insignificant. I knew the trauma had to be dealt with head-on and resolved. But I was frightened. I truly believed if I let go of the trauma there would be nothing left of me. It took every ounce of courage and the love I had for my children to face the trauma.

I talked with a therapist who "called me out" on my

erroneous beliefs about my Heavenly Father's love. He gave me permission to get off the treadmill. He taught me to let my husband become my safe and strong place. He saw past all my "stuff" to the divine part of me. He didn't judge or condemn me for hiding behind the coping skills I had developed over time.

The most difficult part was allowing myself to be weak, or to appear weak to anyone else. I had to admit there was a problem and let go of control. Once I let myself be weak, then I could turn it over to the Savior. I was the one who had to face my trauma, but Christ stood on the other side and beckoned me through.

Because so much of my attempts to cope with the dark and evil parts of the abuse had covered up my divine self, I believed it was gone—taken and unrecoverable. But through therapy and through the Savior, I began to heal from my trauma.

I distinctly remember the moment I caught my first glimpse of that divine part of me. I couldn't even remember ever having felt that part of me. Seeing that sliver of the "divine me" gave me hope. I was surprised at how familiar it felt. *I know this person,* I thought. *This is really me.* That divine part of me felt clean, pure, unburdened, and completely connected to my Heavenly Father. I hadn't believed that I could have felt that again in my lifetime.

As I felt that sliver of divinity, I realized that Christ knew that divine part of me too. As soon as I could feel Christ, then the hope came. Before, I had believed in the Atonement and testified of the Atonement, but somehow I felt it was for everyone else but me. The hardest part for me was to hand my burden over to my Savior. When I realized He was willing to take it, I finally believed that His love and His Atonement were for me. I knew that through Him that tiny sliver of my divine self could become the whole part of me.

Christ became essential to my healing. As the Atonement began to take hold in my life, that divine part of me grew and grew. My feelings of being unclean and unworthy from the abuse had created a wall that had separated me from my Heavenly Father. As I cleared out the trauma, the wall disappeared and the pure relationship that was always there became accessible. I didn't wonder where my Father had been. I knew He had been there all along, seeking me out and blessing me. As the wall came down, I felt His unconditional love, and I no longer had to prove to Him that I was clean and worthy of it.

As I let go of the abuse, and as my divine self grew into its wholeness, I was surprised that I was no longer being defined by my abuse. And yet, when I got rid of the evil and dark parts of that abuse, I still kept the things I had learned from it.

Now I stand with hope. I have found my true self. I can live a happy life. I still have challenges, but now I can access my Heavenly Father's love and gain strength. I have been able to give my real self—my whole self—to my husband and children. I now know that I can take care of myself and my family and serve in the Church without running faster than I have strength. I know that what I can give is enough. I no longer have to earn my Heavenly Father's love. He loves me and I am enough.[1]

---

## Note

1. Manuscript in possession of the author. Used by permission.

*All things shall be in commotion;*
*and surely, men's hearts shall fail them;*
*for fear shall come upon all people.*

DOCTRINE AND COVENANTS 88:91

# CHAPTER FIVE

# THE REALITIES OF LIFE IN THE LAST DAYS

———— ✠ ————

## The Good Old Days

I WAS BORN eleven days after the beginning of World War II—the greatest conflict in history in terms of number of combatants, number of countries involved, and number of civilian populations affected. I was barely toddling when Pearl Harbor was attacked fifteen months later. One would hardly call that an auspicious time to be born. And yet . . .

My elementary school was about a mile and a half from our house. Along with most others kids, I walked back and forth to school—a three-mile round trip—every day except when the weather was really bad. The only warnings I ever got from my mother each morning were, "Watch out for cars," or "Be sure to come right home."

Today, streets and parking lots around elementary schools are clogged morning and afternoon with parents waiting for their children. Some parents live only a block or two from the school, yet dare not let their children walk alone even that far. Now parental warnings go something like this: "Never talk to strangers," or "Never get into a car with someone you don't know." It is not safe to let young children go into public restrooms alone, and parents even have to be watchful of trusted friends and family members.

I don't remember ever hearing about any kind of "drugs" in my high school. Some kids smoked cigarettes, but they left the school grounds to do so. Today, we read of high schools with designated smoking areas, metal detectors at every entrance, and full-time security guards. Police officers are hired to patrol athletic games so rival gangs don't turn them into battlegrounds. Stabbings, gang fights, drive-by shootings, and in-school violence regularly make headlines. Drugs are peddled in school restrooms and on school playgrounds, and some school districts distribute condoms to students as young as eleven because of the high rate of sexually transmitted diseases.[1] We hear of campuses coming under siege as students kill faculty members and fellow students.

When I was a boy (a phrase that always brings a collective groan from my children and grandchildren), after our chores were done, we played. None of this play was sophisticated or elegant or store-bought, but it didn't matter. We made "flippers" from tree crotches and cut-up rubber inner tubes. We played "night games" almost every summer evening. We'd play a game of "rounders" using flattened tin cans, pieces of cardboard, or garbage can lids to make a baseball diamond. It wasn't much, but we sure had a lot of fun.

Today's kids have T-ball, basketball, golf, swim teams, tennis, soccer, lacrosse, volleyball, football, rugby, ballet, clogging, children's theater, children's choirs, cheerleading camps, drill team, school musicals, skiing, snowboarding, four-wheeling, jet-skiing, and bungee jumping—just to name a few. They have their own computers, their own cell phones filled with "apps," and they play sophisticated "games" on their computers or televisions. They have access to hundreds of television channels, including on-demand programming.

They attend megaplex theaters, theme parks, professional sporting events, and big-name concerts and other shows.

Is that bad? Of course not. My grandchildren participate in many of those activities and are the richer for it. But life is certainly more complicated, more structured, and more over-programmed now than it ever was in my day.

One last example: I worked at our local movie theater during my high school years. In 1954, a movie that was already making national headlines came to our theater. For the first time in movie history, actors used certain words that had never before been heard on the big screen. When the movie finally arrived at our little theater, I can still remember hearing the audiences gasp as these "shockers" were spoken aloud. What words were so scandalous? "Mistress." "Seduce." "Pregnant." "Virgin." Considering where we are now, that sounds so quaint as to be almost unbelievable.

## The Times in Which We Live

Someone once said that much of the good-old-days syndrome is caused by a poor memory. Maybe so, but I can testify that the realities of growing up for me were very different than the realities my grandchildren are facing. Don't get me wrong. I don't believe we are on the verge of the end of the world as we know it. I don't believe the United States is going to collapse and cease to exist. Nor do I believe that things are in a terrible state overall.

In so many ways, our lives are better off today than when I was a kid. We live in a world of comfort and convenience. Advances in communication, technology, global commerce, education, science, and medicine have blessed all of us tremendously. (Think what Brigham Young would have given to have cell phones and a GPS navigating device in each wagon company.)

On the other hand, I see evidence all around of growing moral decay and an increasing dissolution and devaluation of the family. But even things which are not inherently evil, such as the sheer complexity of our lives, are bringing their own set of challenges. In these difficult economic times, many have lost or are losing their homes. Many are unemployed. Even those who have a job find their employers demanding more hours and more travel, and putting them under greater stress. Retirement funds and savings accounts have taken huge hits, causing many people to return to a job market that is already glutted with too many people looking for work. In so many ways I believe we face circumstances that are darker, more pervasive, more dangerous, and more challenging than they have been for a very long time.

The Savior said that His disciples would be "in the world" (John 13:1), and He also said, "In the world *ye shall have tribulation*" (John 16:33). We certainly seem to be seeing some of that tribulation, and that directly contributes to our anxiety, fear, and depression. Even the good things we enjoy bring a new set of problems. The Internet brings pornography. Social networking allows Internet stalking. Predators who used to prowl the streets at night now prowl cyberspace. We have so many opportunities that our parents didn't have, and yet the complexity of life leaves us feeling overwhelmed, exhausted, and struggling to cope.

About now you may be saying, "I thought this was supposed to be a book on hope. Why all of this negative stuff?" That's simple to answer. It is the "negative stuff" that brings despair and hopelessness in its wake. No wonder we need hope! As we seek it, we have to recognize the realities around us.

## Perilous Times

The Apostle Paul said, "This know also, that *in the last days perilous times shall come*" (2 Timothy 3:1). I believe he saw our day. I believe that we are now living in those perilous times. Here are some comments on our day and age from those whom we sustain as prophets, seers, and revelators:

*President Howard W. Hunter.* All dispensations have had their perilous times, but our day will include genuine peril (2 Timothy 3:1).[2]

*President Boyd K. Packer.* Your generation is filled with uncertainties. A life of fun and games and expensive toys has come to an abrupt end. We move from a generation of ease and entertainment to a generation of hard work and responsibility. We do not know how long that will last.[3]

*President Boyd K. Packer.* The world is spiraling downward at an ever-quickening pace. I am sorry to tell you that it will not get better. . . .

. . . These are days of great spiritual danger. . . .

I know of nothing in the history of the Church or in the history of the world to compare with our present circumstances. . . . Nothing happened in Sodom and Gomorrah which exceeds in wickedness and depravity that which surrounds us now. . . .

. . . Unspeakable wickedness and perversion were once hid in dark places; now they are in the open, even accorded legal protection.

At Sodom and Gomorrah these things were localized. Now they are spread across the world, and they are among us.[4]

*President Gordon B. Hinckley.* Wonderful as this time is, it is fraught with peril. Evil is all about us. . . . We live in a season when fierce men do terrible and despicable things.[5]

*President Gordon B. Hinckley.* I do not know what the future holds. I do not wish to sound negative, but I wish to remind you of the warnings of scripture and the teachings of the prophets. . . . The time will come when the earth will be cleansed and there will be indescribable distress.[6]

The scriptural picture is equally grim.

- "There shall be great pollutions upon the face of the earth; there shall be murders, and robbing, and lying, and deceivings, and whoredoms, and all manner of abominations" (Mormon 8:31).
- "Evil men . . . shall wax worse and worse, deceiving, and being deceived" (2 Timothy 3:13).
- "Peace shall be taken from the earth, and the devil shall have power over his own dominion" (D&C 1:35).
- There will be "wars and rumors of wars, and the whole earth shall be in commotion" (D&C 45:26).
- "Iniquity shall abound" (D&C 45:27).
- "There shall be earthquakes also in divers places, and many desolations; . . . men will . . . take up the sword, one against another, and they will kill one another" (D&C 45:33).
- "Plagues shall go forth . . . until I have completed my work" (D&C 84:97).

### The Earth in Commotion

In the Doctrine and Covenants, the Lord warned that if the world would not listen to the voice of His servants, then He would call upon the world "by the voice of thunderings, and by the voice of lightnings, and by the voice of tempests, and by the voice of earthquakes, and great hailstorms, and by the voice of famines and pestilences of every kind" (D&C 43:25) and by "the voice of the waves of the sea heaving themselves beyond their bounds" (D&C 88:90).

There have always been great natural disasters, of course, but here are just some of those "voices" that have sounded recently:

- Of the sixteen strongest earthquakes in the world since 1900, five—or one-third—of them have happened since the year 2004.[7]

- On December 26, 2004, an earthquake in the Indian Ocean—the third largest ever recorded to date—triggered an enormous tsunami that swamped coastal areas of several countries. Estimates of the dead ranged from 230,000 to 280,000 people.

- Hurricane Katrina, which occurred in September 2005, emptied a city of half a million people and became the costliest natural disaster in the history of the United States. Katrina is ranked as the third-most intense hurricane in the United States.[8]

- On January 12, 2010, the island nation of Haiti was hit by the strongest earthquake to occur there since 1770, killing about 250,000 people. It is one of the top ten deadliest earthquakes in history.

- Less than two months later, on February 27, 2010, the sixth strongest earthquake ever recorded struck the nation of Chile, causing widespread destruction and moving the entire city of Concepción about ten feet to the west.

- Throughout December 2010 and January 2011, as a result of the heaviest rainfall in its recorded history, Australia experienced extensive flooding over an area *the size of France and Germany combined!*[9] This flood became Australia's costliest natural disaster in history.

- On March 11, 2011, an 8.9 earthquake, one of the top five strongest in recorded history, struck near the east coast of Japan's Honshu Island, causing widespread damage and sending a tsunami smashing its way inland for several miles and rupturing a nuclear power plant. One news commentator said: "Today will surely be recorded among the world's most destructive natural disasters ever."[10]

- In 2004, 1,717 tornadoes were reported in the United States. But within the first eleven months of 2011, 1,836 tornadoes had been reported in the United States.[11]

- In one four-day period of the 2011 tornado season—April 25 through April 28—there were 336 confirmed tornadoes. That is an average of 84 tornadoes per day![12]

Mormon noted that human nature is such "that except the Lord doth chasten his people with many afflictions, yea, except he doth visit them with death and with terror, and with famine and with all manner of pestilence, they will not remember him" (Helaman 12:3). I don't believe God sends down these disasters as a means of punishing His children. I believe they are the result of natural forces which God controls and uses for His own purposes.

Unfortunately, natural disasters impact the good as well as the evil. Righteous individuals and families are caught in earthquakes and floods and tornadoes and tsunamis. But these events can serve as "wake-up calls" for all of us, reminding us of the fragile nature of our lives. We can use them to reassess where we are and reevaluate our priorities. This can sharpen our focus on things that matter most and motivate us to bring our lives into closer alignment with the Lord.

## The Agency of Others

We know that the war in heaven was fought when Satan sought to destroy man's agency (see Moses 4:3). We know that agency was an absolute necessity if we were to prove ourselves (see Abraham 3:25; 2 Nephi 2:13–14). And we also know that it is through man's use of individual agency that much tragedy is brought into the world. Man-made disasters are far more frequent, and in many cases, far more devastating than the natural ones.

In the last few years, the effects of greed, poor management, foolish decisions, and well-intentioned but misguided attempts to "fix" things have led to the near bankruptcy of our nation and the loss of employment for millions. How many people in the world have been killed by suicide bombers or in other terrorist attacks over the last decade? How many millions suffer under the hand of tyranny? How many thousands of children face starvation as the leaders of their countries battle for political supremacy or siphon off billions of dollars into hidden bank accounts? How much suffering has war brought upon families around the world throughout all of history?

It is because of the misuse of agency that we see an increasing plague of social, emotional, and physical abuse. It is because of the misuse of agency that marriage covenants are broken, the hearts of spouses and children are shattered, and families are torn apart. It is through the misuse of agency that young girls become pregnant and are then abandoned by their partners to deal with the consequences. Who can possibly catalog the sorrow and despair brought into the world through the misuse of moral agency?

Why does God allow such things? Why doesn't He interfere or intervene? The truth is that He does intervene many times and in many ways—softening the effects, blessing those who suffer, answering earnest prayers—but the only way He could totally eliminate such suffering would be to remove the agency of man, and He won't do that. Agency is too fundamental to our happiness. It is too basic to the plan of salvation.

## The Nature of Life

While these lists naturally raise anxieties in our hearts, let us keep in mind three things. First, this is the nature of life as we know it. Life is, by its very nature, filled with opposition, or opposites. While many enjoy a high standard of wealth, millions of others live in crushing poverty. Along with good health comes sickness, disease, infections, congenital birth defects, and injuries that can leave us crippled or paralyzed for life. We enjoy much that is good, but evil grows ever more virulent. We see virtue under attack by vice. Marriage too often dissolves through divorce. We are promised that we will have joy and rejoicing in our posterity, but children can also be the cause of some of the most intense sorrow we can experience. A lifetime career can abruptly end. A natural disaster can destroy a lifetime of work in seconds.

The second thing to remember is this: What makes all of this especially difficult is that these kinds of problems and challenges are usually random, unpredictable, and beyond our control. They strike without warning and with shocking swiftness. If they affected only the wicked—i.e., those who "deserved" it—they might be easier for us to accept. But there is this blind unfairness about life sometimes. Even the best preparations, the most careful planning, or the most faithful obedience are not guarantees that we will stay below the "tragedy radar." Wouldn't it be wonderful if we had some kind of "early warning tragedy system" in place as we do with storms so we could prepare ourselves or flee?

Here is a third thing to keep in mind. These terrible things may be a natural part of life, but they are not the defining influences. The nature of life also includes a myriad of blessings and goodness and happiness. We must learn to counterbalance the grimmer things with the good things of life we enjoy each day—family, food, health, life. Even in the prophetic picture of the future, we are reminded that there are great things ahead. Remember, the last days are called both "great and dreadful" (D&C 110:16).

We know, for example, that along with increased wickedness, the gospel and the kingdom of God "shall roll forth unto the ends of the earth, . . . that the kingdom of heaven may come" (D&C 65:2, 6). Even as Satan's power seems to be on the increase, the time long prophesied "when temples will dot the earth"[13] is now being fulfilled, and that "'every foundation stone that is laid for a Temple, and every Temple completed . . . lessens the power of Satan on the earth, and increases the power of God and Godliness.'"[14]

Here are a few other things which yet lie in the future:

- The New Jerusalem will be built in Jackson County (see D&C 84:2–5).
- The ten tribes shall return from their long exile (see D&C 133:26–34).
- Babylon, which is the symbol of all that is evil, wicked, and impure in the world, shall be utterly overthrown (see Revelation 18:2, 19–20).
- In the great Millennium there shall be no more war. Peace, love, harmony, progress, and rest shall prevail. Satan will be bound for a thousand years (see D&C 43:30–31).

When we contemplate these promises instead of saying, "I hope I die before all the judgments come," I find myself thinking, "Oh, how wonderful it would be to live in such times." My anxiety turns to anticipation. Remember this statement by Joseph Smith?

> The building up of Zion is a cause that has interested the people of God in every age; it is a theme upon which

prophets, priests and kings have dwelt with peculiar delight; they have looked forward with joyful anticipation to the day in which we live; and fired with heavenly and joyful antici-pations they have sung and written and prophesied of this our day; but they died without the sight; we are the favored people that God has made choice of to bring about the Latter-day glory; it is left for us to see, participate in and help to roll forward the Latter-day glory.[15]

## Finding Hope in These Latter Days

I find it interesting that among the prophecies of the last days, two emotional conditions are predicted: "And there shall be weeping and wailing among the hosts of men" (D&C 29:15). "Weeping and wailing" is another phrase to describe our emotional reactions to the realities of life. They also describe our reaction when we lose hope. We bemoan our condition, sorrow over our circumstances, weep with frustration that life seems so unfair. But "weeping and wailing" is not predicted to be a condition found among only the wicked. Even those of strong faith and deep commitment can be brought to their knees and made to weep.

That is the nature of life. It is wonderful, and it is hard. It is filled with countless blessings, but they come mixed with sorrow and pain. Thanks be to God that He has given us a way to spiritually navigate our way through these difficulties. Through faith, hope, and charity, we can stand steadfast and be filled with hope even in the darkest of circumstances.

There are many reasons for losing hope in this life, and some of the reasons are pretty compelling. We lose hope because the world around us grows increasingly dark and difficult. We lose hope when we are not all that we would like to be. We lose hope because the future—either for the world in general or for ourselves personally—looks increasingly bleak. We lose hope when a difficult situation continues for years on end without relief. We lose hope because it seems as though there are no solutions, no way out, no escape. We lose hope because life, by its very nature, is hard. That is our reality.

Earlier we shared the story of a Christian missionary couple who were transporting tons of equipment across the interior of Africa. They spoke of raging rivers and streams filled with poisonous snakes and crocodiles. In a way, that is what the world is. I see nothing that suggests that, in the foreseeable future, the journey is going to get easier or that our loads will be lightened. Thanks be to God that He has shown us how to strengthen the bridges through hope and faith.

Citing lessons we can learn from Joseph Smith's time in Liberty Jail, Elder Jeffrey R. Holland noted:

> Everyone, including (and perhaps especially) the righteous, will be called upon to face trying times. When that happens we can sometimes fear God has abandoned us, and we might be left, at least for a time, to wonder when our troubles will ever end. . . .
>
> But whenever these moments of our extremity come, we must not succumb to the fear that God has abandoned us or that He does not hear our prayers. He *does* hear us. He *does* see us. He *does* love us. . . . He *is* there. Our prayers *are* heard. And when we weep He and the angels of heaven weep with us.[16]

Knowing that, let us lift up our heads, even in these most difficult of times, and say, as did the Prophet Joseph Smith: "Brethren [and sisters], shall we not go on in so great a cause? Go forward and not backward. Courage, brethren; and on, on to the victory!" (D&C 128:22).

## Notes

1. Sarah Lenz, "How far is too far in sex education?" *Deseret News,* 21 April 2011; http://www.deseretnews.com/article/700129063/How-far-is-too-far-in-sex-education.html.

2. Howard W. Hunter, *The Teachings of Howard W. Hunter,* ed. Clyde J. Williams (Salt Lake City: Bookcraft, 1997), 200.

3. Boyd K. Packer, "Counsel to Young Men," *Ensign,* May 2009, 52.

4. Boyd K. Packer, "The One Pure Defense," Address to CES Religious Educators, 6 February 2004; http://www.ldsces.org/training/live/Packer%20Pure%20Defense%20Final.pdf.

5. Gordon B. Hinckley, "Living in the Fulness of Times," *Ensign,* November 2001, 5–6.

6. Gordon B. Hinckley, "The Times in Which We Live," *Ensign,* November 2001, 73–74.

7. United States Geological Survey Earthquake Information Center, "Largest Earthquakes in the World Since 1900"; http://earthquake.usgs.gov/earthquakes/world/10_largest_world.php.

8. See Eric S. Blake, Christopher W. Landsea, and Ethan J. Gibney, *The Deadliest, Costliest, and Most Intense United States Tropical Cyclones from 1851 to 2010 (and Other Frequently Requested Hurricane Facts)* (Miami, FL: National Weather Service, 2011), 15; www.nhc.noaa.gov/pdf/nws-nhc-6.pdf.

9. The Big Picture, "Australian flooding," 3 January 2011; http://www.boston.com/bigpicture/2011/01/australian_flooding.html.

10. "Tsunami in Japan: What Are the 5 Worst Tsunamis of All Time?" 11 March 2011; http://www.aol.news.com/2011/03/11/tsunami-in-japan-what-are-the-5-worst-tsunamis-of-all-time/.

11. See http://en.wikipedia.org/wiki/Tornadoes_of_2011.

12. "April 25–28, 2011 tornado outbreak"; http://en.wikipedia.org/wiki/April_25-28,_2011_tornado_outbreak.

13. Bruce R. McConkie, *Mormon Doctrine,* 2d ed. (Salt Lake City: Bookcraft, 1966), 781.

14. George Q. Cannon, as cited in *Preparing to Enter the Holy Temple* (Salt Lake City: The Church of Jesus Christ of Latter-day Saints, 2002), 36.

15. Joseph Smith, *Teachings of Presidents of the Church: Joseph Smith* (Salt Lake City: The Church of Jesus Christ of Latter-day Saints, 2007), 186.

16. Jeffrey R. Holland, "Lessons from Liberty Jail," *BYU Magazine* (Winter 2009): 36–37.

# "Life Is Fragile, but Eternity Is Forever"

⚜

WE OFTEN TALK about trials and tribulations in terms of how they impact the individual who is experiencing them. But, as is so often the case, those who are close to the suffering individuals are also affected. The tragedy experienced by a loved one may be different for those who love them, but it is, nevertheless, still very real.

I asked Jon and Quinn Silcox of Sandy, Utah, if they would share their story. They both immediately agreed, but Jon struggled when it came time to write it. The pain was too real for him to be completely open about it yet. Then, while on a road trip together, late at night while their children were asleep, Quinn took out her laptop and began asking him questions. In the darkness of the car, he was able to push aside the barriers and be completely honest about his perspective of their experience. Here then is their story as they tell it together.

**Quinn:** November 1, 2007, started out like any other day for me. Jon was busy in his third and final year of his orthodontic residency. Our four- and two-year-old boys were active and delightful, and the baby on the way was taking up more and more space in my growing tummy. But then I got *the* phone call, the call that redefined our family, the call that caused our beautiful little world to crumble.

**Jon:** I went to the doctor because I knew something was wrong. I suspected bad news, but I wasn't prepared for when he said, "I don't know for sure, but I think you have leukemia." All I could think was, *What am I going to do? How is my family going to make it? We've started this journey together, but how will it end if what they are telling me is true and this disease is fatal?*

**Quinn:** Heavenly Father blessed me to stay calm while I was on the phone with Jon. I immediately found a babysitter for the boys and called a friend to meet us at the hospital to give Jon a blessing. And to pray. Absolutely pray. I needed every bit of faith and strength possible.

Cancer is always scary, but it was especially so to me. When my dad was thirty-one—the exact same age as Jon—he was diagnosed with cancer, and he died two years later. I was six years old. Jon's phone call brought back my greatest fear—only this time, instead of being the child, I was the wife and mother. I was not shielded by some naïve hope that the Lord wouldn't allow such a caring husband and attentive father to die. But there was also comfort in knowing the Lord would prepare a way for us if Jon indeed was called to his heavenly home. I had witnessed such a miracle while growing up. I desperately did not want to be a single mother, but I knew I could do it because I had watched my mom do it.

**Jon:** After three days we finally had a diagnosis: Myelodysplastic Syndrome (MDS), a rare type of blood cancer where the bone marrow stops producing blood. If left untreated, it would turn into leukemia. My MDS was so far advanced that the only treatment option was a bone marrow transplant. My doctor delivered the news in our hospital room. After he left, Quinn and I wept in each other's arms.

My cancer was not a "good" type of cancer, at least not in my stage. *If* a donor could be secured quickly and I received a transplant, my chance of living five years was still only 50 percent. When we had no more tears left to cry, the despair started to lift. At least we knew what we were fighting, and we knew how to do it. We hoped our prayers for a donor would be answered through one of my three sisters. They were my best chance of being a match for my transplant.

**Quinn:** A few days after we received Jon's diagnosis, we went to the park on a beautiful autumn day to take pictures. We did it for all the reasons we couldn't yet talk about. After receiving so much blood, Jon looked really good again, and we knew these might be our last family pictures with him.

**Jon:** There was one particular picture that captured my boys perfectly. They were standing with their arms around each other. My oldest has a look of somber innocence on his face, while my younger son is perfectly content clinging to his older brother. To this day, that picture means the world to me. I can look at that picture and know that together they'll make it. They'll survive and help each other. To me, that picture was hope—hope that it would be okay if I died, and hope that I could live to see them grow up together. A lot of what made things all right was remembering all the things I had learned in Primary that I knew were true. Because of our Savior's Atonement I would still be a part of their lives even if I died. I'd see them from somewhere and I'd be with them again.

**Quinn:** As difficult as the diagnosis was, there was peace in having something specific to pray for. Our first step was to secure a donor. There was a tangible spirit of comfort that we felt as everyone who knew us, or even knew about us, united in our behalf to fast and pray for a miracle.

Four weeks later, Jon's mom called us on the phone. She was crying. "Jadi's a match." Our prayers had been answered.

**Jon:** I didn't always believe that I would live, at least not initially. Shortly after I was released from the hospital, but before the transplant, I had some rare and severe side effects from the medications. I had cramps in my legs so bad I could barely walk. Then the cramps would shift to my abdomen and breathing became painful.

My hope began to wane. I began to question whether my first hopes were realistic. There were lots of nights and evenings when I laid in bed, overcome with sadness and unable to hold back the tears. I had built a life with my wife. How could it come to an end?

I worried about being a burden to her as my illness progressed. I also hoped for simpler things. I wanted to be present at the birth of our baby. And I was! I was the one who got to say, "It's a girl!" And as time drew closer for the transplant, I continued to feel better and dared to hope for more.

**Quinn:** Six weeks after our baby was born, Jon went into the hospital for his transplant. I remember one particularly hard day shortly thereafter. I was so tired. I was worried about Jon. Life was difficult without him as I cared for our three children.

I left the hospital with what seemed like an overwhelming amount of grief and worry. As I walked across the bridge to the parking garage, I stared at my feet and realized that one foot always managed to be placed in front of the other. A phrase from my favorite hymn came to me, and I said it in my mind: "As thy days may demand." Then the Spirit finished the phrase: "So thy succor shall be." How I clung to that promise!

**Jon:** I always had my eye on graduation. Maybe not originally, but now it seemed doable and a huge milestone. I wanted to finish my orthodontic residency. I wanted that moment to be a symbol, a way for me to say, "I have survived this far, and I've got more to go."

**Quinn:** The times that were the most difficult were when we encountered something unexpected. When the test results weren't normal, or the doctors couldn't figure out what was wrong, it seemed to chip away at my resolve, and I became vulnerable to fear. But every time we experienced setbacks, it was an opportunity for the Lord to remind me of the things that I knew in spite of the uncertainty: that God loved us, that He was aware of us, and that things were in His hands.

**Jon:** I knew the answer to a prayer is sometimes "no," but I am grateful that many times it is "yes." I am now five years post-transplant [2012] and doing amazingly well. Enough time has passed that I fear I am sometimes guilty of taking for granted all the blessings that I swore I would never take for granted again. But what always brings me back to that state of "remembering" is looking at that picture of my boys. I believe that in some ways we became what the photograph of them represents to me—that we hold on to each other. Life is fragile, but eternity is forever, and that's what life is all about.

*And he beheld Satan; and he had a great chain in his hand, and it veiled the whole face of the earth with darkness.*

MOSES 7:26

CHAPTER SIX

# Satan Is Real

—————◆◆◆—————

## The Reality of Satan

As a priesthood leader, I once dealt with a difficult situation concerning a couple under my jurisdiction. The couple's relationship had deteriorated to the point where it was filled with an endless series of arguments and screaming battles. The contention was negatively affecting the children, as well as both the husband and wife. After marriage counseling failed, the wife finally decided to file for divorce. That only made matters worse. The husband abandoned her, taking most of their financial assets with him. You could see in her face the toll this took on her.

One night, as we were counseling together, she suddenly burst out and said, "This week has been a really bad time for me. And now Satan is working very hard on me." (She didn't elaborate on what that meant.) Then she said, "I am so vulnerable right now. Can't he just leave me alone until I get through this?"

I had never heard it put quite that way before. I looked at her for a long moment, feeling her sorrow and her desperation. Then I said something like this: "You speak of Satan as though he were some kind of a gentleman. Do you really think that because you are spiritually exhausted, he will agree to a time-out so you can rest up and regain your strength? My dear sister, there is no fairness or decency in his nature. I am sure right now he is exulting in your weakness and despair. And he will do anything he can to capitalize on your vulnerability and bring you down even farther."

I immediately regretted being so blunt. It didn't seem like a comforting approach to someone in such pain. But I was wrong. For a long moment she just looked at me. Then her shoulders squared. Her head came up. "You're right," she said. "That's exactly what he wants of me. And I will not give him the satisfaction of getting it." I was touched by her courage and her resolve, especially as I watched her continue to work through a very difficult situation.

Here is another reality of life. There is a very real and powerful force for evil among us. It has become fashionable in this secular world of ours to dismiss the idea that there exists a real being out there—a fallen angel, if you will—who is totally and irrevocably dedicated to evil. Either Satan is rejected outright as sort of an adult "boogeyman" used to frighten us into doing what's right, or he is merely the personification of an abstract concept we call evil, or "the dark side of the Force," as one moviemaker put it.

But Satan is real. He can play a significant and potentially devastating role when it comes to how we cope with the challenges of life. When we talk of hope versus despair, or discouragement versus determination, or surrender versus conquest, or depression versus happiness, we have to be aware of the influence of Satan and his followers in the equation.

Odd as it may seem, studying what the prophets have taught us about Satan and his followers can actually be an enlightening experience. We are at war in this life, and he is the archenemy, the commander of the opposing forces. It is a war that began before the foundations of the world were laid (see Revelation 12:7). It started in the premortal existence, moved to earth millennia ago, and continues with ever-increasing ferocity in our day. It shall continue until Christ comes to earth again.

## What Motivates Satan?

President Spencer W. Kimball gave this powerful—and chilling—description of Satan:

The arch deceiver has studied every way possible to achieve his ends, using every tool, every device possible. He takes over, distorts, and changes and camouflages everything created for the good of man, to make it desirable to men so he may take over their minds and pervert their bodies and claim them his.

He never sleeps—he is diligent and persevering. He analyzes carefully his problem and then moves forward diligently, methodically to reach that objective. He uses all five senses and man's natural hunger and thirst to lead him away. He anticipates resistance and fortifies himself against it. He uses time and space and leisure. He is constant and persuasive and skillful. He uses such useful things as radio, television, the printed page, the airplane, and the car to distort and damage. He uses the gregariousness of man, his loneliness, his every need to lead him astray. He does his work at the most propitious time in the most impressive places with the most influential people. He overlooks nothing that will deceive and distort and prostitute. He uses money, power, force. He entices man and attacks at his weakest spot. He takes the good and creates ugliness. He takes beautiful art and gives it sensualness. He takes divine music and changes it to excite passion and lewdness. He uses sacred things to divert. He uses every teaching art to subvert man.[1]

After reading that description, one has to ask, "So why does Satan do what he does? What's in it for him?" The scriptures give us some clues as to his motivation.

Lehi, speaking of Satan, said:

> He became a devil, having sought that which was evil before God.
>
> And because he had fallen from heaven, and had become miserable forever, he sought also the misery of all mankind. . . .
>
> Wherefore, men are free . . . to choose captivity and death, according to the captivity and power of the devil; for he seeketh that all men might be miserable like unto himself. (2 Nephi 2:17–18, 27)

And in the account of the Great Council in Heaven where Lucifer stepped forth in opposition to the Father's plan, Satan is quoted as saying, "I will redeem all mankind, that one soul shall not be lost, and surely I will do it; wherefore give me thine honor . . . and also [the Lord adds], that I should give unto him mine own power" (Moses 4:1, 3; see also D&C 29:36).

So here we have two primary motives. The first is the ultimate expression of the old saying, "Misery loves company." Because Satan himself is so miserable, he seeks to bring as many souls as possible into that same state of misery as he is in. Misery is the opposite of joy, and evidently he cannot stand the thought that others have joy when he has none.

The second motive is pride—the ultimate case of unbridled egotism. Satan had such a high opinion of himself that he wanted God to step down and let *him* be God, receiving all the power and glory and honor for himself. We get another clue about Satan's pride when we read of his appearance to Moses. In one of the greatest lies in the history of the world, Satan declared that he was "the Only Begotten," and then demanded of Moses, *"Worship me"* (Moses 1:19).

## Satan's Nature and Character

It is instructive to examine the names and titles that are applied to Satan, for they too give us insights into what he is and how he works. Here are some of them:

- *Lucifer.* This is Satan's premortal name, just as Jehovah was Christ's premortal name. Lucifer comes from a Hebrew root meaning "'brightness,'"[2] *"the Shining One,"* or *"Lightbringer."*[3] We know from latter-day revelation that in his premortal state, Lucifer was "an angel of God who was in authority" (D&C 76:25). His name suggests that he was filled with intelligence—or "light and truth" (D&C 93:36). He is also called a "son of the morning" (Isaiah 14:12).

- *Perdition.* After Satan rebelled against God, his name was changed to "Perdition" (D&C 76:26). Perdition comes from a Greek word meaning "'perishing, destruction,'" and includes the idea of great misery.[4]

- *Satan.* This is the formal name for the devil and the one most commonly used in the scriptures. It comes from the Hebrew word *satana,* which literally means "adversary," or "opponent,"[5] or one who makes false accusations against others.[6] Thus John the Revelator called him "the *accuser* of our brethren" (Revelation 12:10).

- *The Devil.* This is one of the most frequently used terms for Satan in the scriptures. The word comes from the Greek *diabolos,* which means "slanderer."[7] A slanderer is someone who makes false statements (or accusations) about others, so this is similar to the meaning of Satan.

- *Beelzebub.* Jesus said that Satan was Beelzebub (Luke 11:18). This name or title is found only in the New Testament, but provides an interesting insight into Satan's nature. Originally Beelzebub was a heathen deity who was considered to be the god of the dung heap. It is a term "of the utmost *contempt.*"[8] How apt. He rules over everything filthy and unclean.[9]

- *The Father of All Lies.* (See Alma 5:25; D&C 93:25; Moses 4:4.) Jesus said of Satan that he "abode not in the truth, because there is no truth in him. When he speaketh a lie, he speaketh of his own: for he is a liar, and the father of it" (John 8:44).

- *Destroyer.* (See D&C 61:19; 101:54; 105:15.) President Brigham Young said: "The Devil delights in the work of destruction—to burn and lay waste and destroy the whole earth. He delights to convulse and throw into confusion the affairs of men, politically, religiously and morally."[10]

What a résumé! It is important for us to understand this nature of Satan, as it endlessly drives him to try to destroy or weaken hope.

## The Power of the Destroyer

All of those negative attributes are bad enough, but we also need to realize that Satan has great power. It is not greater than the power of God, but it is a force to contend with nevertheless. Over and over we find references in the scriptures which refer to Satan in what might be called "power terminology." Here are just a few of the more direct examples of that language.

- Satan seeks "to lead [men] captive at his will" (Moses 4:4).
- "And they that will harden their hearts . . . are taken captive by the devil, and led by his will down to destruction. Now this is what is meant by the chains of hell" (Alma 12:11).
- "[The wicked are] chained down to an everlasting destruction, according to the power and captivity of Satan" (Alma 12:17).
- If we have procrastinated the day of our repentance, Amulek warned that we "become subjected to the spirit of the devil, and he doth seal you his; therefore, the Spirit of the Lord hath withdrawn from you, . . . and the devil hath all power over you" (Alma 34:35).

We are not saying that we are helpless before him. The Prophet Joseph taught that "the devil has no power over us *only as we permit him*."[11] Nevertheless, it is important for us to remember that we are dealing with a formidable enemy here. Comparing him to the Big Bad Wolf, as one well-intentioned blogger did,[12] seems like a woefully inadequate description of his work, his dedication, and his power.

## Satan Is a Liar, a Deceiver, a Slanderer, and a False Accuser

Here are two important truths to remember about Satan. First, Christ said of him, "There is no truth in him" (John 8:44). We are not talking about a person who lies on occasion. By nature, Satan is totally dishonest and untrustworthy. He is the father of lies. There is nothing truthful about him. He accuses us falsely and slanders us in every way possible.

Second, we know that Satan and his followers can give us false revelation (see, for example, D&C 28:11; Alma 30:53). Though they live in a different sphere than we do, and we cannot see them or openly hear their voices, evil spirits can and do communicate with us. That is a concept of great importance. Let me say it again. Satan and his followers can communicate with us and do so regularly. We can receive "the promptings of Satan,"[13] just as we receive promptings from the Holy Spirit. And because of his nature, these promptings will all come with the intent to deceive.

Elder Boyd K. Packer warned: "Be ever on guard lest you be deceived by inspiration from an unworthy source. You can be given false spiritual messages. There are *counterfeit spirits* just as there are counterfeit angels."[14] His choice of words is interesting. A counterfeit is a copy of something that so closely resembles the original that it usually takes an expert to tell the difference. Satan is so cunning that it is easy for us to be deceived when he sends us his promptings. Elder Mark E. Petersen of the Quorum of the Twelve put it this way:

> We are enticed by the good, and we are enticed by the evil. . . . This enticement is just as real as can be, and just as surely as the Lord, by his power, puts good ideas into our minds and entices us by them, so does Satan put evil ideas into our heads and entices us by them. . . .
>
> . . . Satan is definitely a revelator, devilish and evil as he is.[15]

Remember what we said about hope being a battle of the mind, the heart, and the spirit? Satan understands this perfectly and works hard to destroy our faith, our hope, and any tendencies we have to emulate the love of Christ. He is constantly whispering in our ears, feeding us a litany of lies aimed at destroying hope. Here is just a sampling of what are outright lies:

- "Eat, drink, and be merry, for tomorrow we die; and it shall be well with us" (2 Nephi 28:7).
- "'Just try it once. One beer or one cigarette or one porno movie won't hurt.'"[16]
- This isn't a sin. You're not doing anything wrong. "'I am no devil. There is no evil one. There is no black. All is white.'"[17]
- "[The] commandments restrict your freedom, . . . they are oppressive and unpleasant, . . . they prevent you from finding happiness."[18]
- "'It doesn't really matter,' or . . . 'One more time won't make a difference.'"[19]
- "God is hard to reach."[20]

Elder Jeffrey R. Holland noted one of Satan's most cunning and insidious lies:

> If there is one lament I cannot abide—and I hear it from adults as well as students—it is the poor, pitiful, withered cry, "Well, that's just the way I am." . . . I've heard that from too many people who wanted to sin and call it psychology. And I use the word . . . to cover a vast range of habits, some seemingly innocent enough, which nevertheless bring discouragement and doubt and despair.[21]

Satan is also a slanderer and a false accuser. Slander is another form of lying, but in this case it takes the form of a personal attack on someone's character. Here are some examples of how he attempts to slander us so that we lose hope:

- You are a loser.
- How could anyone like someone such as yourself?
- You are not good enough to do that.
- You have gone too far down the path to change now.
- You are not perfect; therefore, you are failing.
- After what you've done, you are not worthy to approach God in prayer.
- Even though you were the victim of sexual abuse (or a sexual assault), you must have been partially responsible.
- God could not possibly love someone like you.

Often these kinds of comments can come from those around us who unwittingly serve as voice to Satan's lies. For example, I think of a woman, who after listening to the complaints of her best friend about her husband's behavior—and without ever hearing the husband's side of things—said, "You don't have to take that. Just divorce him."

If we are standing on firm ground, these accusations are mostly annoying little barbs which we try to ignore. They are not fatal, but they can wear us down. If they come when we are particularly vulnerable—which somehow Satan seems to be able to sense—then they become what the scriptures call the devil's "shafts in the whirlwind" (Helaman 5:12) or "the fiery darts of the adversary" (D&C 3:8). They can strike deep enough that they weaken our faith, drain our hope, and discourage us from taking positive action. This is especially effective because faith, hope, and charity are our three great navigational beacons on our spiritual journey back home. If we are not careful, the wounds inflicted by Satan fester and become toxic, bringing hopelessness, discouragement, disillusionment, and despair in their wake. And that, of course, is his desire.

## Satan Wants Us to Lose Hope

Hope is contrary to Satan's nature. When it is present, it thwarts his work. Hope is a gift of the Spirit—one that strengthens the heart and lifts the spirit—and is therefore a form of light and truth. It also leads to other gifts such as courage, patience, and endurance. But Satan cannot abide light and truth, because there is no truth in him.

Satan wants us to despair, because one of his driving motivations is to make all men as miserable and as filled with darkness as he is. He rejoices when we lose hope.

He understands perfectly that despair and discouragement weaken our faith. Tragedy, by itself, cannot weaken our faith, but with a little nudge from Satan, tragedy opens the door to these feelings.

He also understands perfectly that despair and hopelessness make us more vulnerable to temptation and sin by lowering the threshold of our resistance.

Satan understands something else about this mortal life that we sometimes forget. Trials, tragedy, adversity, and tribulation are all part of our mortal experience. If we meet such experiences with faith and hope, they help us grow and progress. Satan does not want us to grow.

## "O Remember, Remember"

In this book about hope, we have taken the opportunity to remind ourselves of him who opposes hope in any form, and who tries to strip it away from us. We have done so in order to remember that we are dealing with a being of endless cunning, a being of implacable purpose who labors tirelessly to bring our souls into captivity and to destroy the work of God.

Let us remember that there is no mercy in Satan, no softness, no fairness or justice. He thrives on misery and exults in the destruction of the human soul. He knows our soft spots, our weaknesses, our vulnerabilities, and he exploits them to the max. He always goes for the jugular, because his ultimate goal is our destruction. And when he gets us to do his will, his reward is to drag us down to misery and destruction, laughing in triumph as he does so (see Moses 7:26).

If we are to maintain hope, we must vigorously combat his insidious whisperings. We must stand up and respond with faith, and with hope in our hearts let us shout out: "These are lies. What you say is not true. Life is not hopeless. God has not forsaken me. I can be clean. I can be forgiven. He does hear my cries. He does love me. I can find power in Him to conquer. I can endure this suffering. This is not too hard for me to bear."

Let us also remember that hope is an abiding trust in the Lord's promises. Some of those promises have to do with Satan and his opposition. For example:

- "My wisdom is greater than the cunning of the devil" (D&C 10:43).
- "Pray always, . . . yea, that you may conquer Satan, and that you may escape the hands of the servants of Satan that do uphold his work" (D&C 10:5).
- "If God be for us, who can be against us?" (Romans 8:31).

Those are the promises. If we hold onto hope, keeping an abiding trust in those promises, then hope will help us see our way through this perilous, wonderful, difficult, marvelous, and endlessly fascinating journey we call mortality.

## Notes

1. Spencer W. Kimball, "How to Evaluate Your Performance (Part 1)," *Improvement Era,* October 1969, 12.

2. Merrill F. Unger, *The New Unger's Bible Dictionary* (Chicago: Moody Press, 1957), s.v. "Lucifer," 787.

3. LDS Bible Dictionary, s.v. "Lucifer," 726; emphasis in original.

4. Unger, *New Unger's Bible Dictionary,* s.v. "Perdition, Son of," 984.

5. William Wilson, *Old Testament Word Studies* (Grand Rapids, MI: Kregel Publications, 1978), 367; Unger, *The New Unger's Bible Dictionary,* s.v. "Satan," 1133.

6. Wilson, *Old Testament Word Studies,* 5.

7. Marvin R. Vincent, *Word Studies in the New Testament* (New York: Charles Scribner's Sons, 1901), 1:27.

8. Adam Clarke, *The New Testament of Our Lord and Saviour Jesus Christ: A Commentary,* 3 vols. (Tennessee: Abingdon, n.d.), 3:122.

9. See Unger, *New Unger's Bible Dictionary,* s.v. "Beelzebub," 151.

10. Brigham Young, *Discourses of Brigham Young,* comp. John A. Widtsoe (Salt Lake City: Deseret Book, 1978), 69.

11. Joseph Smith, *Teachings of Presidents of the Church: Joseph Smith* (Salt Lake City: The Church of Jesus Christ of Latter-day Saints, 2007), 214.

12. See College Kid, "Satan, Big Bad Wolf, Walls, and Jesus," 19 April 2011; http://belovedinspiration.wordpress.com/2011/04/19.

13. Marion G. Romney, *Look to God and Live: Discourses of Marion G. Romney,* comp. George J. Romney (Salt Lake City: Deseret Book, 1973), 8; see also Bruce R. McConkie, *Mormon Doctrine,* 2d ed. (Salt Lake City: Bookcraft, 1966), 714.

14. Boyd K. Packer, "Speaking Today: The Candle of the Lord," *Ensign,* January 1983, 55.

15. Mark E. Petersen, "Revelation," at the Convention of Teachers of Religion on the College Level, Brigham Young University, 24 August 1954, 3–4.

16. Dallin H. Oaks, "Be Not Deceived," *Ensign,* November 2004, 44.

17. Spencer W. Kimball, in Conference Report, October 1967, 30.

18. Ezra Taft Benson, *The Teachings of Ezra Taft Benson* (Salt Lake City: Bookcraft, 1988), 402.

19. M. Russell Ballard, *When Thou Art Converted: Continuing Our Search for Happiness* (Salt Lake City: Deseret Book, 2001), 32.

20. Henry B. Eyring, *To Draw Closer to God: A Collection of Discourses* (Salt Lake City: Deseret Book, 1997), 154.

21. Jeffrey R. Holland, "For Times of Trouble," in *1980 Devotional Speeches of the Year* (Provo, Utah: Brigham Young University Press, 1980), 42; emphasis in original.

# II

# The Need for Alignment

*Why were we then happy [in the premortal
existence]? I think it was because good had
triumphed over evil and the whole human family
was on the Lord's side. We turned our backs on
the adversary and aligned ourselves with the
forces of God, and those forces were victorious.*

*But having made that decision,
why should we have to make it again and again
after our birth into mortality?*

*I cannot understand why so many
have betrayed in life the decision they once made
when the great war occurred in heaven.*

Gordon B. Hinckley

*It is not . . . enough for us to be convinced
by the gospel; we must act and think
so that we are converted to it. In contrast
to the institutions of the world, which
teach us to know something, the gospel of
Jesus Christ challenges us to
become something. . . .*

*. . . The commandments, ordinances,
and covenants of the gospel are not a list
of deposits required to be made in some
heavenly account. The gospel of Jesus Christ
is a plan that shows us how to become
what our Heavenly Father desires us to become.*

❧❧❧

DALLIN H. OAKS

# CHAPTER SEVEN

# CONVERSION: ALIGNING OUR LIVES WITH GOD

I N THIS CHAPTER we begin a discussion on aligning ourselves with the Lord in order to get greater power in our lives so that we can have more of God's promises. This alignment creates greater hope, because when our lives are in harmony with His will, then the Spirit comes freely into our lives. Remember, hope is a gift of the Spirit, and greater hope is what we so urgently need in these difficult times in which we live.

## Alignment

The word *alignment* represents the state of someone or something being in line with someone or something else. *Alignment* is a noun; *align* is a verb. The dictionary gives several definitions for *align* or *alignment* which are relevant to our discussion:

- *"To arrange in a straight line."* I like that. We are to follow Christ as though we are directly behind Him, in line always with His teachings and His example. The world—and even some religions—would have us believe that we can be wandering all over the map—that we can pretty well do as we please—and still be following Him. The scriptures clearly teach that His path is "a strait and narrow" one (1 Nephi 8:20; see also Jacob 6:11; Matthew 7:13–14).

- *"To bring into cooperation or agreement with; to join with others in a cause."* Here the idea of alignment is harmony and unity. This requires an acceptance of what God asks of us. Only as we are in harmony with His will—only to the degree that our will is "swallowed up in the will of the Father" (Mosiah 15:7)—are we aligned with Him.

- *"The proper adjustment of the components of an electrical circuit, machine, etc., for coordinated functioning."* Though this technical definition may not seem to have application to us at first, think of it as being in tune, like having a radio receiver so perfectly aligned with the signal source that we can clearly receive whatever message is being transmitted.

Alignment with God involves each of these aspects. It is an alignment of our thoughts, our attitudes, our values, our motives, our choices, our actions, and our desires. When we bring these things into harmony with His will, then we become more like Him, which is our ultimate goal.

## Moving into Alignment

Before answering how we do that, let me share a statement by Thomas Jefferson. He was speaking of the tremendous influence that George Washington and Benjamin Franklin had during the drafting of the United States Constitution during the Constitutional Convention. Explaining why he felt they had been so influential, Jefferson said, "They laid their shoulders to the great points, knowing that the little ones would follow of themselves."[1] That concept carries significant implications. When it comes to bringing about change, some things matter more than others. If we can put those things in place, then other things will come along with them. I believe that is also true for drawing closer to God.

However, the very complexity of living the gospel can become its own problem. Those of us who desire to be more like the Father and the Son may become discouraged as we contemplate all of the commandments, requirements, and expectations. We may feel overwhelmed by how far short we have fallen of the mark. It is enough to cause us to lose heart and give up.

But we should never forget that we don't have to do this alone. We have the Spirit with all of its gifts. We can draw upon power from on high.

That's why I love the statement by Jefferson. When we focus on the fundamentals, other things will fall into line. Conversion is the first "great point" we shall examine, because it is the natural result of our having experiences with the Spirit.

"But wait," some of you may be saying, "I am already converted. I believe in God. I'm actively serving in the Church. I'm trying to do what is right."

True enough. But my response to that is twofold. First, we are reviewing the "great points" that are pivotal in our quest for hope. This review does not mean I am assuming my readers have not experienced conversion.

Second, conversion is not an either "you are or you are not" proposition. There are different levels of conversion. There were pioneers who were converted enough that they left their homes in Europe and came to America. But somewhere along the way, their commitment waned, their faith faltered, and they turned away.

This is happening today as well. Members who have been faithful and active in the Church for years suddenly begin to wonder whether it is all worth it, especially when life turns sour and things get rough. For others, they are still living the gospel, but as one stake president said, "The joy is gone."

I've pondered what he meant by that. I don't believe we're expected to have our lives be filled with nearly endless joy and happiness. We all have things that challenge us, or make life a drudgery at times. But have we lost sight of the joy of the gospel? Have we lost hope and decided that the life of discipleship is only another burden to be borne until we leave this life? If so, we need to renew our conversion, expand our vision, rekindle our faith, and rediscover the joy. We should all be asking ourselves, "Is my level of conversion deep enough to see me through whatever hard times I am going through now, or those that yet lie ahead?"

I believe all of us can sharpen our alignment with the Lord, like carefully adjusting the dial on a radio, or using a GPS device to find our way.

## Conversion: Mental Assent or Spiritual Conviction

Many years ago, while I was serving in a bishopric in Southern California, one of the Twelve came to preside at our stake conference. In the priesthood leadership meeting, he taught a concept very similar to what Thomas Jefferson said.

He asked the leaders of the stake if we were having problems with the numbers of marriages in our wards and stakes that were outside of the temple. Was the level of our home teaching not where we wanted it to be? Were too many of our young men not going on missions? Everyone was nodding, of course. Then he said, "Let me give you a solution for all of these problems. *Focus on seeing that your people are converted* and these other problems will also be reduced."[2]

President Gordon B. Hinckley spoke of conversion and said this:

*In the work of the Lord there is a more appropriate motivation than [external] pressure. There is the motivation that comes of true conversion.* When there throbs in the heart of an individual Latter-day Saint a great and vital testimony of the truth of this work, he will be found doing his duty in the Church. . . . *It is conversion that makes the difference.*[3]

There are many reasons why able young men don't go on missions, but the root problem is that they are not truly converted. Some members of the Church choose not to marry in the temple because they are not convinced that the promises of an eternal marriage are that significant. And some individuals are knocked off their bearings when tragedy strikes. In times such as these, we desperately need "a great and vital testimony" throbbing in our hearts. It is in the trials of life that conversion is tested to its limits.

Some years ago, my wife and I were in an informal setting where Elder M. Russell Ballard shared some counsel from President Gordon B. Hinckley.

There is concern that some people in the Church have mental but not spiritual conversion. The gospel appeals to them, but real conversion is when they *feel something in their hearts* and not just in their minds. *There is mental assent, but not spiritual conviction.* They must be touched by the power of the Holy Ghost, which creates a spiritual experience. The power and deep conversion of the Spirit is needed by our members to get into their hearts to confirm what they agreed to in their minds. *This will carry them through every storm of adversity.*

Then Elder Ballard concluded with this:

> The great task, the great challenge of the First Presidency and the Twelve is to *get the spirit of the gospel from people's minds into their hearts,* to where they have *spiritual experiences,* and *those spiritual experiences are enough that they change feelings,* they change our view of life.[4]

## "I've Been on Vacation from the Lord"

I am reminded of an experience I had many years ago. My wife was in the Young Women presidency in our ward, with responsibility for the fourteen- and fifteen-year-old girls. One night, she had about a dozen of them in our home working on a project. The children were in bed, and I was in an adjoining room, out of sight. They were unaware of my presence, but I could clearly hear what was going on.

I wasn't paying much attention until a snippet of conversation caught my ear. One of the girls asked a question: "So, Kristen, are you still dating Allen?" I was teaching seminary at that time, and we were emphasizing President Spencer W. Kimball's request that youth not date until they were sixteen. The conversation continued something like this:

Kristen: "We're not really dating."

Girl 1: "What do you mean you're not dating? You're with him almost every night."

Kristen: "Yes, but we don't go on *formal* dates."

Girl 2: "So what do you do?"

Kristen: "I go over to his house. Sometimes we go to a movie."

**Girl 1:** "And that's not dating? How do your parents feel about this?"

**Kristen:** "Oh, they don't know. They don't like me spending that much time with him."

**Girl 3:** "They don't know? How can they not know?"

**Kristen (sheepishly):** "I tell them that I'm doing homework with one of you, or sleeping over at your house. Or something like that."

**Girl 1:** "So you lie to them?"

**Kristen (defensive now):** "Not really. I did come and sleep at your house last Friday after Allen and I had been together. And I do a little homework before I see him."

The conversation broke off then. I thought about what Kristen had said. I was a little surprised because I knew her family well, and they were a strong, active family. But then, this wasn't some shocking revelation of deep sin. I had been around youth enough to know this kind of thing was not unusual. The moment passed, and I quickly forgot about the conversation.

A few weeks later, in a fast and testimony meeting, Kristen came up to the pulpit. As I watched her walk forward, I was curious about what she would say. It was a sweet and humble testimony, said with great fervor—and tears—as she ended. Her expressions included things like this: "I love my Heavenly Father and Jesus. I know that President Spencer W. Kimball is a true prophet. I love my mother and father." I didn't detect any pretense in her words. She seemed sincere and genuinely touched. But as she spoke, the conversation I had heard a few nights earlier came back to my mind. It seemed to me there was some degree of disconnect between what she was saying now and what I had heard then.

A short time later in that same meeting, a sudden hush came over the congregation. A young man in his early twenties was coming forward from the very back of the hall. The hush came because of his appearance. It was definitely not the traditional dress seen in sacrament meetings. He wore Levis and tennis shoes—without socks—and a T-shirt. He had a scraggly beard. His hair was full and long enough that it was braided in a ponytail down his back. As he came forward, every eye was on him.

What happened next was almost stunning. He came to the pulpit and gripped it tightly with both hands. His head was down, and he stood there, rigid as a fence post, for several moments. Then his head came up and he looked out at us. "I have been on a vacation from the Lord," he said in a low voice. His head dropped again. His whisper was barely audible. "And I've missed Him." Head up again, stronger now. "And I want to come back." He turned and looked at the bishop. "Bishop," he said, "I'll be in to see you." And with that he walked back to his seat.

Several months later he was back at that same pulpit—hair cut short, dressed in a suit and tie—where he gave his farewell address before leaving on a mission.

## Spiritual Experiences and True Conversion

The point I'm making is not really about Kristen. I don't believe she was in a state of deep apostasy at that point. She was not yet sixteen and was still learning and growing. She probably went on to be married in the temple, raise her own family, and is now a grandmother somewhere. If she happens to read this story, I'm guessing she won't even recognize that it is about her at all.

But the contrast between her and the young man that day was startling. Outwardly, all seemed to be in order with her, yet there was a disconnect between what she believed and what she was doing.

Clearly she had mental assent, but it hadn't touched her deeply enough to bring obedience to what she knew was right. On the other hand, the young man outwardly appeared to be far from the Lord. Yet something had happened deep in his heart that impelled him to want to bring his life back in alignment with the Lord.

So which of the two was truly converted?

President Gordon B. Hinckley not only described what true conversion is (or is not), he also described the *process* which brings it about. Note again what he and Elder Ballard said: "They must be touched by the power of the Holy Ghost, which creates a spiritual experience." The problem is "to get the spirit of the gospel from people's minds into their hearts, to where they have spiritual experiences, and those spiritual experiences are enough that they change feelings, they change our view of life."[5] That's the process. Here is a diagram so we can see more clearly how it works.

1. HOLY GHOST → 2. SPIRITUAL EXPERIENCES → 3. TRUE CONVERSION → 4. LIVE THE GOSPEL → 5. GAIN ETERNAL LIFE

Following the process backward helps us see how one thing leads to the next. Our ultimate goal is eternal life (5). To achieve that goal, we must live the gospel so we will "do our duty" and all that that implies (4). The motivation to live the gospel comes from true conversion, a conversion of the heart and not just the head. And what leads to true conversion (3)? According to President Hinckley, it is spiritual experiences (2). Spiritual experiences provide the confirming witness that strengthens faith and deepens hope, and also leads us to act as God would have us act. Finally, spiritual experiences come from receiving some form of revelation from the Holy Ghost (1).

It is feeling the influence of the Holy Ghost and receiving the gifts He has for us that helps us move from intellectual assent to emotional and spiritual commitment. Elder Dallin H. Oaks said that true conversion was in and of itself a spiritual experience: "A true conversion is a spiritual experience based on the individual communication of the Spirit."[6]

## Peter Neilson

Elder Jeffrey R. Holland shared a little-known story of an early pioneer who exemplified this quiet determination to do one's duty.

> I attended church [as a boy] in the grand old St. George Tabernacle. . . . During very lengthy sermons I would amuse myself by . . . counting the window panes—2,244 of them—because I grew up on the story of Peter Neilson. . . .
>
> In the course of constructing that tabernacle, the local brethren ordered the glass for the windows from New York and had it shipped around the cape [of South America] to California. But a bill of $800 was due and payable before the panes could be picked up and delivered to St. George. . . . After painstaking effort, the entire community, giving virtually everything they had to these two monumental building projects, had been able to come up with only $200 cash. On sheer faith Brother Cannon [who was in charge of raising the funds] committed a team of freighters to prepare to leave for California to get the glass. He continued to pray that the enormous balance of $600 would somehow be forthcoming before their departure.
>
> Living in nearby Washington, Utah, was Peter Neilson, a Danish immigrant who had been saving for years to add on to his modest two-room adobe home. On the eve of the freighters' departure for California, Peter spent a sleepless

night in that tiny little house. He thought of his conversion in far-off Denmark and his subsequent gathering with the Saints in America. . . . As he lay in bed that night contemplating his years in the Church, he weighed the sacrifices asked of him against the wonderful blessings he had received. Somewhere in those private hours he made a decision.

Some say it was a dream, others say an impression, still others simply a call to duty. However the direction came, Peter Neilson arose before dawn on the morning the teams were to leave for California. With only a candle and the light of the gospel to aid him, Peter brought out of a secret hiding place $600 in gold coins. . . . His wife, Karen, aroused by the predawn bustling, asked why he was up so early. He said only that he had to walk quickly the seven miles to St. George.

As the first light of morning fell on the beautiful red cliffs of southern Utah, a knock came at David H. Cannon's door. There stood Peter Neilson, holding a red bandanna which sagged under the weight it carried. "Good morning, David," said Peter. "I hope I am not too late. You will know what to do with this money."

With that he turned on his heel and retraced his steps back to Washington, back to a faithful and unquestioning wife, and back to a small two-room adobe house that remained just two rooms for the rest of his life.[7]

Note that he considered "the wonderful blessings he had received." That's another way of saying that he had been truly converted by the spiritual confirmations he had received.

If spiritual experiences are what lead us to that kind of conversion, the next question becomes: How do we get our own spiritual experiences? Elder Richard G. Scott gave this very specific answer to that question:

> Stated simply, true conversion is the *fruit* of *faith, repentance,* and *consistent obedience. Faith* comes by hearing the word of God and responding to it. You will receive from the Holy Ghost a confirming witness of things you accept on *faith* by willingly doing them. You will be led to *repent* of errors resulting from wrong things done or right things not done. As a consequence, your capacity to *consistently obey* will be strengthened. This cycle of *faith, repentance,* and *consistent obedience* will lead you to greater conversion with its attendant blessings. *True conversion will strengthen your capacity to do what you know you should do, when you should do it, regardless of the circumstances.*[8]

A few months ago, I would have said, "Spiritual experiences come from faith." Now, I would amend that in this important way: "Spiritual experiences are the direct result of faith, *hope,* and charity working together in perfect harmony with each other."

Conversion is one of the "great points" that will strengthen the bridges of our lives, lift up our heads when they hang down, and help us navigate our way through this life. It is one of the surest ways to achieve alignment. And if we make that alignment, so many other things will follow naturally.

However, we must not think that true conversion is some kind of self-improvement formula that, if we fulfill each step in proper sequence, will mean we are converted. True conversion is a gift of the Spirit. It is a "mighty change in us, or in our hearts, that we have no more disposition to do evil, but to do good continually" (Mosiah 5:2).

## Notes

*Part II Epigraph.* Gordon B. Hinckley, "The Dawning of a Brighter Day" *Ensign,* May 2004, 81.

*Chapter 7 Epigraph.* Dallin H. Oaks, *With Full Purpose of Heart* (Salt Lake City: Deseret Book, 2002), 37–38; emphasis in original.

1. Thomas Jefferson, quoted in *Three Centuries of American Poetry and Prose,* ed. Alphonso G. Newcomer, Alice E. Andrews, and Howard J. Hall (Chicago: Scott, Foresman and Company, 1917), 170.

2. From the author's personal notes.

3. Gordon B. Hinckley, Regional Representatives' seminar, 6 April 1984; as cited by Mack M. Lawrence, "Conversion and Commitment," *Ensign,* May 1996, 75; emphasis in original.

4. Transcribed by the author from a recording made of M. Russell Ballard speaking to a group gathered at Martin's Cove, Wyoming, 11 July 2001. The transcript was approved by Elder M. Russell Ballard and is used with his permission.

5. Ibid.

6. Dallin H. Oaks, *The Lord's Way* (Salt Lake City: Deseret Book, 1991), 88.

7. Jeffrey R. Holland, "As Doves to our Windows," *Ensign,* May 2000, 76.

8. Richard G. Scott, "Full Conversion Brings Happiness," *Ensign,* May 2002, 25; emphasis in original and added.

# CONVERSION AND DOING ONE'S DUTY

HERE ARE TWO other examples of individuals whose lives exemplified the concept of true conversion, which then led to their "doing their duty,"[1] as President Gordon B. Hinckley said. The first was related by President Dieter F. Uchtdorf in the October 2008 general conference. The second was shared by President Henry B. Eyring about his father.

## John Rowe Moyle

This year marks the 200th anniversary of the birth of John Rowe Moyle. John was a convert to the Church who left his home in England and traveled to the Salt Lake Valley as part of a handcart company. He built a home for his family in a small town a valley away from Salt Lake City [Alpine, Utah]. John was an accomplished stonecutter and, because of this skill, was asked to work on the Salt Lake Temple.

Every Monday John left home at two o'clock in the morning and walked six hours in order to be at his post on time. On Friday he would leave his work at five o'clock in the evening and walk almost until midnight before arriving home. He did this year after year.

One day, while he was doing his chores at home, a cow kicked him in the leg, causing a compound fracture. With limited medical resources, the only option was to amputate the broken leg. So John's family and friends strapped him onto a door and, with a bucksaw, cut off his leg a few inches from the knee.

In spite of the crude surgery, the leg started to heal. Once John could sit up in bed, he began carving a wooden leg with an ingenious joint that served as an ankle to an artificial foot. Walking on this device was extremely painful, but John did not give up, building up his endurance until he could make the 22-mile . . . journey to the Salt Lake Temple each week, where he continued his work.

His hands carved the words "Holiness to the Lord" that stand today as a golden marker to all who visit the Salt Lake Temple.[2]

## Waiting on the Lord

I want to tell you a story about waiting on the Lord. My father once told it to me with the intention of chuckling at himself. It's a story about his trying to do his duty, just the way you try to do your duty.

Now, you have to know a little bit about my father. His name was Henry Eyring, like mine. His work in chemistry was substantial enough to bring him many honors, but he was still a member of a ward of the Church with his duty to do. To appreciate this story, you have to realize that it occurred when he was nearly eighty and had bone cancer. He had bone cancer so badly in his hips that he could hardly move. The pain was great.

Dad was the senior high councilor in his stake, and he had the responsibility for the welfare farm. An assignment was given to weed a field of onions, so Dad assigned himself to go work on the farm. He never told me how hard it was, but I have met several people who were with him that day. I talked to one of them on the phone, and he said that he was weeding in the row next to Dad through much of the day. He told me the same thing that others who were there that day have told me. He said that the pain was so great that Dad was pulling himself along on his stomach with his elbows. He couldn't kneel. The pain was too great for him to kneel. Everyone who has talked to me about that day has remarked how Dad smiled and laughed and talked happily with them as they worked in that field of onions.

Now, this is the joke Dad told me on himself afterward. He said he was there at the end of the day. After all the work was finished and the onions were all weeded, someone said to him, "Henry, good heavens! You didn't pull those weeds, did you? Those weeds were sprayed two days ago, and they were going to die anyway."

Dad just roared. He thought that was the funniest thing. He thought it was a great joke on himself. He had worked through the day in the wrong weeds. They had been sprayed and would have died anyway.

When Dad told me this story, I knew how tough it was. So I asked him, "Dad, how could you make a joke out of that? How could you take it so pleasantly?" He said something to me that I will never forget, and I hope you won't. He said, "Hal, I wasn't there for the weeds."

Now, you'll be in an onion patch much of your life. So will I. It will be hard to see the powers of heaven magnifying us or our efforts. It may even be hard to see our work being of any value at all. And sometimes our work won't go well.

But you didn't come for the weeds. You came for the Savior. And if you pray, and if you choose to be clean, and if you choose to follow God's servants, you will be able to work and wait long enough to bring down the powers of heaven.

I was with Dad in the White House in Washington, D.C., the morning he got the National Medal of Science from the president of the United States. I missed the days when he got all the other medals and prizes. But, oh, how I'd like to be with him on the morning he gets the prize he won for his days in the onion patches. He was there to wait on the Lord. And you and I can do that, too.[3]

---

## Notes

1. Gordon B. Hinckley, Regional Representatives' seminar, 6 April 1984; as cited by Mack M. Lawrence, "Conversion and Commitment," *Ensign*, May 1996, 75.

2. Dieter F. Uchtdorf, "Lift Where You Stand," *Ensign*, November 2008, 55.

3. Henry B. Eyring, *To Draw Closer to God: A Collection of Discourses by Henry B. Eyring* (Salt Lake City: Deseret Book, 1997), 101–2.

*Every foundation stone that is laid
for a Temple, and every Temple completed
according to the order the Lord has revealed for
His holy priesthood, lessens the power of Satan
on the earth, and increases the power of God and
Godliness, moves the heavens in mighty power in
our behalf, invokes and calls down upon us the
blessings of the Eternal Gods, and those who
reside in their presence.*

GEORGE Q. CANNON

CHAPTER EIGHT

# ENDOWED WITH
# POWER FROM ON HIGH

❧

### Blessings for This Life

MANY YEARS AGO, I was with a group of Church Educational System teachers for an in-service training meeting. One of the Seventy had been invited to speak to us. He spoke about the temple. His introductory comment has stuck with me over the years. He said, "Usually when we talk about the blessings of the temple, we speak of the eternal blessings that come from temple work, both for the dead and for ourselves. Today, I am going to speak only about the blessings of the temple *in this life.*"[1]

My first reaction was that it would be a short talk. I was wrong. It opened up new perspectives for me that I have never forgotten.

I'm not suggesting that the blessings of creating eternal families and becoming "saviors on Mount Zion"[2] for the dead are less important. Rather, the focus for this chapter is about finding hope in *this life.*

I have come to understand that we can find much hope in the temple. President Harold B. Lee spoke of the "wealth of eternal riches" to be found in the temples, but then added, "The temple ceremonies are designed by a wise Heavenly Father who has revealed them to us in these last days *as a guide and a protection throughout our lives*."[3] Not just eternity. Throughout our lives.

It's a simple chain of reasoning. Our hope will be greatly strengthened as we bring our lives into closer alignment with the Lord. The temple and its ordinances provide a significant way for us to achieve that alignment. Therefore, the temple is a significant source of hope for us in *this life*. Here are some of the ways that hope can come to us now.

## Temple Ordinances and the Second Coming

In the last book of the Old Testament, the prophet Malachi asked these questions: "Who may abide the day of [Christ's] coming? and who shall stand when he appeareth?" (Malachi 3:2). It's not just who will *survive* the day, but who will *abide* the day. I like the word *abide*. It sounds so much more positive than just surviving. Malachi's questions take on added significance when we read his description of what that day will be like: "The day cometh, that shall burn as an oven; and all the proud, yea, and all that do wickedly, shall be stubble: and the day that cometh shall burn them up" (Malachi 4:1). Who wouldn't like to "abide" that experience?

The answer to the question comes directly from the Lord: "Behold, I will send you Elijah the prophet before the coming of the great and dreadful day of the Lord: and he shall turn the heart of the fathers to the children, and the heart of the children to their fathers, lest I come and smite the earth with a curse" (Malachi 4:5–6).

By the time of Malachi, Elijah had been dead for several centuries. Why would the Lord send him back? And how is his return tied to the Second Coming? This is not the place for a full discussion of Elijah and the keys that he restored, but here are few statements that help us see that there are blessings for this life to be found in the temple.

- Elijah appeared, along with Moses and Elias, to Joseph Smith and Oliver Cowdery in the Kirtland Temple on April 3, 1836. The Lord then reaffirmed that "by this [i.e., by Elijah's coming] ye may know that the great and dreadful day of the Lord is near, even at the doors" (D&C 110:16).

- The Prophet Joseph explained that the word *turn* as used by Malachi "should be translated *bind,* or seal."[4]

- The Prophet also said: "The spirit, power, and calling of Elijah is, that ye have power to hold the key of the revelation, ordinances, oracles, powers and *endowments* of the fullness of the Melchizedek Priesthood and of the kingdom of God on the earth."[5]

Conclusion: Elijah came back to earth to restore the keys of the sealing power, which include power and authority to institute temple ordinances.

Why is that important? An obvious answer is that it is in the temple where we seal husbands, wives, and children together into eternal family units. But that's not all. There is another promise of great value as well.

Joseph Smith gave us more information on why Elijah's return is important to us. In the dedicatory prayer for the Kirtland Temple—which the Prophet said was given to him by revelation[6]—we find these words:

> Let the *anointing* of thy ministers be *sealed* upon them with power from on high. . . .
>
> . . . And prepare the hearts of thy saints for all those judgments thou art about to send . . . *that thy people may not faint in the day of trouble.* . . .
>
> We know that thou hast spoken by the mouth of thy

prophets terrible things concerning the wicked, in the last days—that thou wilt pour out thy judgments, without measure;

Therefore, O Lord, deliver thy people from the calamity of the wicked; enable thy servants to *seal* up the law, and bind up the testimony, *that they may be prepared against the day of burning.* (D&C 109:35, 38, 45–46)

Joseph Smith also said the following four statements:

In the days of Noah, God destroyed the world by a flood, and He has promised to destroy it by fire in the last days: but before it should take place, Elijah should first come and turn the hearts of the fathers to the children.[7]

How shall God come to the rescue of this generation? He will send Elijah the prophet. . . . Elijah shall reveal the covenants to *seal* the hearts of the fathers to the children, and the children to the fathers.[8]

Four destroying angels [hold] power over the four quarters of the earth until the servants of God are *sealed* . . . , which signifies *sealing* the blessing upon their heads, meaning the everlasting covenant.[9]

The Saints have not too much time to save and redeem their dead, and gather together their living relatives, that they may be saved also, before the earth will be smitten, and the consumption decreed falls upon the world.

I would advise all the Saints to go with their might . . . that they may be *sealed and saved,* that they may be prepared against the day that the destroying angel goes forth.[10]

Here is a blessing we don't often speak about. We don't know exactly what it means, or how it will be done, but there is *a direct and clear promise of divine help and protection* in these latter days for those who partake of the blessings of the temple.

The endowment is another blessing, and one that may help us understand how the protection comes.

## An Endowment of Power

One of the central ordinances of the temple is called the endowment. It is a word with special meaning for Latter-day Saints, but the word is not unique to the temple. Its basic meaning is a gift, but "gift" doesn't capture its fullest meaning. An endowment is a gift that provides continuing benefits to the receiver long after it is given. We often hear of a wealthy person giving an endowment to a university or endowing a trust fund. The word *dowry* comes from the same root. A woman's dowry is meant to bless the marriage for many years to come. Thus, an endowment is truly "the gift that keeps on giving."

Over the years, I have asked groups of endowed members this question: "If endowment means a gift, what gift are we given in the temple endowment?" I am not surprised that many seem puzzled by the question and are not sure how to answer it. I didn't understand it for many years.

The scriptures make it clear what that gift is: "Ye are to be taught from on high. Sanctify yourselves and ye shall be *endowed with power*" (D&C 43:16), "power from on high" (D&C 38:32, 38; 105:11). Truly, the blessing of power from heaven is of great worth to us in this life.

Joseph Smith once said, "You need an endowment, brethren, in order that you may be prepared and able to overcome all things."[11] Notice that he says we can overcome "all things." What are some of the things that require God's power to overcome?

Before we answer that, let's note something else about the endowment.

Elder John A. Widtsoe called the endowment "the story of man's eternal journey."[12] President Gordon B. Hinckley referred to the endowment as "the odyssey of man's eternal journey from premortal existence through this life to the life beyond."[13] There's an important clue for us in those statements. In the endowment, we are taught about our eternal journey. We are taught how to receive and utilize power from on high so we can make that journey safely and return to God's presence.

Currently we are living the mortal part of that journey. We have already discussed how dangerous it is. Satan is in our midst, working hard to destroy us. We live amid crime, violence, war, disease, evil, natural disasters, and many other dangers. That is why we need this gift of power from on high. We need power to resist Satan. We need power to overcome temptation. We need strength to endure adversity, suffering, and tribulation. We need help from a higher power to overcome doubt, discouragement, distress, depression, and despair. We need power to overcome death. We need divine help to be perfected.

Elder Russell M. Nelson spoke of the power we receive through making and keeping covenants as "both *protective* and *enabling*."[14] And Brigham Young actually used the word *enable* in his definition of the endowment:

> Your endowment is, to receive all those ordinances in the house of the Lord, which are necessary for you, after you have departed this life, to *enable* you to walk back to the presence of the Father, passing the angels who stand as sentinels, being *enabled* to give them the key words, the signs and tokens,

pertaining to the holy Priesthood, and gain your eternal exaltation in spite of earth and hell.[15]

We are not talking about power in some metaphorical sense. We are talking about a very real protective and enabling power to which we can turn for help. Other prophets have described this power in greater detail:

*President Harold B. Lee.* The temple ceremonies are designed by a wise Heavenly Father who has revealed them to us in these last days as a guide and a *protection* throughout our lives that you and I might not fail of an exaltation in the Celestial kingdom where God and Christ dwell.[16]

*Elder John A. Widtsoe.* The men and women who have come with this power out of the Lord's holy house will be hedged about by divine protection and walk more safely among the perplexities of earth. . . . Spiritual power accompanies all who marry in the temple, if they thenceforth keep their sacred covenants.[17]

The Lord Himself made this promise:

This greater priesthood [of Melchizedek] . . . holdeth the key of the mysteries of the kingdom. . . .

Therefore, in the *ordinances thereof* [i.e., the temple ordinances], *the power of godliness is manifest.*

And without the ordinances thereof, and the authority of the priesthood, the power of godliness is not manifest unto men in the flesh. (D&C 84:19–21)

If these promises do not fill our hearts with greater hope, then I don't know what can.

## A House of Prayer, Learning, and Order

In one of the early revelations on temples, the Lord described His temple as "a house of prayer, a house of fasting, a house of faith, a house of learning, a house of glory, a house of order, a house of God" (D&C 88:119). Need an additional motivation to go to the temple? Just look at that list and consider the implications of each of those.

Let's briefly explore some of them in greater detail.

*"A house of prayer."* One of the blessings for temple worthy, endowed members is the privilege of going to the temple when we are seeking answers to questions, or solutions to problems. In the quiet and holy sanctity of the temple, we can get away from the noise and hectic rush of the world and become more sensitive to the promptings of the Spirit. If we come in a spirit of seeking—as many do—we can be taught both by the ordinances themselves and also by the Spirit in that quiet and sacred setting.

Elder John A. Widtsoe said:

> I believe that the busy person on the farm, in the shop, in the office, or in the household, who has his worries and troubles, can solve his problems better and more quickly in the house of the Lord than anywhere else. If he will leave his problems behind and in the temple work for himself and for his dead, he will confer a mighty blessing upon those who have gone before, and *quite as large a blessing will come to him,* for at the most unexpected moments, in or out of the temple will come to him, as a revelation, the solution of the problems that vex his life.[18]

*"A house of learning."* Diana Harman and her brother, Dan, of Twin Falls, Idaho, are two people who can testify that the temple is a house of revelation. Diana had a bright future when she graduated

from high school in 1968. She had received a four-year scholarship to BYU. Then suddenly her kidneys failed. In the sixties, treatment for kidney disease was far behind where it is now.

Diana became critically ill. She lost weight as her kidneys failed. She was given massive doses of steroids, and her body became bloated with fluids even as she began to lose muscle mass. "They sent me home to die," she said. This became a difficult time emotionally as well as physically for her. During this time, her parents were not active in the Church, so Diana turned to her brother, Dan, for comfort. After he returned home from his mission, they grew close, and he gave her numerous priesthood blessings. Diana is convinced those blessings kept her alive.

They tried dialysis for a time. It helped, but only marginally. "I was very ill," Diana remembers. "I got down to 85 pounds. I was anemic. I had bone disease. I had congestive heart failure. I was wasting away. I realized this was not the answer."

Sometime later, the doctors recommended a kidney transplant, a procedure that was still somewhat controversial at the time. It came with a lot of risk, and many people felt it was morally wrong. Dan and Diana wondered if this was what she should do. It was a very difficult decision.

Here's what happened next:

> Dan fasted and took the matter to the temple. He received a spiritual experience* confirming the choice for a transplant. He was [also] impressed to suggest to Diana's bishop that she receive her endowment. The speed with which the suggestion was approved surprised him: in a week,

---

\* In chapter 7, we read that President Gordon B. Hinckley taught that spiritual experiences lead to true conversion. Here we see a good example of how that works.

she was endowed. She credits her endowment with providing the spiritual insight and strength for the blessings which were to come. . . .

The night before the surgery, Diana received a priesthood blessing from Dan that confirmed this, saying simply, "This is what the Lord wants and this will work.

"It wasn't that we believed the Lord could; it was that *we knew* He would." . . .

. . . The organs were a perfect match. Not long after the last stitch was in place, Diana's blood cleared up permanently. She regained her health. And her sense of the future. Returning to BYU, she received her bachelor's degree in dietetics in three years, graduating as co-valedictorian. She went on for a master's degree in nutritional science and began a career teaching. That was interrupted by marriage and children. She and William McGuire, a young attorney . . . were married. After their five children were born—all delivered by cesarean section—she was the subject of an article in a medical journal for having the most children of a kidney transplant patient.[19]

It is significant that Dan went to the temple seeking to know if Diana should have a transplant. He got the answer, but he was also told that Diana needed to be endowed. What followed thereafter is evidence of the additional measure of spiritual power she received.

*"A house of order."* For those of us who live in modern, industrialized, technology-rich, opportunity-laden societies, our lives are typically hectic and filled with stress. There are so many demands on our time. There are so many wonderful opportunities for us and our families, all of which impact our time and complicate our lives. There are so many good choices available to us that it can make choosing

the best ones a serious challenge. How do we know where to put our time and how to best spend our resources?

The Lord has declared: "My house is a house of order" (D&C 132:18). Could it be otherwise? I find it hard to picture God as running about hither and thither, trying to keep His priorities straight, breathlessly trying to fit everything in, clutter all around Him, falling exhausted into bed at the end of the day wondering if He got everything done. Order is one of God's divine attributes.

This also applies to His temples; they are houses of order. This is true in at least two ways. Temple presidents go to great lengths to see that things are orderly and organized for the patrons. No detail is overlooked to make sure things are carefully scheduled, confusion is eliminated, and order is maintained.

But I believe there is another way that temples are houses of order. In the covenants we make as part of the temple ordinances, we are taught how to achieve order in our lives. We are taught which things in life matter most and which things can bring us sorrow. In the temples—because they are houses of learning—we can receive specific revelation on how to order our lives—what to emphasize, and what we can let go of. In the temples we can be shown how to prioritize the "good, better, and best" things in our lives.[20] The temple is a house of order and therefore also a source of hope.

## The Temple Garment

Much of what happens in the temple ordinances is taught with symbols. An excellent example of this is the temple garment. It is a tangible symbol of the promise of power and protection. The *Encyclopedia of Mormonism* has this to say about the temple garment:

> The white garment symbolizes purity and helps assure modesty, respect for the attributes of God, and, to the

degree it is honored, *a token of what Paul regarded as taking upon one the whole armor of God* (Eph. 6:13; cf. D&C 27:15). It is an outward expression of an inward covenant, and symbolizes Christlike attributes in one's mission in life. Garments bear several simple marks of orientation toward the gospel principles of obedience, truth, life, and discipleship in Christ.[21]

In an article on temple blessings, Elder Russell M. Nelson recommended reviewing another article on the temple garment written by Elder Carlos E. Asay of the Seventy.[22] With that endorsement, and due to the sacred nature of this topic, I include excerpts from Elder Asay's article without further comment:

> We are at war! . . . We are engaged in a life-and-death struggle with forces capable of thrashing us inside out and sending us down into the depths of spiritual defeat if we are not vigilant. . . .
>
> There is, however, [a] *piece of armor* worthy of our consideration. It is the special underclothing known as the temple garment, or garment of the holy priesthood, worn by members of The Church of Jesus Christ of Latter-day Saints who have received their temple endowment. This garment, worn day and night, serves three important purposes: it is a reminder of the sacred covenants made with the Lord in His holy house, a *protective covering* for the body, and a symbol of the modesty of dress and living that should characterize the lives of all the humble followers of Christ. . . .
>
> . . . The real battles of life in our modern day will be won by those who are clad in a spiritual armor—an armor consisting of faith in God, faith in self, faith in one's cause, and faith in one's leaders. The piece of armor called the temple garment

not only provides the comfort and warmth of a cloth covering, it also strengthens the wearer to resist temptation, fend off evil influences, and stand firmly for the right. . . .

I fear that too many Church members take for granted the promise of protection and blessings associated with the temple garment. Some wear it improperly, and others remove it to suit whims of circumstance. In such cases, the instructions of modern prophets, seers, and revelators are ignored and spiritual protection placed in jeopardy.

In a letter from the First Presidency dated 3 July 1974 [which has since been renewed and sent out again], Church members were reminded of the sacred nature of the garment: "The sacredness of the garment should be ever present and uppermost in the wearer's mind; . . . *the blessings which flow from the observance of our covenants* are sufficiently great to recompense for any mere inconvenience. To break our covenants is to forfeit the protection and blessings promised for obedience to them."[23]

## Blessings of a Temple Marriage

At the laying of the cornerstone for the Atlanta Georgia Temple, President Ezra Taft Benson shared yet another way in which the endowment brings power into our lives and increases our hope:

There is a power associated with the ordinances of heaven—even the power of godliness—which can and will thwart the forces of evil if we will be worthy of those sacred blessings. This community will be protected, *our families will be protected, our children will be safeguarded* as we live the gospel, visit the temple, and live close to the Lord.[24]

Again I affirm that this is not speaking of power as an abstract metaphor. And I believe strongly that the promised endowment of spiritual power extends to our marriage as well. I believe there is a measure of protection, enlightenment, and other spiritual blessings that "distill[s] upon [our souls] as the dews of heaven" (D&C 121:45) when we are faithful to our covenants.

I'm not suggesting that if a couple marry in the temple all will be well with them forever after, nor am I saying that without a temple marriage there is no hope for happiness. But when a couple is sealed in the temple and remain faithful, they can call down promised blessings upon their marriage.

Here is another blessing related to our families. Joseph Smith said, "When a seal is put upon the father and mother, it secures their posterity, so that they cannot be lost, but will be saved by virtue of the covenant of their father and mother."[25] That is a remarkable statement and takes on deeply poignant significance for parents who have seen their children do as Lehi saw in his vision of the tree of life: "They fell away into forbidden paths and were lost" (1 Nephi 8:28).

This concept raises many questions in our minds: "Is this true even if a child has sinned gravely?" "How is it possible that he or she won't be punished?" "When will this occur?" "Doesn't this, to some degree, do away with the justice of God?" "If men cannot be punished for someone else's sins, how can they be rewarded for someone else's goodness?"

I don't know the answers to those questions, and I'm not sure that we can fully comprehend the implications of the Prophet's statement. For example, what did the Prophet mean by "lost"? By "secures their posterity"? By the word "saved"? He doesn't say. But this is not an isolated doctrine taught only by Joseph Smith. Others of those whom we sustain as prophets, seers, and revelators have spoken in similar fashion over the years. I share their statements without further comment, leaving the reader to contemplate what they mean:

*President Lorenzo Snow.* You that are mourning about your children straying away will have your sons and your daughters. If you succeed in passing through these trials and afflictions and receive a resurrection, you will, by the power of the Priesthood, work and labor, as the Son of God has, until you get all your sons and daughters in the path of exaltation and glory. . . . Inasmuch as we succeed in securing eternal glory, and stand as saviors, and as kings and priests to our God, we will save our posterity.[26]

*Elder Orson F. Whitney.* You parents of the willful and the wayward! Don't give them up. Don't cast them off. They are not utterly lost. The Shepherd will find his sheep. They were his before they were yours—long before he entrusted them to your care; and you cannot begin to love them as he loves them. . . . Our Heavenly Father is far more merciful, infinitely more charitable, than even the best of his servants, and the Everlasting Gospel is mightier in power to save than our narrow finite minds can comprehend. . . .

The Prophet Joseph Smith declared—and he never taught more comforting doctrine—that the eternal sealings of faithful parents and the divine promises made to them for valiant service in the Cause of Truth, would save not only themselves, but likewise their posterity. . . . They will have to pay their debt to justice; they will suffer for their sins; and may tread a thorny path; but if it leads them at last, like the penitent Prodigal, to a loving and forgiving father's heart and home, the painful experience will not have been in vain. Pray for your careless and disobedient children; hold on to them with your faith. Hope on, trust on, till you see the salvation of God.[27]

***President Boyd K. Packer.*** The measure of our success as parents, however, will not rest solely on how our children turn out. That judgment would be just only if we could raise our families in a perfectly moral environment, and that now is not possible.

It is not uncommon for responsible parents to lose one of their children, for a time, to influences over which they have no control. They agonize over rebellious sons or daughters. They are puzzled over why they are so helpless when they have tried so hard to do what they should.

It is my conviction that those wicked influences one day will be overruled. [He then quotes Orson F. Whitney.]

We cannot overemphasize the value of temple marriage, the binding ties of the sealing ordinance, and the standards of worthiness required of them. When parents keep the covenants they have made at the altar of the temple, their children will be forever bound to them.[28]

***President James E. Faust.*** There are some great spiritual promises which may help faithful parents in this church. Children of eternal sealings may have visited upon them the divine promises made to their valiant forebears who nobly kept their covenants. Covenants remembered by parents will be remembered by God. The children may thus become the beneficiaries and inheritors of these great covenants and promises. This is because they are the children of the covenant. [Then he, too, cites Orson F. Whitney as a reference.][29]

## Unacceptable to the Lord

These are just some of the promises for this life found in the temple. I take great comfort in them, and find my hope lifted and strengthened by them. However, we have been reminded again and again that these promises are tied to our obedience, to whether or not we keep the covenants we make in the temple.

God has said that He will not be mocked (see Galatians 6:7; D&C 124:71). We enter into those covenants of our own free will and choice. If we then treat those covenants lightly or violate them, the consequences are serious and can bring a loss of the very power and blessings promised to us.

This is so important for us to remember that I would like to share an experience of the late Carlfred Broderick, a prominent LDS marriage and family therapist. Through him, the Lord rebuked a couple who had forgotten the covenants they had made. They weren't violating the law of chastity or in open apostasy, but their failure to honor their covenants with the Lord and to each other had resulted in a loss of spiritual power in their lives.

Brother Broderick was the priesthood leader of this couple, and they were also his good friends. He described them as "fine Latter-day Saints who loved the Lord." They came to him for counsel and also a priesthood blessing because their marriage of twenty years was on the verge of breaking up. In all that time, the wife had viewed her husband as "passive and resistant to her suggestions." The husband's strategy, when things started getting rough, was to "withdraw and leave her to handle things."

Both admitted that there was some truth to the accusations but told Broderick that they were "just too emotionally exhausted to cope with each other anymore." Recently, the husband had gotten himself in over his head financially in a business and was now in a crisis. Because he didn't have the energy to deal with his wife anymore, he moved in with a friend. The wife reported that she "had just about reached bottom and had even considered taking her own life."

Broderick said that normally his approach with people in pain was "to be empathetic and gentle and to help them feel accepted and understood." But in this case, he said, the Lord took the issue out of his hands.

> I was prompted by the Spirit to remind the couple that they were *not* released from their responsibility for the marriage because they were weary and discouraged. It was unacceptable to the Lord that they offer *any* excuse for not doing the things that they knew perfectly well they must do in order to make their marriage work. In the blessing that followed, I heard myself telling the husband that he was like a reluctant Jonah, attempting to flee from Nineveh. He was reminded that he had made no eternal covenants with his business associates or lawyers or bankers, but that before God and authoritative witnesses he had taken a most holy oath to be the husband of this woman and to shepherd her and his children born under that covenant back to the kingdom. He was told that in the Lord's eyes, this was by far his most serious stewardship. For this purpose he had come to this earth. His eternal salvation depended on his faithful fulfillment of that duty. His business was only a means of supporting his material needs, and the Lord would not abandon him in that if he gave priority to the things that deserved his full energy and commitment.[30]

Without realizing it, this couple had decided they could rewrite the requirements of their temple marriage, or be excused from them altogether. Thus, they lost power—in their marriage, in their business, and in their personal lives.

Brother Broderick does not say if the couple accepted his counsel or not, but one thing is clear. If they both decided to repent and earnestly strived to live by those covenants, the promise of power would return—in their marriage, in their business, and in their personal lives.

## A House of Hope

As we have seen, the Lord describes the temple as His house, and a house where there are many blessings to be had. It is a house of learning, a house of prayer, a house of glory, a house of order. In it, we find increased protection in these last days before the coming of the Son of Man. In it, we receive the ordinances and covenants that endow us with spiritual power and protection so needed in these perilous times in which we live. It is where we bring ourselves into closer alignment with God. It is a place of peace where we can put off the world and partake of the stillness (see D&C 101:16) that allows revelation to come more easily.

Because we find so many wonderful promises in the temple and the work done therein—both for this life and the life to come—and because hope is defined as trusting in the promises of the Lord, I believe we can also rightly consider the temple to be *a house of hope.* It is a place of refuge from the storms of life. It brings enlightenment when we struggle in the darkness. It brings clarity when all around us is confusion. It brings protection for us and our families in an increasingly dangerous world. It is the place where we create eternal family units—one of the fundamental reasons for coming to earth.

Truly there are many blessings of the temple promised for us in *this life* as well as for the next. Why wouldn't we turn our hearts toward the temple when we are struggling to find and maintain hope in times of difficulty, or even despair?

## Notes

*Epigraph.* George Q. Cannon, in "The Logan Temple," *Millennial Star,* 12 November 1877, 743; see also *Preparing to Enter the Holy Temple* (Salt Lake City: The Church of Jesus Christ of Latter-day Saints, 2002), 36.

1. Notes in possession of the author.

2. Joseph Smith, *Teachings of Presidents of the Church: Joseph Smith* (Salt Lake City: The Church of Jesus Christ of Latter-day Saints, 2007), 473.

3. Harold B. Lee, "Enter a Holy Temple," *Improvement Era,* June 1967, 144.

4. Smith, *Teachings of Presidents of the Church: Joseph Smith,* 472; emphasis in original.

5. Ibid., 311.

6. See heading to D&C 109.

7. Smith, *Teachings of Presidents of the Church: Joseph Smith,* 311.

8. Ibid., 313.

9. Joseph Smith, *Teachings of the Prophet Joseph Smith,* comp. Joseph Fielding Smith (Salt Lake City: Deseret Book, 1977), 321.

10. Smith, *Teachings of Presidents of the Church: Joseph Smith,* 473–74.

11. Smith, *Teachings of the Prophet Joseph Smith,* 91.

12. John A. Widtsoe, comp., *Priesthood and Church Government* (Salt Lake City: Deseret Book, 1962), 333.

13. Gordon B. Hinckley, *Teachings of Gordon B. Hinckley* (Salt Lake City: Deseret Book, 1997), 635.

14. Russell M. Nelson, "Prepare for Blessings of the Temple," *Ensign,* March 2002, 21.

15. Brigham Young, *Discourses of Brigham Young,* comp. John A. Widtsoe (Salt Lake City: Deseret Book, 1954), 416.

16. Harold B. Lee, *Decisions for Successful Living* (Salt Lake City: Deseret Book, 1973), 141.

17. John A. Widtsoe, *Evidences and Reconciliations,* ed. G. Homer Durham (Salt Lake City, Bookcraft, 1960), 300–301.

18. John A. Widtsoe, "Temple Worship," *The Utah Genealogical and Historical Magazine,* April 1921, 63–64.

19. John L. Hart, "A brother's gift," *Church News,* 16 September 2006, 11–12.

20. Dallin H. Oaks, "Good, Better, Best," *Ensign,* November 2007, 107.

21. "Garments," in *Encyclopedia of Mormonism,* ed. Daniel H. Ludlow (New York: MacMillan Publishing Co., 1992), 2:534.

22. See Nelson, "Prepare for Blessings of the Temple," 20.

23. Carlos E. Asay, "The Temple Garment: 'An Outward Expression of an Inward Commitment,'" *Ensign,* August 1997, 22.

24. Ezra Taft Benson, *The Teachings of Ezra Taft Benson* (Salt Lake City: Bookcraft, 1988), 256.

25. Smith, *Teachings of the Prophet Joseph Smith,* 321.

26. Lorenzo Snow, *The Teachings of Lorenzo Snow,* ed. Clyde J. Williams (Salt Lake City: Bookcraft, 1984), 195.

27. Orson F. Whitney, in Conference Report, April 1929, 110.

28. Boyd K. Packer, "Our Moral Environment," *Ensign,* May 1992, 68.

29. James E. Faust, "The Greatest Challenge in the World—Good Parenting," *Ensign,* November 1990, 35.

30. Carlfred Broderick, *One Flesh, One Heart: Putting Celestial Love into Your Temple Marriage* (Salt Lake City: Deseret Book, 1986), 16–17; emphasis in original.

*The word of the Lord is so clear to us,*
*and his laws so plainly designed for our happiness,*
*that it is difficult to understand why some people feel*
*their own judgment is superior, and disregard God's*
*laws and bring upon themselves misery and*
*unhappiness by so doing.*

N. ELDON TANNER

# Chapter Nine

# "Seek Not to Counsel Your God"

I N THIS SECTION, we are speaking about alignment. The premise we are trying to establish is this: Only as we bring our lives into closer alignment with God's will for us will we find sufficient hope to endure whatever challenges life may bring upon us. Our purpose in this chapter is to look at another aspect of alignment. At first glance, this concept may seem a trivial thing, but as we shall see, it can be a serious problem that can have a devastating effect on hope. Let us begin with a quick review of a concept taught earlier.

## There Is Divine Purpose in Suffering

In chapter 3, we briefly discussed why it "must needs be" (2 Nephi 2:11) that we live in a world of opposites where things which cause us sorrow and suffering permeate our existence. We concluded that not only was this necessary to our growth and learning, but was also required if we wanted to prove ourselves worthy to return to God's presence. Life with God before we were born did not provide that kind of environment. Neither did the Garden of Eden. Steel is forged in the fire, and gold is purged in the flame, and that is, it seems, part of the design.

Though short in duration compared to our premortal and post-mortal experiences, mortality may prove to be one of the most critical times in our entire existence. How we deal with the more difficult times of mortality is part of our testing process. The good times have their own kinds of challenges, but when life serves up intense pain or prolonged suffering, a very human response is to cry out, as much in frustration as in anguish, "Why, God? Why?" It is a good question. If He is all-powerful then why can't He remove the pain, solve the problem, send a cure, or deflect the danger? But such questions can trigger a crisis of faith and undermine the hope of even the strongest and most stalwart of believers.

## Counseling God

The prophet Jacob taught a principle in the Book of Mormon that captures the essence of a very human tendency. He said: "Wherefore, brethren, *seek not to counsel the Lord,* but to take counsel from his hand. For behold, ye yourselves know that he counseleth in wisdom, and in justice, and in great mercy, over all his works" (Jacob 4:10).

Perhaps our first reaction is to say, "But I would never seek to counsel God. I know better than that." But in reality, it happens all too frequently. This is understandable in a way. After all, who knows better than we do what we need and what is best for us? Who else can know so intimately and perfectly our inner longings, desires, and needs? And, by the way, it is our life, so shouldn't we have a say in what happens to us?

If we are not careful, this self-centered perspective can bring impatience with God. Why can't He see things our way? Why isn't He meeting our needs? Perhaps He needs some nudging to "bring Him around." This flawed perception seems to come easily to us, and even the most faithful can fall into the trap.

While these may be natural reactions to tribulation and adversity, when you think about it, by their very nature these ideas challenge the wisdom and judgment of God. We decide that He's not doing His duty, or that He doesn't care, or that maybe He's not there after all.

There are two things to say about this. First of all, this attitude, whether conscious or not, is a form of pride. It comes because we believe our wisdom and understanding is superior to God's. This can put us in grave spiritual danger because pride grieves the Spirit and distances us from the Lord. Some people are even bold enough to decide that if that's the way God's going to be, then we'll just "show Him." We'll stop praying to Him. We'll stop believing in Him. We may even decide to "get even" and convince others to reject Him as well. "That'll teach Him," we think.

The second point is that if bitterness and despair actually made things better, it would make more sense to give way to them, but they don't. They only worsen the situation. *Despair is not a solution.* Despair actually contributes to the problem. Despair is not only destructive to the spirit, but it can also profoundly affect both our mental and emotional state. It can even contribute to a worsening of our physical health.[1]

The bottom line is that we—finite, sinful, erring, imperfect, selfish beings, with limited vision, knowledge, power, and wisdom—undertake to tell God—an infinite, perfectly loving and caring Father with all power and all knowledge—how to do His business. This attitude represents such astonishing audacity and utter folly as to take one's breath away. And yet that is exactly what we do again and again. Sometimes this spiritual shortsightedness is shown in relatively harmless ways. Other times, it blinds our vision and may become a serious obstacle to our progress.

Here are three actual examples of how we can slip into the mode of seeking to counsel our God without realizing it. The first story is of a couple who had a deep faith and trust in God and who were trying to do God's will. Yet, without realizing it, they were also trying to tell the Lord what had to happen. In the other two situations, individuals were caught up in deep and trying circumstances, including great personal suffering. Here too, the Lord taught them a gentle lesson about His wisdom, His perfections, and His love.

## "We Have to Know by Friday"

While I was serving as a bishop, a couple came to me one Wednesday evening, looking for counsel about their current employment situation. They had been unemployed for a couple of months, but now two different companies had offered them employment in widely separated locations in the country. Since both jobs were nearly equal in salary, benefits, and potential job satisfaction, the couple decided that the determining factor for them would be to go where the Lord would like them to be. They began to fast and pray to know what to do. They had been seeking an answer for more than a week. But earlier that day, one company had called and said they needed a decision by four o'clock on Friday afternoon or the offer would be withdrawn.

The couple was frustrated. They were trying to do what God wanted them to do. So why couldn't they get an answer? The husband said to me, "Bishop, we've told the Lord that we have to know by Friday. *We have to!* What do we do?"

Remembering a principle I had been taught by a wise priesthood leader, I opened the Doctrine and Covenants. "Let me read you something the Lord has said about sending us revelation," I said. "'It shall be in his own time, and in his own way, and according to his own will' (D&C 88:68).

"The Lord may very well answer you before your deadline," I went on, "but don't be surprised if He ends up saying, 'No, you really don't have to know by Friday afternoon, and I'll prove that to you.'"

As it turned out, that's exactly what happened. No answer came, and the offer was withdrawn, much to the dismay of this couple. The decision was taken out of their hands. But by Sunday evening, a deep feeling of peace had come over both of them, and they knew that the other job was the one they were supposed to take.

"In his own time, and in his own way, and according to his own will" is a good lesson for all of us.

## "It's the Only Humane Thing to Do"

I knew a man who had begun to self-medicate with drugs and alcohol to try to ease the inner hell he was experiencing due to a long-term mental illness. He quickly became addicted, which only brought additional problems and suffering. He lost his job, and he was in and out of jail several times. He had his life threatened by drug dealers demanding payment. He tried suicide more than once and failed. When his mother made him promise that he would never try suicide again because it would absolutely devastate her, he reluctantly agreed to her wishes.

About this same time, his beloved dog was growing old and suffering with considerable pain. Finally, he had a veterinarian put the dog to sleep. That opened up a new line of reasoning for him. His thoughts turned to euthanasia. This led to almost an obsession with assisted suicide. He read articles on it, could name places where it was legal and experts who endorsed it. He talked about it all the time.

One day, after a particularly long and difficult stretch of adversity, he burst out in despair and said to one of his sisters, "I can't stand it anymore. I had the vet put my dog to sleep because I loved him too much to let him suffer. It's the only humane thing to do. So why won't my family let me be put out of my misery?"

In one of those instant flashes of inspiration, his sister quietly answered, "Because dogs can't learn from their suffering, and you can."

The truth of what she said resonated with him so strongly that he never spoke of euthanasia again with the family.

Now here's the lesson. Through the help of a loving family, a carefully balanced medication regimen, competent psychiatric and clinical counseling, and a lot of just "hanging in there," he gradually began to turn his life around. He's been off alcohol and drugs for nearly three years now. The other day he told his mother that he's happier than he's been in twenty-five years. How grateful he should be that the Lord didn't let him have his way. How many lessons would he have missed? What lessons did his parents and siblings who nurtured him back to normalcy learn about charity, and hope, and faith, and patience?

## Closets of the Mind

While I was in the midst of writing this book on hope, I received a letter out of the blue from a woman I did not know. (Some people might call it a coincidence, I like to call it a "divine signature.") Her name is Jelean Reynolds. She titled her letter "Closets of the Mind," which is also the title of a book she has written.

She told me that she had written her story for the *Ensign* many years before, which would give me some background on her life. She said that reading it would help me better understand what she wanted to share with me in her letter.

Here is an excerpt from that article which summarizes her situation:

The words "God can heal anything" seemed to jump back at me from the page as I read another faith-promoting story in the *Ensign*. My eyes welled up with tears, and bitterly I muttered to myself, as I had done a thousand times before, "Then why hasn't he healed me?"

I had been ill for ten years. The doctors were baffled. My

husband and I had spent thousands of dollars, seen many physicians, tried many prescribed medications.

Our families and our ward had fasted several times in my behalf. I had been administered to a number of times, and we had pleaded with the Lord to make me well. Still, relief had not come. . . .

. . . I was unable to function as a wife and mother. . . . Each day was a nightmare for me and a struggle for [my husband].

It was a test of my faith to learn to endure when relief did not come, when it seemed as though my prayers had not been answered.[2]

That was written in 1987, and the prayers that her illness be cured and removed from her have still not been answered. For thirty-five years—the greater portion of her life—she has lived with constant pain and suffering.

As we corresponded, she shared additional insights into her life and this lifetime learning process she has endured. One particular incident is a wonderful illustration of why we shouldn't seek to counsel God. I express my gratitude to Jelean for allowing me to share her story.

In daily prayer, our family supplicated Heavenly Father: "Please bless Mom to get better. And bless her that she will be able to have a baby." When I turned thirty-eight, I told my family that I was too sick and too old. "No more prayers for babies!" I insisted.

A short time later I unexpectedly became pregnant. I hid from our children the shock and panic I was feeling. Thirteen-year-old Bret explained, "I didn't stop praying for a new baby, Mom." He had disobeyed and prayed behind my back. We joked about that. But Bret's prayer had been answered. In utter agony and exasperation, I winced, realizing that the pregnancy would only add to my suffering with indescribable pain.

It had been eight years since our last child. We had thought we were through having babies. Why would Heavenly Father answer the prayer of a thirteen-year-old boy that would cause his mother to experience misery and suffering? Why would God do that to me? I had been continually praying for relief for many years; now my suffering had deepened. How could I go on believing that my Father in Heaven loved me? Would I live to give birth? Would the baby survive? Would I survive?

The pregnancy did have a negative effect on her, interacting with other chemicals in her body—in her words, "torching my brain and teasing my sanity." The effects on her mind were more painful than a bleeding wound. Yet she determined she would not take any medication while she was pregnant. She rejected suggestions that she should abort the child, and added that "with strict determination I resisted the ever-present thoughts to rid myself of me forever."

May 6 arrived. My water broke. I trembled in pain and in fear for my infant. I went through labor and delivery drug free. She was born healthy! I sobbed in relief. She was bright-eyed, pink, and beautiful. The children gently touched her face and cuddled her. We gathered around her, united in our love for her.

We named her Jeanie, which means "God's gracious gift." I understand now that my son's prayers were answered for a reason. Though our infant child brought sweetness and love to all of us, the answer to Bret's prayer was not for him, the answer was for *me.* Heavenly Father knew the love of this child would console me and soothe my pain. Jeanie's hallowed countenance continued to bless me through her childhood, youth, and adulthood. Now she is a mother. . . .

I had endured appalling mental pain and survived a pregnancy, during which *I had thought I knew more than the God* who had listened to and answered the prayer of a thirteen-year-old boy.[3]

As I read Jelean's account of her experience, the words of Isaiah came to my mind: "For my thoughts are not your thoughts, neither are your ways my ways, saith the Lord. For as the heavens are higher than the earth, so are my ways higher than your ways, and my thoughts than your thoughts" (Isaiah 55:8–9).

## "This Life Is an Experience in Profound Trust"

It is an astonishing blind spot in our spiritual vision to think that we can counsel God. To plead for understanding, courage, patience, and strength to endure is legitimate. It is even all right to hope for a cure, escape, or deliverance. The test is whether or not that is all we ask for. It is when we demand it—or else—that we cross the line and counsel the Lord.

Let us close with some wise counsel from two ordained apostles on this matter:

*Elder Joseph B. Wirthlin.* You may feel singled out when adversity enters your life. You shake your head and wonder, "Why me?"

But the dial on the wheel of sorrow eventually points to each of us. At one time or another, everyone must experience sorrow. . . .

Learning to endure times of disappointment, suffering,

and sorrow is part of our on-the-job training. These experiences, while often difficult to bear at the time, are precisely the kinds of experiences that stretch our understanding, build our character, and increase our compassion for others.[4]

*Elder Richard G. Scott.* This life is an experience in profound trust—trust in Jesus Christ, trust in His teachings, trust in our capacity as led by the Holy Spirit to obey those teachings for happiness now and for a purposeful, supremely happy eternal existence. To trust means to obey willingly without knowing the end from the beginning. . . . To produce fruit, *your trust in the Lord must be more powerful and enduring than your confidence in your own personal feelings and experience.*[5]

## Notes

*Epigraph.* Nathan Eldon Tanner, "The Laws of God," *Ensign,* November 1975, 84.

1. As just one example see Michael F. Scheier and Charles S. Carver, "Effects of Optimism on Psychological and Physical Well-being," *Cognitive Therapy and Research* 16, no. 2 (1992): 201–28.

2. Jelean Vaughn Reynolds, "A Test of Faith," in "Mormon Journal," *Ensign,* August 1987, 41.

3. Letter in possession of the author. Used by permission.

4. Joseph B. Wirthlin, "Come What May, and Love It," *Ensign,* November 2008, 27.

5. Richard G. Scott, "Trust in the Lord," *Ensign,* November 1995, 17.

# "Trust in the Lord"

THE WRITER OF Proverbs offers this simple yet profound observation: "Trust in the Lord with all thine heart; and lean not unto [or *on*] thine own understanding" (Proverbs 3:5). Wise counsel, but when things start to fall apart, it is difficult to keep that in mind.

Troy and Rebecca Belliston have five children ranging in age from 15 to 2½ years old. Troy went straight to the Detroit area after graduating from Utah State University in mechanical engineering. He works as a design engineer for one of the big suppliers to the automotive industry. They have lived with their family in Michigan for nearly fourteen years now. He was caught in the financial crash that began in 2008 and hit the automotive industry so hard.

I asked Rebecca and Troy if they would be willing to share their story. They agreed. Though Rebecca serves as voice in their narrative, she has incorporated Troy's perspective as well.

## "It's Interesting How the Lord Works"

We should have known it was coming. Everyone was losing their jobs around us in Michigan, and cuts were still coming. Troy had only been at his company two years and as such

179

was one of the newest employees. As Troy's company started looking at cutting their work force, we figured he would be one of the first to go. The company was offering everyone a voluntary severance package—in Troy's case, six months' pay and benefits—but when we prayed about whether to accept the voluntary severance package, the answer was a firm no. To us, we thought that meant he was going to keep his job, and we relaxed a little. We were wrong!

It's interesting to see how the Lord works. Before Troy lost his job, we kept hearing messages about how hard times were coming, but we felt it would be okay and that the Lord would not forget us. Those feelings came to us at church, while reading the scriptures, even through songs—"How Firm a Foundation" comes to mind.

We kept thinking, "Yes, hard times are coming in general, but not for us personally. We are paying our tithing. We have several demanding church callings; Troy is serving in the bishopric. We have family home evening each week and try to read scriptures with the kids." We weren't perfect by any stretch of the imagination, but we were trying to keep up on our LDS checklist. "The Lord will protect us," we kept telling ourselves.

The day before Troy lost his job, the Lord was still trying to warn us. My visiting teacher came over and said, "I was planning on giving you the Relief Society message in the *Ensign* for this month, but I was reading this article in the BYU alumni magazine, and I thought you might like it." The article was a talk given by Elder Jeffrey R. Holland entitled "Lessons from Liberty Jail." The summary of the article identifies the message perfectly. It read, "As did the Prophet Joseph, you can have sacred, revelatory, profoundly instructive experiences—even in the most miserable times of your life." And I would now add, even *because* of the most miserable times of your life.

Within twenty-four hours of that visiting teaching message, Troy called me to say he had just been "walked out the door."

There we were, suddenly with no income and five young children, in an economy that was brutally wiping out automotive engineers everywhere. He was offered another severance package, only this time it was for six weeks, not six months.

We checked our kids out of school and broke the news to them. I can't describe the emotions we had sitting on the couch and telling our children that Dad no longer had a job. Laura and Michael (ages 13 and 11) asked us, "What did we do wrong? I thought we prayed and Dad wasn't supposed to take the severance package. Why did this happen?" We didn't know what to say. Katelynn (age 5) even went so far as to ask if we were all going to die. We assured her that we weren't, but that if worse came to worst, we'd go back to Utah and move in with Grandma and Grandpa for a time. At that point Andrew (age 9) said, "That's the *worst* thing that can happen?" Then he jumped off the couch and went into another room, totally fine with everything.

We knew we were facing a difficult and uncertain time. The evening news kept saying it would be years before the automotive industry would recover. We knew that Troy had been blessed to have received even six weeks of severance pay, and we calculated that with that money, plus our savings—and with some scrimping and prudent use of our food storage—we could make our house payments for a year. But for two or three years? There was no way.

Troy lost his job on the Friday before general conference in April 2009. I remember talk after talk during that conference about how things are tough, but it's okay, the Lord will not abandon you.

In between listening to the comforting words of the prophets, we brainstormed on who Troy could call or where he could start looking for a job, knowing he was now one of the thousands of people all fighting for the same jobs. We knew networking was the way to go and, as such, thought back to his old company. He had left that company two years previously because even back then, they weren't very secure. Troy had heard that they, too, were laying off a substantial number of engineers. Going back there seemed fruitless, yet we kept feeling like he should call. He had really liked his previous boss, Dave, and so Troy decided to call him first thing Monday morning just to let him know that, if things turned around down the road, he was available.

But Monday was one of those "when it rains, it pours" days. As Troy tried to get onto the computer Monday morning to find Dave's telephone number, the computer crashed over and over again. Then our dryer broke. The kids were fighting, and a hundred other tiny things seemed to hit us in the space of about thirty minutes. It was uncanny.

I was so overwhelmed, I finally threw myself on my bed and burst into tears. I basically said in my mind, "Okay, Lord. I give up. I can't do this. You take over."

The Lord did. And then the miracles began.

The kids were so shocked to see me totally lose it that they climbed onto the bed with me and just sat there, thankfully no longer fighting. Troy finally got the computer to work long enough to retrieve Dave's number. Troy called his old boss, who confirmed that the company was doing horribly and they were laying off engineers. There was no way he could get Troy a job there.

But then he said, "However, I haven't told anyone else this yet, but I have just taken a position as vice president of a new company." The job was in the automotive industry, but in an area that was still doing pretty well. Dave explained that he had just given his two weeks' notice, and after he settled into his new position, he would definitely be needing engineers—especially engineers with the mind-set and work ethic that Troy had. "I just need a little time to make it happen," he said. "Can you hang on until then?"

As Troy came upstairs to report, we began to realize just how miraculous the timing was. There was the tiniest window of time where Dave would still be at his old job—at the only phone number Troy had for him—and yet he had already been hired as VP in the new company, where he was able to give Troy hope for a new job. But even further, we realized that if Troy had stayed with his old company instead of leaving two years earlier, Dave wouldn't have been able to take Troy to the new company because of likely "no-compete" restrictions. Suddenly we were all emotional again. And it was only Monday. Troy hadn't even spent one full workday out of a job.

Needless to say, our little family of seven fell on our knees and cried our way through a prayer of thanks.

The next two and a half months weren't always easy, and there were still dark, hard times when we didn't hear anything from Dave and began to wonder if things were actually going to work out. It was scary because, despite our daily efforts to find other jobs, there was literally nothing else. But Dave came through, or more accurately, the Lord came through and gave us our miracle.

The Lord has blessed us beyond measure. There were things we got to do as a family that we never could have done if Troy had been working.

A few weeks after losing his job, Troy was asked to teach a lesson to all the adults on the fifth Sunday—a lesson that had been scheduled several months previously—about how the Lord will help us through our trials. Needless to say, he and I cried through most of it.

Looking back now, it's amazing to see how the hand of the Lord came into our lives during that difficult time. I can testify that we had the very experiences Elder Holland promised. They were sacred times, revelatory times, and I am certain that the experience had a profound effect on all of us, including our five children. They, along with Troy and me, were taught about answers to prayer and how closely the Lord orchestrates our lives. We are closer to each other and the Lord for it.

Looking back, I can also see how the Lord continued to send us messages of hope. We came to know the reality of the promise in John 14:18: "I will not leave you comfortless." Though the tunnel was dark, and felt, at times, very long, He never took away the light at the end of it. I always knew He had us in His hand and that He would get us through stronger, and the better for it.[1]

### "Why Not Me?"

This story and others like it might raise a question in the minds of some readers: "Why him, and not me? Why them, and not us?" I'm sure there are many faithful, striving Latter-day Saints who have lost their jobs in these rough economic times. They prayed. They fasted. They paid their tithing. They served faithfully in the Church. So why didn't they find jobs the Monday following their termination? Some people have gone months and months without finding employment. Others have lost their homes or their businesses and been forced to move in with relatives or face bankruptcy. What are they doing wrong?

But when we are trusting in the Lord, we must have a larger perspective. It would be nice if there was a simple and clear correlation between adversity and spiritual worthiness. If only it was the wicked who always suffered and the righteous who were always blessed. But that is not the case, and so we must be careful else we berate ourselves for what we think might be our failings, or blame God for what we perceive to be His.

Isaiah reminds us, "For my thoughts are not your thoughts, neither are your ways my ways, saith the Lord. For as the heavens are higher than the earth, so are my ways higher than your ways, and my thoughts than your thoughts" (Isaiah 55:8–9). Our vision and understanding is so limited, so finite, that we cannot see all that He sees or know all that He knows.

But one thing is for sure. We are not the only ones involved in, or affected by, our circumstances. We are so different. Why should it surprise us that our prayers for deliverance from similar circumstances should be answered in so many different ways?

That is why we are talking about hope. Hope is an abiding trust in God's goodness, and the promises He extends to us enlarge our perspective, deepen our courage, extend our patience, and help us endure faithfully.

---

Note

1. Troy and Rebecca Belliston of Milford, Michigan. Material in possession of the author. Used by permission.

*When in situations of stress we wonder
if there is any more in us to give, we can be
comforted to know that God, who knows our
capacity perfectly, placed us here to succeed.
No one was foreordained to fail or to be wicked.
When we have been weighed and found wanting,
let us remember that we were measured before and
we were found equal to our tasks; and, therefore,
let us continue, but with a more determined
discipleship. When we feel overwhelmed, let us recall
the assurance that God will not overprogram us; he
will not press upon us more than we can bear.*

NEAL A. MAXWELL

# CHAPTER TEN

# PATIENCE, COURAGE, AND ENDURANCE

—◦—ᴧᴑᴖ◦ᴖ—◦—

## Enduring Well

WHILE TEACHING THE Twelve about the signs of the times—certainly not the happiest of topics—the Savior said, "But he that shall endure unto the end, the same shall be saved" (Matthew 24:13). Considering the judgments that are to come before Christ's Second Coming, an exhortation to endure is not surprising. But it seems that life itself must require a considerable measure of endurance, because the exhortation to endure to the end is found more than a dozen times throughout the scriptures. In addition to enduring, we are exhorted to "bear our burdens," to "press forward," to "be steadfast," to "take patiently," or to "wait patiently."

The scriptures not only talk about *what* we are to endure—

- "affliction or persecution" (Mark 4:17)
- our own burdens, as well as each other's burdens (see Galatians 6:2, 5)
- "hardness" (i.e., hardships, difficulty) (2 Timothy 2:3)
- the chastening of the Lord (see D&C 101:5)

- the grief which comes from suffering wrongly (see 1 Peter 2:19)

—but *how* we are to endure it:

- endure *diligently* through prayer (see Moroni 8:26)
- wait *patiently* on the Lord (see Psalm 27:14)
- "press forward with . . . *steadfastness*" (2 Nephi 31:20)
- "endure in *faith*" (D&C 101:35)
- "endure *valiantly*" (D&C 121:29)

There it is. Our challenge. Not only are we to endure trials and setbacks, but we are to endure them well. There is no question that patience, courage, and endurance are required if we are to bring our hearts into alignment with the Lord's will. These three qualities are closely related to the idea that we don't seek to counsel the Lord. A loss of patience generally means we are quite put out with God—or fate, or Providence, or destiny—whatever we may choose to call it. After all, it is really quite annoying when the world doesn't align itself with our needs and wishes.

## More Synergy

Earlier, we talked about synergy. The combination of patience, courage, and endurance is another synergistic relationship of great importance. As I think about the relationship of these three, I picture them this way: Patience and courage are the *driving attributes,* and the strength to endure is the *outcome.* If that's so, then where do patience and courage come from? They come from faith, hope, and charity, all gifts of the Spirit given to us when we strive to put our lives in harmony with God. They are the byproducts of true conversion. They are part of the endowment of power we receive in the temple. They come as part of the boundless love and mercy of the Father and the Son.

In most cases of adversity, we cannot significantly alter the external circumstances which are causing the pain or the suffering. What we can do is choose *how we will respond* to those circumstances. And courage and faith are choices we can make. This is where faith and hope and conversion work together to stiffen "the spiritual spine"[1] or temper our "soul-steel,"[2] as Elder Neal A. Maxwell puts it.

## Oil for the Lamp of Hope

What we have just said may not be very satisfying to some. It may actually be frustrating. Why? Because if we haven't been developing those gospel qualities over the years, we may in trouble when the crisis strikes. We may find ourselves in a situation similar to the parable of the Ten Virgins (see Matthew 25:1–13). It may turn out that we have insufficient oil in our "hope lamps." We know that the oil in the parable represents the light of the Spirit (see D&C 45:56–57). If we don't have that Spirit, it's not just personal revelation that we lack. Hope and faith and courage and patience are all gifts of the Spirit too. If our spiritual oil is low when the crisis strikes, then we may lack the courage and patience to endure. The problem is complicated by the fact that at midnight it is unlikely that we'll find anyone selling jars of "endurance" at the local convenience store.

This is the real "oil crisis" of our generation, not the one at the gas pumps. If we, or people we love, are facing a crisis or a tragedy or prolonged suffering, and our own oil reserves are low, leaving us short on patience and courage, we may be led to exclaim, "Then what hope is there for me?" I believe there are two answers for that.

First, *start now!* If we are not in the midst of a crisis at this moment, then now is the time to start building up those reserves. As President Spencer W. Kimball said:

In the parable, oil can be purchased at the market. In our lives the oil of preparedness is accumulated drop by drop in righteous living. Attendance at sacrament meetings adds oil to our lamps, drop by drop over the years. Fasting, family prayer, home teaching, control of bodily appetites, preaching the gospel, studying the scriptures—each act of dedication and obedience is a drop added to our store.[3]

As President Ezra Taft Benson reminded us, "Becoming Christlike is a *lifetime pursuit* and very often involves growth and change that is slow, almost imperceptible."[4] And Elder Neal A. Maxwell added this insight:

> It is our stubborn use of our agency that slows us, not God's desire for delay. *The eternal attributes require time for their development and expression.* Instant forgiveness is not always given, though it is desperately wished for. Instant compassion is not always generated, though it is so needed. . . . And, of course, *instant patience is a contradiction in terms.*[5]

The promise is clear: "He that seeketh me early shall find me, and shall not be forsaken" (D&C 88:83).

But suppose the crisis *is* upon us. Then what? This answer is equally simple. *Start now!* That's right, the second answer is the same as the first. Where you are at the moment doesn't change the need. The best solution for getting more oil in our lamps is to start now. It is never too late to start. We are *always* better off if we turn to God. May I recommend for those who might be struggling with this particular aspect of hope that you take a moment right now and study carefully the three parables found in Luke 15. I call them the "parables of the lost"—the lost sheep, the lost coin, the lost son.

In each of these three parables, the promise is always the same.

Whether we wandered away seeking greener grass, were dropped and lost through someone's carelessness, or openly rebelled against the Father, whenever the lost were found, there was great rejoicing, for, as the Savior said, "There is joy in the presence of the angels of God over one sinner that repenteth" (Luke 15:10).

Also note that in the case of the prodigal son (see Luke 15:11–32), when he finally "came to himself" (Luke 15:17) and started back home, he didn't have to come all the way back before his father responded. "When he was yet *a great way off,* his father saw him, and had compassion, and ran, and fell on his neck, and kissed him" (Luke 15:20). I love that imagery, because the only way the father could have seen him a great way off was if the father was watching for his son.

## Hope for the Hopeless

When Alma and his sons, along with Amulek and other missionaries, went to teach the Zoramites, they found that most of the people were haughty, proud, self-righteous, and practicing a sterile form of religious worship (see Alma 31). The missionaries were mocked, ridiculed, and rejected. Then a large group of Zoramites sought them out. These were people who were wretchedly poor. They had been rejected and scorned by the rich, who had exploited them. They believed they had lost any chance to worship God and therefore find relief (see Alma 32:1–5).

Alma's response provides a wonderful answer to the dilemma of being caught in a crisis when our reserves of spiritual oil are low. "When Alma heard this, . . . he beheld with great joy; for he beheld that *their afflictions had truly humbled them,* and that they were in a preparation to hear the word" (Alma 32:6).

Did you catch that? Our afflictions can humble us. Tragedies can soften our hearts. Our challenges can bring us up short so that we turn around to face the Lord again. And with that softened heart, we begin the process of gaining—or regaining—our faith, hope, and testimony. And these bring spiritual power back into our lives.

Here's another promise that gives me great hope. When Alma finished his masterful discourse on faith, Amulek came forward and began to teach the people about Christ and His Atonement—the source of all hope. He also taught them about prayer and repentance. Then he made this rather startling statement: "Yea, I would that ye would come forth and harden not your hearts any longer; for behold, now is the time and the day of your salvation; and therefore, if ye will repent and harden not your hearts, *immediately* shall the great plan of redemption be brought about unto you" (Alma 34:31).

Immediately? What does that mean? If I've turned away from the Lord for a long time, does that mean that all I have to do is be sorry and everything will be immediately resolved? Will tragedy turn into instant triumph? Will deep despair be dispelled by deliverance? Of course not. We're not promising dramatic miracles, or instant turn-arounds—though sometimes they do happen. I believe what Amulek is saying is that as soon as we humble ourselves and turn back toward God, then spiritual power immediately begins to come back into our lives. No matter where we are in our spiritual development, starting that process of turning to God will always be the best thing we can do to deal with a crisis.

## "A Mighty Change of Heart"

I know a man in Latin America whose life had become such a wreck that one day he woke up from a drunken stupor in a city far from his home. He had no idea where he was or how he had gotten there. Alcohol had become such a problem that his marriage was on the rocks. He had lost his job. His children were afraid of him. His life was in shambles.

At that moment of deep despair, he decided he had to do something with his life. He had to change. He fell to his knees and begged God to help him. He went back to his family and asked for their forgiveness. He pleaded for another chance. He sought treatment for his alcoholism. A few months later, when two missionaries knocked on his door and said they had a message about how he and his family could find real joy in life, he invited them in, listened, and was baptized with his family a few weeks later.

When he told me his story, it had been nearly fifteen years since he had decided to change his life. I just stared at him. I couldn't believe what he was telling me. This man, in my opinion, epitomized all that the gospel asks of us. He was a righteous patriarch in his family, beloved by his wife and children and grandchildren. He was humble and submissive, always seeking ways to bless others. He had served as a branch president, bishop, stake president, and eventually as an Area Seventy. He had been a seminary and institute teacher and had touched many lives. It was a miraculous transformation. I came to better appreciate what Alma meant when he said, "There was a mighty change wrought in his heart" (Alma 5:12). That change began immediately when my friend turned to the Lord and asked for help. It took years for him to come to the point where he was when I first met him, but the *process* began immediately. The process is always the same. It just works at a different level and at a different pace, depending on our hearts and our desires and our willingness to change.

### The Lord Makes an Escape

Here's another promise to hold onto when we are struggling in the depths of despair: "There hath no temptation* taken you but such

---

* The basic meaning of the Greek verb used here is "to test, try, prove, . . . testing

as is common to man: but God is faithful, who will not suffer you to be tempted [tried or tested] above that ye are able; but will with the temptation also *make a way to escape,* that ye may be able to bear it" (1 Corinthians 10:13).

Elder Neal A. Maxwell, in that wonderful way of his, expressed it like this:

> The thermostat on the furnace of affliction will not have been set too high for us—though clearly we may think so at the time. Our God is a refining God who has been tempering soul-steel for a very long time. *He knows when the right edge has been put upon our excellence and also when there is more in us than we have yet given.* One day we will praise God for taking us near to our limits—as He did His Only Begotten in Gethsemane and Calvary.[6]

And here is how Elder Richard G. Scott expressed it:

> When you face adversity, you can be led to ask many questions. Some serve a useful purpose; others do not. To ask, Why does this have to happen to me? Why do I have to suffer this, now? What have I done to cause this? will lead you into blind alleys. It really does no good to ask questions that reflect opposition to the will of God. Rather ask, What am I to do? What am I to learn from this experience? *What am I to change?* . . . When you pray with real conviction, "Please let me know Thy will" and "May Thy will be done," you are in the strongest position to receive the maximum help from your loving Father.[7]

---

as permitted by God" (see W. E. Vine, *Vine's Expository Dictionary of Old and New Testament Words* [Old Tappan, NJ: Fleming H. Revell Company, 1981], 4:116).

## Life Is So Daily!

We have been talking about finding the courage and strength to endure adversity or tragedy. But there is another kind of patience and courage required of us. It is the patience and courage to simply face life.

When I was growing up, my mother wore an apron with the statement that said, "The problem with cooking is that it is so daily!" I would like to amend that to read: The problem with *life* is that it is so daily!

In chapter 1, I cited some quotes I had heard from people who were struggling to find hope. I shall repeat some of them here. They reflect not great tragedy or terrible loss but the daily struggle to keep going with some hope in life:

- A woman to the teacher just before a gospel instruction class was to begin: "Just thought I'd warn you. If you tell me one more thing I'm supposed to be doing to be a better person, I'm going to stand up in the middle of your lecture and scream."

- A young single adult to her institute instructor after class: "Thank you so much for that lesson, Brother Jones. It was so inspiring, and I'm so depressed."

- A stake president describing a concern about some of his faithful members: "They know the gospel is true. They serve faithfully. But the joy is gone."

- An elderly couple: "Life grows increasingly difficult as our pains increase and our capacities diminish."

Life is so daily!

They are not talking about major crises in their lives; they're talking about life. That's why I love the quote of a wise widow I know:

"It's rarely the big trees that get you. It's pushing your way through the undergrowth."

Very seldom are our days filled with euphoria and bliss—not just perfect bliss—*any* bliss. Many things in life are boring, tedious, and monotonous. Often they are pretty dreary, and sometimes they can be downright awful. There are a thousand ways that daily life can diminish our hope or test our faith. It doesn't have to be something as dramatic as losing a leg, or losing our life's savings, or having terminal cancer. The daily realities of life can also leave us feeling discouraged, disillusioned, dissatisfied, or even in despair. These feelings may come from growing old or being stuck in a monotonous, dead-end job. Some people are terribly lonely; some struggle with a loveless and lifeless marriage. Others remain single for life. Some seem unable to catch a break of any kind, failing in one endeavor after another.

Such times require courage and patience and endurance as surely as the greater crises do.

## Mother's Day

In the April 2009 general conference, Elder Dallin H. Oaks spoke about why there is a growing tendency for people to have fewer children than they did before.

> Mothers suffer pain and loss of personal priorities and comforts to bear and rear each child. Fathers adjust their lives and priorities to support a family. The gap between those who are and those who are not willing to do this is widening in today's world. One of our family members recently overheard a young couple on an airline flight explaining that they chose to have a dog instead of children. "Dogs are less trouble," they declared. "Dogs don't talk back, and we never have to ground them."[8]

Though we are promised that we shall have joy and rejoicing in our posterity—which I can testify from personal experience is true—nevertheless our posterity also bring us frustration, exasperation, agitation, humiliation, privation, aggravation, abdication, and a dozen other -ations. Like it or not, for all the joy our families can bring, when we talk about the day-to-day challenges of life, that frequently involves our children. They provide much of the "undergrowth" that parents have to push through on a daily basis. (And in a teenager's bedroom, that may be more literal than metaphorical.)

To illustrate, let me share with you an experience I had many years ago when my wife and I were in the midst of raising a young family. I was asked by the bishopric to speak in sacrament meeting on Mother's Day and to focus specifically on the importance of motherhood. About a week before, in a setting where there were four other couples, I told the women about my assignment and asked, "You're the mothers. Tell me what you would like me to say."

Without a moment's hesitation, one of them shot right back, "Please don't tell us how wonderful we are." Surprised, I mumbled something about that being exactly what I was thinking of doing. "Well, don't!" she snapped.

I guess she saw the bewilderment in my eyes, because she then went on. "Let me describe last Mother's Day so you will understand." Then she told me how her husband was in the bishopric, so he was gone by six on Sunday mornings. It was up to her to get their five children ready for church. That was usually a running battle, but on this day it was particularly bad. By the time they got to church, everyone was angry and not speaking to each other. She was in a bad enough mood that she decided she wouldn't partake of the sacrament that day, but as the bread started down the row, her youngest child tossed a bag of Cheerios into the air, and she forgot her vow and took a piece of bread as she tried to clean up the mess.

"It was about then," she went on, "that the speaker stood up and said things like 'Motherhood is the grandest and most important calling a woman can have in this life' and 'The hand that rocks the cradle rules the world' and 'A mother's influence on her children affects them for this life and the eternities to come.' That did it," she concluded. "I started to bawl right there in Church."

To my surprise, as she finished, the other women at the table were all nodding in agreement. This was her challenge in life, and maintaining the patience to endure that life was proving to be very difficult.

## "Give Us This Day Our Daily Bread"

Whether we talk of major challenges or the daily grind, the need for patience, courage, and endurance is real. And if that is real, then so is the need for hope.

On January 9, 2011, just as a new year was beginning, Elder D. Todd Christofferson spoke to young adults worldwide in a fireside broadcast. His counsel given to them is of great value to all of us:

> We do not live in the future—we live in the present. It is day by day that we work out our plans for the future; it is day by day that we achieve our goals. It is one day at a time that we raise and nurture our families. It is one day at a time that we overcome imperfections. We endure in faith to the end one day at a time. . . .
>
> Included in the Lord's Prayer is the petition "Give us this day our daily bread" (Matthew 6:11) or "Give us day by day our daily bread" (Luke 11:3). I believe that we would all readily acknowledge that we have needs each day that we want our Heavenly Father's help in dealing with. For some, on some days, it is quite literally bread—that is, the food

needed to sustain life that day. It could be spiritual and physical strength to deal with one more day of chronic illness or a painfully slow rehabilitation. . . .

Jesus is teaching us, His disciples, that we should look to God each day for the bread—the help and sustenance—we require in that particular day.[9]

Speaking of the day-to-day nature of life, Elder Christofferson went on:

In reality, there aren't very many things in a day that are totally without significance. Even the mundane and repetitious can be tiny but significant building blocks that in time establish the discipline and character and order needed to realize our plans and dreams. Therefore, as you ask in prayer for your daily bread, consider thoughtfully your needs—both what you may lack and what you must protect against. As you retire to bed, think about the successes and failures of the day and what will make the next day a little better. . . . Your reflections will increase your faith in Him as you see His hand helping you to endure some things and to change others. You will be able to rejoice in one more day, one more step toward eternal life.[10]

### When Hope Is Part of the "Problem"

Before we complete our discussion on the attributes of patience, courage, and endurance, we should make note of one other situation that can try the soul. In these cases, the challenge is not that we doubt, but that we believe. It is not so much that we wonder if God is there, it's *knowing* that He's there but wondering *why* He's not doing anything. That is its own kind of challenge.

Take for example, a woman who never marries in life. Let's say she been faithful all her life. She served an honorable mission, graduated from a respected university, has served in many callings in the Church. She studies the scriptures, pays her tithing, attends the temple, says her prayers. *And she is still single.* Here is a conversation she might have with herself from time to time.

> From the time I was a little girl, my greatest wish and dream has been to be a successful wife and mother like my mom. I have been praying for that since I was in my mid-teens and started to date. I dated through high school and college, and I believed that someone was waiting for me just around the corner. But it never happened. My life is full and rich, but often my days are filled with loneliness, and at night I feel an aching hope that there may still be a chance for a husband and children in this life.
>
> I know these blessings will come in the next life. I don't doubt that in any way. But that is so far in the future that it only marginally eases my pain now. I try to push the questions away, but I can't help wondering: Have I done something wrong? Is there something more I should be doing? How can this be what's "best" for me? I know it is, but that doesn't stop the pain.

It's ironic, isn't it? One of life's great contradictions is that deep adversity and prolonged suffering test the very core of our faith and hope. But it is faith and hope that gives us the strength to endure deep adversity and prolonged suffering. And sometimes our faith and hope may even add to our suffering, as it did in the case of so many of the early Saints.

All I can say in answer to these difficult questions is this: The way back to the Lord is strait and narrow. It doesn't skirt around the rough stretches or detour past the steepest climbs. Nor does God always prepare safe crossing of the numerous canyons, chasms, ravines, rivers, and streams that lay before us. We must build many of the bridges for those crossings ourselves as part of this grand learning experience we are engaged in. What God has promised to do on this journey along the strait and narrow path is to help us strengthen the bridges until they are capable of bearing whatever load it is we are asked to carry. He has also offered us a spiritual navigation system called faith, hope, and charity to help us find our way.

Virginia H. Pearce, daughter of President Gordon B. Hinckley, said this of her father: "President Gordon B. Hinckley had a personal motto that is quite practical. He taught it in many settings: *'Things will work out. If you keep trying and praying and working, things will work out. They always do.'*"[11]

Elder Neal A. Maxwell put it this way:

> We are not merely to exist to the end. Rather, we are to persist "in following the example of the Son of the living God." . . .
>
> Especially it may be so for Latter-day Saints, who have great expectations and then must endure the difference between what we could be and what we are, all the while trying to make use of the divine discontent within us.
>
> Our emphasis, therefore, should be on "doing" and "becoming," not just on surviving; on serving others, not just serving time.[12]

It is from that "doing" and "becoming" that we gain the courage and patience sufficient to endure to the end. There seems to be no other way.

I would exhort you to have patience, and that ye bear with all manner of afflictions. . . .

. . . Have patience, and bear with those afflictions, with a firm hope that ye shall one day rest from all your afflictions. (Alma 34:40–41)

---

## Notes

*Epigraph.* Neal A. Maxwell, "Meeting the Challenges of Today," *1978 Devotional Speeches of the Year* (Provo, Utah: Brigham Young University Press, 1978), 156.

1. Neal A. Maxwell, *One More Strain of Praise* (Salt Lake City: Bookcraft, 1999), 74.

2. Neal A. Maxwell, *All These Things Shall Give Thee Experience* (Salt Lake City: Deseret Book, 1979), 46.

3. Spencer W. Kimball, *Faith Precedes the Miracle* (Salt Lake City: Deseret Book, 1972), 255.

4. Ezra Taft Benson, *The Teachings of Ezra Taft Benson* (Salt Lake City: Bookcraft, 1988), 72.

5. Neal A. Maxwell, *Even As I Am* (Salt Lake City: Deseret Book, 1982), 47.

6. Maxwell, *All These Things Shall Give Thee Experience,* 46.

7. Richard G. Scott, "Trust in the Lord," *Ensign,* November 1995, 17.

8. Dallin H. Oaks, "Unselfish Service," *Ensign,* May 2009, 93.

9. D. Todd Christofferson, "Give Us This Day Our Daily Bread," CES Fireside for Young Adults, 9 January 2011, 1.

10. Christofferson, "Give Us This Day Our Daily Bread," 5.

11. Virginia H. Pearce, "Prayer: A Small and Simple Thing," in *By Small and Simple Things: Talks from the 2011 BYU Women's Conference* (Salt Lake City: Deseret Book, 2012), 236.

12. Neal A. Maxwell, *"Not My Will, But Thine"* (Salt Lake City: Deseret Book, 1988), 115.

# Patience and Prayer

IN THE 2011 Women's Conference at Brigham Young University, Virginia H. Pearce spoke on the power of prayer. From her words we can also learn much about patience, courage, and endurance.

### Prayer Works

In October of 2008, my husband and I were busily preparing to respond to a mission call. It had been a year of perpetual motion for us. My father [President Gordon B. Hinckley] had died in January, necessitating the business of dividing and distributing all of his stuff. Oh, we do leave lots of things behind, don't we? . . .

Responding to some symptoms that were becoming increasingly problematic, my husband went in for tests and was diagnosed with a fatal and untreatable disease. He lived just short of one year from the day of diagnosis.

It was a unique year for us—one of quiet and slow living—of unbusyness. President Dieter F. Uchtdorf explained, "When growing conditions are not ideal, trees slow down their growth and devote their energy to the basic elements necessary for survival." He continued, "It is good advice to slow down a little, steady the course, and focus on the essentials when experiencing adverse conditions."

We did just that.

We talked, we cried, we read and reread verses of scripture, we pored over talks from the brethren, we spent sweet time with family and friends. We went to bed every night and got up every morning. Most of all, though, we prayed. We prayed together, we prayed separately, we prayed vocally, we prayed silently. We prayed with loved ones. We fasted and prayed. We went to the temple and prayed. We prayed constantly. We pled with our Father in Heaven in the name of His Son, Jesus Christ. . . .

. . . Prayer works. It does indeed call down the powers of heaven. It reconciles our will with the will of the Father. It consecrates even our most aversive experiences to the welfare of our souls. Through combined prayer we experience love, unity, and power that is impossible to describe. We may not be granted that which we desire, but we end up grateful with all of our hearts for that which the Lord gives us.

And along the way we experience tender mercies over and over—those unmistakable messages from Him: "I am here. I love you. You are living your life with my approval. Everything will work together for your good. Trust me."

Even though we may not see from minute to minute that we are moving forward and making progress, I believe we will be able to one day look back at our lives and see that we were, in fact, doing just what we needed to be doing at just the right time in just the right place. We can trust that the Lord will work in and through us.[1]

## Note

1. Virginia H. Pearce, "Prayer: A Small and Simple Thing," in *By Small and Simple Things: Talks from the 2011 BYU Women's Conference* (Salt Lake City: Deseret Book, 2012), 237–38.

*Desires dictate our priorities,*
*priorities shape our choices,*
*and choices determine our actions.*
*The desires we act on determine*
*our changing, our achieving,*
*and our becoming.*

DALLIN H. OAKS

# Chapter Eleven

# "According to Their Desires"

---❧❧❧---

## Aligning Our Hearts with God

WE SHALL CONCLUDE this section on the need to align our lives with God by examining the desires of our heart. This discussion is a critical one. Desire ranks right up there with faith, hope, charity, patience, courage, and endurance in determining how strong our hope will be.

In chapter 2, we spoke a great deal about the importance of the condition of our hearts. If we are hard-hearted or stiff-necked, the process of developing faith and hope is stopped. If our hearts are softened and teachable, then the learning and growing process can move forward.

One word which is often used to describe the proper condition of the heart is humility. For example, the Lord says, "Be thou humble; and the Lord thy God shall lead thee by the hand, and give thee answer to thy prayers" (D&C 112:10). Here is another choice that is ours to make. Humility is an act of personal will, as is indicated by the phrase "humble yourself," which is found more than a dozen times in the scriptures. In the *Encyclopedia of Mormonism,* we find this beautiful description of humility: "True humility is the recognition of one's imperfection that is acquired only as one joyfully, voluntarily, and quietly submits one's whole life to God's will."[1]

The spiritual condition of our hearts has a profound influence on what we desire. Desire is part of our everyday life, though we typically do not consciously perceive it, nor express it in those terms. How many times a day do we say or think, "I want that," or "I want to do that"? What we desire for ourselves and others becomes the motivating, driving power for most of our actions. We're hungry, so we eat. We're tired, so we go to bed. We want to be able to support our families, so we work long hours. We want to better ourselves, so we spend years getting an education.

Since desire also works in a similar fashion in the spiritual realm, *what* we desire has a major effect on determining what we do and who we are. Let me say that again. What we desire in our hearts will profoundly affect what we do and who we are. There may be all kinds of external influences which stimulate (or repress) our desires, but we are the ones who choose if, how, and when we will let those outside influences become a driving desire in our lives.

The temptation of pornography is an excellent example of how this works. Two individuals can see the exact same external stimulus—a website that pops up unbidden onto the screen of one's computer, for example. Both individuals know it is wrong, but the first person harbors secret desires to see such images. Making sure he is alone, he opens the website. Ironically, what he sees only stimulates his desires. So he returns again. Finds other sites. The second person is also tempted to look at the site, but he has a strong desire to have the Spirit in his life, so he leaves the site without looking.

Desire and choice—together they determine so much of what we do. Having Satan along with us for the ride in such situations is not helpful, for, as Helaman noted, the devil keeps whispering in our ears: "Do whatsoever your heart desireth" (Helaman 13:27).

Here's another example. We often use Nephi as an example of great faith and obedience. But evidently, when Lehi first announced that the Lord had commanded him to take his family into the wilderness, it wasn't just Laman and Lemuel who struggled with the news. Nephi says of himself, "And it came to pass that I, Nephi, . . . *having great desires* to know of the mysteries of God, wherefore, I did cry unto the Lord; and behold he did visit me, and did *soften my heart.*" Was his initial reaction similar to Laman's and Lemuel's? Perhaps so. But his desires made all the difference. Nephi continues, "I did believe all the words which had been spoken by my father; wherefore, *I did not rebel against him* like unto my brothers" (1 Nephi 2:16).

Laman and Lemuel, on the other hand, resented their father and murmured against him because he "had led them out of the land of Jerusalem, to leave . . . their gold, and their silver, and their precious things" (1 Nephi 2:11). As Nephi notes, his brothers "were past feeling" (1 Nephi 17:45). The sharply contrasting desires of Lehi's sons would define the history of their peoples for the next thousand years.

We have talked much about hope being a trust in the promises of God. Here is another promise, this one tied directly to our desires: "Verily, verily, I say unto you, *even as you desire of me so it shall be done unto you;* and, if you desire, you shall be the means of doing much good in this generation" (D&C 11:8).

## We Are Judged According to Our Desires

Isn't it odd how we can read a passage of scripture again and again, and then one day a word or a phrase leaps out at us and the Spirit teaches us something new? That experience happened to me a few years back as I was reading Alma's final counsel to his son Corianton, who had violated the law of chastity while serving as a missionary with his father.

Throughout the scriptures we find passages that tell us we are "judged according to our works" (Alma 12:12; there are actually twenty-eight references to being judged for our works). Since most of us have a keen awareness of our failings, this promise can be somewhat discouraging. Alma warned Corianton that he would be judged for his actions, but added another significant dimension: "It is requisite with the justice of God that men should be judged according to their works; and if their works were good in this life, *and the desires of their hearts were good,* that they should also, at the last day, be restored unto that which is good" (Alma 41:3).

This is an important concept. What we *desire to do* will be considered along with what we *actually do.* The old saying "The road to hell is paved with good intentions" may be true, but evidently, so is the road to heaven.

How often do we undertake something with a desire to do what is right, intending to accomplish something that would please God, and then it all goes wrong? I think of a husband who, after a contentious argument with his wife, decided he had been wrong and wanted to make it right. When he went in to the bedroom—where she had fled in tears—things were still tense and awkward. He went in wanting to say that he realized he had been completely wrong; he wanted to apologize to her. But unfortunately, groping for words, he said, "Look, dear, I know neither one of us is perfect, so . . ." The look she gave him stopped him cold. It took another full day before she was calm enough for him to apologize with a little more wisdom. The point of the story, though, is that he went in *wanting* to do the right thing.

It is deeply gratifying to me that the Lord doesn't just judge us only on what we do. Consider the young mother who didn't want to be told how wonderful she was on Mother's Day. She was not perfect in her mothering skills—and she was keenly aware of that—but she longed to be! The *desires of her heart were good,* even though *her performance fell short.*

Once I grasped that concept, I began to find it elsewhere in the scriptures. I quoted only one verse of what Alma taught Corianton. Here is more: "All things shall be restored to their proper order. . . . The one raised to happiness according to his desires of happiness, or good according to his desires of good" (Alma 41:4–5).

Here are some similar promises:

- The Lord said that the gifts of the Spirit "are given for the benefit of those who love me and keep all my commandments, and him that seeketh so to do" (D&C 46:9).
- Speaking of the trumps that will sound at the Second Coming of Christ, the Savior said, "Then shall the second angel sound his trump, and reveal the secret acts of men, and the thoughts and intents of their hearts" (D&C 88:109).
- "I, the Lord, will judge all men according to their works, according to the desire of their hearts" (D&C 137:9).

## A Promise and a Warning

For those striving to do good, these are wonderful promises. For those whose hearts desire evil, the same passages contain a sobering warning. For the hard of heart, there will be no protestations of innocence, no hiding behind the mask of hypocrisy, no denial of selfish motives, no claims of being unable to remember what we did. We are told that at the judgment we shall have "a perfect remembrance of all [our] wickedness" (Alma 5:18) and "a bright recollection of all our guilt" (Alma 11:43). In short, if our desires are good, it is a wonderful promise. However, if our desires have been evil—*even if we do not always carry those desires into full action*—then our perfect recollection will convict us.

Alma, speaking of his own desires, taught us an important principle. After saying that he wished he were an angel so he could declare the gospel as with the voice of a trump (which is a pretty righteous desire), he immediately caught himself:

> But behold, I am a man, and do sin in my wish; for I ought to be content with the things which the Lord hath allotted unto me. . . .
>
> . . . For I know that he granteth unto men *according to their desire,* whether it be unto death or unto life; yea, I know that he allotteth unto men, yea, decreeth unto them decrees which are unalterable, *according to their wills,* whether they be unto salvation or unto destruction. (Alma 29:3–4)

A careful reading of Alma's words reveals that he's not saying that God grants us evil things, but rather that He grants us "according to our desires." So why did Alma consider that he had "sinned" in his wish? To be a more powerful preacher of the gospel is surely a righteous desire. How could that be a bad thing? Evidently, even as Alma spoke, the Spirit reminded him to be careful about his desires. It may not seem like a bad thing for him to desire to be an angel so he could preach more effectively, but there is a deeper issue here.

Having angels preach the gospel to the world with voices that blast out like trumpets would surely get more attention than two young missionaries preaching on a street corner. So why doesn't God call angels on missions instead of mortals? (Aside from their effectiveness, you wouldn't have to worry about angels keeping the mission rules.) Here's another question. It was estimated that three to four billion people watched some part of the Beijing Olympics held in 2008. Why not send the angel Gabriel down to hold a press conference with

ABC, NBC, CBS, CNN, FoxNews, the BBC, and other news sta-
tions, along with representatives from all the major newspapers of the
world? Think of the coverage that would get!

So why doesn't God do it that way? I think the answer has to
do with moral agency—the right to choose for ourselves what to
do, what to believe, how to act, what we value, and what we desire.
Agency is so fundamental to the gospel plan of happiness, so essential
to our growth, and so sacred in and of itself that God is very careful never to do anything that would violate our agency. One of our
hymns sums it up very well:

> He'll call, persuade, direct aright,
> And bless with wisdom, love, and light,
> In nameless ways be good and kind,
> But never force the human mind.[2]

I like the word *persuade*. I also like that it's not just that God
doesn't force humans to do good, he is careful not even to force the
mind. He is careful that the invitation to come unto Him is not given
in such a direct and powerful way that it overwhelms us. We are here
to walk by faith, not by sight. Angels knocking on doors would be
pretty compelling. Who would slam the door in the face of an angel?
But no. Instead of blasting us with the volume of trumpets, He entices us with the whisperings of the Spirit. Instead of sending an angel
to convince us it is all true, He says that we receive no witness until
after the trial of our faith.

So in a very real sense, Alma's wish—though well-meant—
reflected a momentary lapse of judgment. Why? Because he desired
something that did not square with God's eternal purposes. I believe
that was why Alma said that he had sinned in his wish. It was a lesson for him, and, thankfully, he taught us that lesson as well. It is
the same principle that Father Lehi taught to his son Jacob: men "are

free to choose." We can "choose liberty and eternal life," or we can "choose captivity and death" (2 Nephi 2:27).

But surely, we say, no rational being would choose captivity and death. Of course not. Not directly. The words of Elder Dallin H. Oaks show an interesting progression that permeates our lives: "Desires dictate our priorities, priorities shape our choices, and choices determine our actions."[3] If our desires—even well-intentioned ones—are out of harmony with God's will, and if we persist in making choices based on those desires, the natural consequence of those choices can lead us to captivity and death. (The opposite is true too, of course, but we are talking now only about the road to spiritual death and destruction.)

Let's return to our example of pornography. When those two individuals see the website, let's assume they both feel the same twinges of temptation. Then something happens. Lehi said it "must needs be" that we be "enticed" by both good and evil. So as this temptation rises, the Spirit immediately tries to the warn them about the consequences of making a wrong choice, or remind them of the *promises* that follow from making the right choice.

The problem is, the Holy Ghost doesn't shout at us. It might simplify our lives if every time we were tempted to do something wrong, the Spirit yelled, "Don't do that!" But His voice is still, and small, and it whispers (see D&C 85:6). It whispers things like "This will bring you sorrow." "If you resist this temptation, I will draw closer to you." "This could destroy your marriage." "Watching these things will corrode your soul." "I will help you resist if you let me."

Satan's approach is very different. In the first place, he tries to keep our focus away from the consequences. "One look won't hurt anyone." "You're strong enough to quit whenever you want." "What's the big deal—it's just a picture. You can't be immoral with a picture."

He too makes promises, but they are for instant fulfillment and gratification—fun, pleasure, satisfaction, stimulation, excitement.

The key concept here is that God, because of the sacred nature of agency, allows us to make these kinds of choices. Then He grants unto us according to our desires. We can choose things which bring liberty and life, or we can choose things which lead to captivity and death. That is what Alma was teaching Corianton when he said, "Therefore, O my son, whosoever *will* come may come and partake of the waters of life freely; and whosoever will not come *the same is not compelled to come;* but in the last day it shall be restored unto him according to his deeds" (Alma 42:27).

## When Good Desires Can Lead Us Astray

Alma caught himself desiring something that sounded really wonderful but that was, in truth, contrary to God's purposes. Fortunately, the Spirit whispered to him and he saw that his desires were not pleasing to the Lord. We must be on guard against making that same mistake. We can't assume that just because our desires are good, we have permission to proceed.

A common example of this happens in the family. German philosopher Friedrich Nietzsche gave this thought-provoking warning: "This is the hardest of all: to close the open hand out of love, and keep modest as a giver."[4] How many parents, motivated by love and a desire to make their children happy, overindulge them with toys, gifts, money, and opportunities, with little or nothing required of them in return? Does giving our children everything, without asking for anything in return, have anything to do with the principle that "he that is idle shall not eat the bread nor wear the garments of the laborer" (D&C 42:42)? Does that apply to our children too?

On the other hand, other parents are so determined to keep their children on the right path—again, a noble desire—that they resort to open coercion to try to force their children to be righteous. In other words, they do to their children what God refuses to do for His children.

Our purpose here is not to answer how we strike a balance between these two parenting dilemmas. The point is, good desires are not enough. What pulled Alma back from his desire to be an angel was a gospel principle. That is a good model for us. We must apply gospel principles to situations and look for both the positive and negative consequences of our actions. We also need the Spirit to give us the wisdom to see what is right, not just what is desirable.

Here is a case where outwardly good intentions actually led a person into decisions that ended in tragedy, not only for himself, but for his family as well. The late Carlfred Broderick was a prominent LDS family therapist. He shares this example of how "people's virtues as well as their vices may play an important part in their infidelity."[5]

Brother Broderick tells the story of a young husband and father who held the calling of a local missionary in his stake. This young man was considered by many to be "intensely spiritual." He was effective in his calling because he was not reluctant to share the gospel with others.

His secretary at work was a young divorcee, still reeling from the painful breakup of her marriage. He began to talk to her, hoping he might bring some joy into her life. They began to have long gospel conversations over lunch. She told him of her unhappy childhood and her difficult marriage. His heart went out to her. He told her that her Heavenly Father loved her and that he believed God had sent her to this place of employment so she could meet him and find the gospel and be healed. He was thrilled to think he might be an instrument in bringing about that purpose.

As time went on, they took long lunches together so they could talk without interruption. Occasionally he stopped off at her apartment so they could continue an unfinished discussion. He called her his "little Goldie," because she was such a "golden contact." He began giving her reassuring hugs so she would know how much he cared for her. She, in turn, was grateful for his concern and help and "saw him almost as her savior."

Brother Broderick describes what happened next:

> On one occasion when he hugged her, she pulled him to her and kissed him. He was overwhelmed with a flood of feelings that washed over him, and before that visit was ended he violated his covenants.
>
> By the time he confessed his sin to his wife and stake president a few weeks later, he was convinced that he loved this woman as he had never loved his wife, and that she and her two young sons needed him more than his own family did. He promised her that after he had divorced his wife and paid the penalty for his sin, he would yet baptize her and take her to the temple. Clear through the Church court, he insisted that although he had been wrong to violate his temple vows, he had been sent to this young woman by God.

Brother Broderick concludes the story with this observation:

> It is difficult to say at exactly what point this man's spiritual pride, ability to rationalize, and poor judgment combined to lead him from righteous sharing of the gospel to unrighteous indulgence and betrayal of his marital vows. Certainly it was early in the relationship. *He was so bemused by the virtue of his own motivation and by the intensity of the "spirit" he felt . . . that he was immune to warnings from his wife, his friends, or even the Spirit.*[6]

I've heard it said that "the mind is a wonderful thing. It can think up a thousand reasons for doing what the heart is already committed to do." It is part of human nature to seek to justify ourselves to ourselves through rationalizing that what we want or what we are doing is good. We must remember that the desires of our heart will determine what we are and what we are becoming. Those desires must be good in God's eyes, not just our own.

## Other Factors Considered in the Judgment

With that, let's move on to a more cheerful aspect of this topic. We know from the scriptures that the Lord also takes other factors into account at the Judgment. Many of those factors are also related to our desires. For example, we are told that those "who died without law" will be judged differently than those who had a knowledge of the gospel (D&C 76:72). How is that related to our desires? Because the law (or the word of God) contains the promises, and these promises are what trigger a desire to win them for ourselves.

We know that those who sin against the greater light receive a greater condemnation (see D&C 82:3). We know that young children can be selfish, cruel, and disobedient, but they are judged by a different standard because they have not yet reached the age of accountability (see D&C 137:10; 18:42; 20:71). Here too our desires are directly affected by the opportunities—or lack of them—which are part of our lives.

Elder Neal A. Maxwell spoke of another mitigating factor that God will take into account when we are judged. He said, "God thus takes into merciful account not only our desires and our performance, but also *the degrees of difficulty* which our varied circumstances impose upon us."[7] I love that concept. Would anything less be fair and just?

I may desire to accomplish great things as an artist, or invent something that will bless all of mankind, but if I grow up in a hut instead of a mansion, if I never learn to read while others go to Harvard or Oxford, my circumstances greatly restrict my desires. Isn't it fair to expect more intellectually from an Einstein than from a person with an average IQ of 100? Shouldn't we expect more from a Mozart than from a normal six-year-old piano student? The Lord's answer to these questions is clear: "For of him unto whom much is given much is required; and he who sins against the greater light shall receive the greater condemnation" (D&C 82:3).

Why, in the parable of the soils, did the good soil differ in the amount of fruit it produced—"some an hundredfold, some sixtyfold, some thirtyfold" (Matthew 13:8)? All the soil was good. What made the difference? Any farmer or gardener can tell you that even good soils differ in quality and productivity.

## Yielding Our Hearts to God

When our hearts are in tune with the Spirit and our desires are aligned with God, we can draw on a great reservoir of hope that can sustain us in any adversity or tribulation we may experience. Here is the promise on which that hope is based, as described by Elder Neal A. Maxwell: "What we insistently desire, over time, is what we will eventually become and what we will receive in eternity."[8]

I close this chapter with three pertinent reminders of the importance of desire.

- "Look not on [a man's] countenance, or on the height of his stature; because I have refused him: for the Lord seeth not as man seeth; for man looketh on the outward appearance, but *the Lord looketh on the heart*" (1 Samuel 16:7).
- "They did fast and pray oft, and did wax stronger and stronger in their humility, and firmer and firmer in the

faith of Christ, unto the filling their souls with joy and consolation, yea, even to the purifying and the sanctification of their hearts, which sanctification cometh *because of their yielding their hearts unto God*" (Helaman 3:35).

- "Delight thyself also in the Lord; and he shall give thee the desires of thine heart" (Psalm 37:4).

---

## Notes

*Epigraph.* Dallin H. Oaks, "Desire," *Ensign,* May 2011, 42.

1. "Humility," in *Encyclopedia of Mormonism,* ed. Daniel H. Ludlow (New York: MacMillan Publishing Co., 1992), 2:663.

2. "Know This, That Every Soul Is Free," in *Hymns of The Church of Jesus Christ of Latter-day Saints* (Salt Lake City: The Church of Jesus Christ of Latter-day Saints, 1985), no. 240.

3. Oaks, "Desire," 42.

4. Frederich Nietzsche, *Thus Spake Zarathustra,* trans. Thomas Common (Calgary, Canada: Theophania, 2011), 92.

5. Carlfred Broderick, *One Flesh, One Heart: Putting Celestial Love into Your Temple Marriage* (Salt Lake City: Deseret Book, 1986), 19.

6. Broderick, *One Flesh, One Heart,* 20.

7. Neal A. Maxwell, "'According to the Desire of [Our] Hearts,'" *Ensign,* November 1996, 21.

8. Ibid.

# A Personal Witness

I<small>N OUR QUEST</small> to gain greater hope, the role that the desires of the heart play is especially meaningful to me because of an experience I had a few years ago. Though it is of a personal nature, I feel that it might help some to better understand the particular role that the desires of our heart can play in the development of faith and hope.

My life's career was with the Church Educational System (CES). After nearly thirty-five years, I took an early retirement in order to pursue a dream of mine. I had long desired to create a media company that would create values-laden media, with the primary focus being the creation of big-screen movies. I felt like this was a righteous desire and hoped the Lord agreed.

Once I retired, the first task I faced was deciding where to start, and how to prioritize the various projects I had considered doing. When I sat down and listed all possible books and media projects, there were twenty-seven items on my list. The challenge was deciding where to begin. I began asking the Lord which project would be most pleasing to Him, and also which might have the greatest chance for success so as to create momentum for additional projects.

For weeks I asked the Lord each day for help and direction. A scripture from the Doctrine and Covenants became an inspiration to me: "Verily, verily, I say unto you, *even as you desire* of me so it shall be done unto you; and, *if you desire, you shall be the means of doing much good* in this generation" (D&C 11:8). I read it over and over, and decided what I really desired was to choose a project that would accomplish good and not just be personally fulfilling for me.

To my surprise, months passed and no answer came. I began to feel frustrated. This seemed like a pretty acceptable desire (at least, that's what I kept telling myself). I wanted to be of service and to do something meaningful and to make a contribution to others. And I was ready to go; I was chomping at the bit to get started. But nothing came. I began to move forward in small steps. I finished one book and started research on another. I called several colleagues who had experience in media and we began brainstorming possibilities. I'd get really excited about something, but by the next morning, it sounded dumber than a pile of rocks.

I decided to jump-start the process by searching in the scriptures, specifically the Doctrine and Covenants. Very quickly I began to notice a pattern popping up in what I was reading. It was the concept of patience. I was a bit irritated, to be honest. I had been retired for several months now, and I was no closer to an answer than before, and He was asking me to be patient? If anything, I was less sure of what I should be doing now than before I started. It didn't come easily, but I finally got the message: "Be patient."

Something else was going on in my life during that same time. Even now, about ten years later, I wince to think about it, because it represented some unwarranted assumptions on my part, assumptions that were actually a bit prideful.

The last decade of my career in CES was working as a zone administrator in central headquarters. There were nine zone administrators, and between us, we supervised the worldwide operations of the Church Educational System. Because of the caliber of these men, during that decade I saw one after another take a three-year leave of absence from CES to serve as a mission president. By the time I retired, I and a couple of others were the only ones who hadn't served in that capacity.

Here is where my pride got the better of me. In the midst of my search for guidance, this thought came to me one day: "Maybe the reason you're not getting answers is that you're going to be called as a mission president." I realize now how presumptuous that was of me, but the more I thought about it, the more certain I was that this was why I wasn't getting an answer. I was not elated by that thought. In fact, the thought brought me great dismay. Being a mission president would ruin everything. Mission presidents don't write books or produce movies while on their missions. It would mean putting all of my plans and dreams on hold for another three years. I was even tempted to pray and ask the Lord that I might be excused from such service. I'm happy to say that I never gave in to that temptation. But I may as well have, because in my heart that desire was pretty close to a prayer.

More time passed with no answers. I began to wonder if the Lord wasn't trying to teach me something. I started adding this phrase to my prayers, "Thy will—and Thy *timing*—be done." I have to admit, though, this additional request frequently came into my thoughts without bidding: *"And please hurry."*

By the next fall—a full year after retirement—I was still no closer to getting an answer. And all that time I kept my fingers crossed that I would not be called as a mission president.

Then came a lesson in priesthood meeting one Sunday. The guest instructor was Elder F. Enzio Busche, of the Seventy. The Busches were members of our ward, and on this Sunday, the high priest group leader invited Elder Busche to teach. To introduce his subject, Elder Busche had all of us turn to Alma 29, where Alma begins by expressing his wish that he could be an angel and declare the gospel as if with a trump. As Elder Busche read the verses, he emphasized certain phrases that struck my mind with great force.

- "I ought to be *content* with the things which the Lord hath allotted unto me."
- "[God] granteth unto men according to their *desire,* whether it be unto death or unto life."
- "It is given according to his *desires,* whether he *desireth* good or evil, life or death, joy or remorse" (Alma 29:3–5).

Talk about taking a shot to the head. It was suddenly as if I were the only person in the room and Elder Busche were speaking directly to me. I don't remember much about the rest of the lesson. My mind was a wild tumble of thoughts. I thought about my grand plans for a media company. I thought of my burning desire to make movies. I thought about my constant dread that I might be called as a mission president. And I was filled with shame. I was fooling myself. I might be saying, "Thy will—and Thy timing—be done," but that wasn't what I *really wanted.*

That night, my prayers changed dramatically, both in content and fervency. I asked for the Lord's forgiveness for my selfishness. Like Alma, my desires weren't evil, but I too did "sin in my wish," because I was not really open to whatever it was the Lord might allot unto me. I had read this scripture from the Old Testament—"Thou shalt rejoice before the Lord thy God *in all that thou puttest thine hands unto*" (Deuteronomy 12:18)—and I humbly promised the Lord that I would put my hand to whatever He wanted me to do. And I would try to rejoice if it was the Lord's will that I be called as a mission president.

Elder Busche's lesson, with its personal and pointed call to repentance, occurred around Christmas. For several more months nothing specific happened, but now I was content to wait. Well, mostly. The one thing I held onto was the absolute trust that God's wisdom was greater than mine, and that His purposes were higher than mine, and that His will for me was superior to my own. Even if His will meant I would be called away for three years.

Then on April 4, 2002, my wife and I received a call from the First Presidency's office asking if we could come to the office of President Gordon B. Hinckley the next day. We did so, and that day changed our lives forever. President Hinckley called me to be a member of the Second Quorum of the Seventy and a General Authority. My wife was asked to be my companion in that calling. I was literally stunned into silence. And one of the thoughts that flashed through my mind in that moment was *Well, there's your answer on which project gets first priority. None of them.*

I was sustained in general conference the next day, and went on to serve *six and a half years* as a Seventy. Three of those years (how's that for irony?) were in the Area Presidency for the Europe West Area. It was the most significant growing experience in my life and in the lives of my family. We saw blessings that had been promised by two patriarchs fifty years earlier fulfilled. We saw rich blessings come to our family. We had many confirming spiritual experiences and our faith grew.

But among all of those blessings came two which caught me totally by surprise. The first had to do with one of the books on my list. For many years, I had been fascinated by the subject of personal revelation—how it comes, what it's like, how we recognize it, how we get it. And several years before I retired from CES, I had begun a serious study of the subject. I began speaking on the topic every opportunity I got. I discovered it was a topic that struck a responsive chord in many people. Many times after a class or a fireside, I was asked if I planned to write a book on it. Deseret Book also encouraged me to do so. I was sorely tempted, but something held me back. My stock answer to those questions went something like this: "Because of the nature of the topic, and its doctrinal importance and sensitivity, I believe that topic should be reserved for a General Authority, perhaps even one of the Twelve."

But as the years passed, my file on personal revelation grew. During the time I had been trying to decide on a project, I considered writing a book on personal revelation several times, but it never felt right. Then came the calling to be a General Authority and our assignment to England. Our schedule was so full with other duties that I didn't have time to even consider writing a book, but I did find myself thinking about the book from time to time and telling myself, *You're a General Authority now. No more excuses.* After our return home to Salt Lake City, our schedule stabilized and I had more time. I began work on *Hearing the Voice of the Lord: Principles and Patterns of Personal Revelation.* It was published in 2007 while I was still serving as a Seventy.

The second blessing was even more ironic. When my call came, I assumed this was the Lord's way of saying, "My son, making movies is not what I have in mind for you." Wrong again. A few months after my call to the Seventy, I received a telephone call from two men who were seeking permission to make a movie based on the Work and the Glory novels that I had written. These two men had the movie-making experience and the personal values that I was looking for. Since my only involvement would be to review the script to make sure there were not any serious concerns, the First Presidency said they had no objection to their moving forward. One year later, with the financial backing of Larry H. Miller, *The Work and the Glory* was released nationwide.

Then they made another movie. *And another!* My dream was one movie; the Lord made it possible for three to be done. All along I had thought I had to be the catalyst in getting a movie made. The Lord—with what feels like a wry touch of humor—seemed to be saying, "If I can just get you out of the way for three years, we can make this all happen."

How grateful I am to Elder Busche for teaching that lesson in our quorum meeting that day. How grateful I am to Alma for teaching a principle that I badly needed to learn. And how grateful I am that the Lord didn't let me have it my way.

# III

# The Value of Perspective

*In those moments when we feel the pain*
*which is a necessary part of the plan of happiness,*
*we can remember that there was an ancient*
*time when that plan was first unveiled.*
*Then the perceptive among us voted not secretly,*
*but audibly—by shouting for joy! (See Job 38:7.)*
*Let us not go back on those feelings now—*
*for we saw more clearly then what we*
*are experiencing now!*

Neal A. Maxwell

*Fear thou not; for I am with thee: be not dismayed;*
*for I am thy God: I will strengthen thee; yea,*
*I will help thee; yea, I will uphold thee with the*
*right hand of my righteousness. . . .*

*For I the Lord thy God will hold thy right hand,*
*saying unto thee, Fear not; I will help thee.*

ISAIAH 41:10, 13

# CHAPTER TWELVE

# THE HAND OF THE LORD

❧❦❧

## Perspective

I N THIS SECTION, we move from the concept of alignment to the concept of perspective as it relates to acquiring greater hope. Two definitions of perspective which are relevant to our discussion are "a mental view or prospect" and "seeing all the relevant data in a meaningful relationship."[1] Some synonyms for perspective would include things like viewpoint, vantage point, outlook, or a way of seeing and thinking about things.

Our perspective of things, especially as it relates to our relationship with God and His plan for us, directly affects how we react to things, what choices we make, how we prioritize our lives, and how we progress spiritually. The "inevitable tragedies of life"[2] can be compelling, demanding, disheartening, and exhausting. We have already talked about people who have been active, faithful believers for all of their lives and yet have changed their perspective as they have faced adverse circumstances and have turned away from the Church. Some even reject God and want no part of Him in their lives. Thus, having a true perspective of things becomes another important way to maintain or fortify hope.

With that introduction, let us begin by examining one of the most important perspectives we can have if we are to stand fast when the storms of life howl around us.

### Seeing the Hand of the Lord in Our Lives

President Joseph F. Smith said this:

> It has not been by the wisdom of man that this people have been directed in their course until the present; it has been by the wisdom of him who is above man, whose knowledge is greater than that of man, and whose power is above the power of man. . . . *The hand of the Lord may not be visible to all.* There may be many who cannot discern the workings of God's will in the progress and development of this great latter-day work, but there are those who see in every hour and in every moment of the existence of the Church, from its beginning until now, the overruling, almighty hand of [God].[3]

Note that President Smith said that the hand of the Lord "may not be visible to all." Normally, God works in our lives in quiet ways, without fanfare or claps of thunder. Some things we experience are so subtle, so "normal," that they pass right by us and we don't "see" them for what they are. Sometimes, even the most faithful miss the evidence before them and do not perceive the Lord's hand or recognize His voice. That is why we need to focus our spiritual eyes more closely on the events of our lives. We may be surprised by how much we have missed or are missing. Remember, one definition of perspective is to see all the relevant data in a meaningful relationship.

In chapter 7, we quoted President Gordon B. Hinckley, who said that true conversion comes when we have "spiritual experiences."[4] When we speak of seeing the hand of the Lord in our lives, that's another way of talking about spiritual experiences. These experiences are what confirm our hope in the promises. This not only strengthens our faith but also deepens our hope to the point where we are truly converted. Remember that, as President Dieter F. Uchtdorf said, to hope is to trust in the promises.[5] When the promises are confirmed, "then shall [we] rejoice; for [we] shall know that it is a blessing . . . *from the hand of God*" (2 Nephi 30:6).

In another book of mine, I referred to some of these "hand of the Lord" experiences as "divine signatures." I defined them in this way:

> Sometimes, the Lord sends His blessings in such a highly unusual, dramatic, or precisely timed manner, that it might be likened to a "divine signature." It is as though the Lord "signs" the blessing personally so that we will know with certainty that it comes from Him.
>
> In doing so, God not only gives us the blessing, but at the same time He strengthens our faith and deepens our testimony of Him.[6]

After pondering and studying the concept of hope, I would amend the last sentence to read: "In doing so, God not only gives us the blessing, *and confirms His promises,* but at the same time He strengthens our faith, deepens our testimony, and *fortifies our hope.*"

We shall focus on just four ways the hand of the Lord is shown in our lives—two in this chapter and two in the next.

### Personal Blessings for Us and Those We Love

It has been my experience that we experience the hand of the Lord most often, and most directly, at the personal, individual level. This is where the Lord's influence can most directly and powerfully affect our faith and our testimony. The blessings come in a variety of ways. Sometimes they are so dramatic and so unmistakable that we call them miracles. Other times they are so subtle and so quiet that we find ourselves asking, "Was that really from God? Or was it just a coincidence?"

But whether grand or small, the blessings are intensely personal. They are tailored for *our* needs, *our* desires, and *our* pleadings. When they come, they confirm to our hearts that God really does live, that He really is a loving and caring Father. They show us that God can and does

- protect us in times of danger—both physical and spiritual (see 3 Nephi 4:30).
- enlighten us by the Spirit of truth (see D&C 6:15).
- ease our burdens (see Mosiah 24:14).
- heal the brokenhearted (see Luke 4:18).
- heal the wounded soul (see Jacob 2:8).
- let all things work together for our good (see D&C 100:15).
- go before our face; be on our right hand and on our left; and place angels round about us to bear us up (see D&C 84:88).

There are many other similar promises of such personal blessings from the hand of the Lord. Sometimes His help comes in times of great personal crisis or personal suffering. In these cases, we tend to view the blessings as remarkable divine signatures that testify of the Lord's love. Here is an example from the handcart pioneers.

Louisa Mellor was sixteen years old when she came across the plains with her family in the Martin Handcart Company. Somewhere between Florence, Nebraska, and Fort Laramie, Wyoming, food ran so low that the members of the company were limited to a few ounces of flour each day. Then the weather closed in. Louisa's mother completely lost heart (another way of saying she lost hope) and refused to go any farther. Here is Louisa's account of what followed.

> The company could not wait for her, so she bade my father goodbye and kissed each one of the children Godspeed. Then my mother sat down on a boulder and wept. I told my . . . sister Elizabeth to take good care of the twins and the rest of the family, and that I would stay with mother.
>
> I went a few yards away and prayed *with faith* that God would help us, that He would protect us from devouring wolves, and asked that He would let us reach camp. As I was going back to where Mother was sitting, I found a pie in the road. I picked it up and gave it to mother to eat. After resting awhile we started on our journey, thanking God for the blessings.[7]

Even if we could explain how a pie had somehow ended up in the road out in the middle of a vast wilderness—especially when no one in the company had sufficient food to make a pie—we would still have to account for the fact that the entire handcart company had passed over that road a short time before and not seen it. However it happened, at a time of complete hopelessness, the Lord extended a tender mercy to this girl and her mother. The pie provided physical nourishment for only a brief time, but far more significant was the fact that the pie nourished their *hope!*

Here is how Louisa concludes her account:

> Many times after that, Mother felt like giving up and quitting, but then she would remember how wonderful the Lord had been to spare her so many times, and offered a prayer of gratitude instead.[8]

By His own declaration, the Lord said, "I . . . am merciful and gracious unto those who fear me, and *delight* to honor those who serve me in righteousness and in truth unto the end" (D&C 76:5). I love to think of the Lord as being delighted when He blesses us. I like to think that leaving a pie in the middle of the trail was a delight to Him.

In many other cases, the blessings are not so dramatic or miraculous. They are simple and sometimes seem unimportant—even trivial—in the great cosmic scheme of things. They seem far beneath the attention of an all-powerful deity. We often refer to these "small" blessings as the "tender mercies of the Lord" (1 Nephi 1:20). I put "small" in quotes because often these blessings can be very important in converting the heart, building testimony, strengthening faith, and deepening hope. Ask any group of children if God has ever heard and answered one of their prayers, and you will probably hear stories like these:

- They lost a treasured item (money, a toy, etc.) and asked Heavenly Father to help them. Immediately they found what they were looking for.
- A sick kitten was healed.
- Daddy made it home in time for an important activity.
- When they were lost, they prayed and were found or else found their way home.
- They received unusual help on a test in school.
- When they were deeply frightened by darkness (or a thunderstorm or a bad dream) at night, they prayed and immediately peace came and they were able to fall asleep.
- They found a friend at school when they asked God to help them do so.

Here's one story I found especially touching. In a fast and testimony meeting, a mother thanked the Lord for a tender mercy that had been given to her son the previous week. His first-grade teacher set aside part of one day each week as "popcorn day." Popcorn was served to a student during recess if all of his or her work had been completed. It was her son's favorite day at school, and he looked forward to it all week.

Because of a doctor's appointment, though, he had been unable to attend school on popcorn day. He was so disappointed, and he asked his mother if she thought they might have popcorn day the next day instead. She said no, explaining that it was always held on the same day of the week. If something came up at school that interfered with the treat, then the teacher simply skipped it for that week.

Nothing she said could dampen her son's hope. As he prepared to leave for school the next day, she warned him again that it likely wouldn't be popcorn day. "It's all right, Mom," he said cheerfully. "I asked Heavenly Father if it could be popcorn day today."

Touched by his faith, she said nothing more, but she worried all day about how he would react when popcorn day didn't happen. When he came home, his mother waited for a few minutes, but he didn't mention anything unusual. Finally, she asked if they had had popcorn day. "Sure," he said, as if it were the most natural thing in the world.

Why would the God of the universe, a deity of infinite power and majesty, concern Himself with something as trivial as popcorn day or a sick kitten? I believe there are two answers to that. First, it is because He is not just God, but our Heavenly Father. Any parent will tell you that they find joy in doing small and trivial things for their children if it brings them joy.

But second, and more important, consider that while popcorn day *is* perhaps of little eternal consequence, a child's testimony is not.

And that little boy's testimony was strengthened that day. A beloved Primary song asks this question:

> Heavenly Father, are you really there?
> And do you hear and answer ev'ry child's prayer?[9]

In my experience, it is older children or adults who are unsure of the answer to that question. Most children don't have to ask. They already know.

Thanks be to God that He realizes that there are times when even adults need to know the answer to that question, even if it is for something that is not one of the great cosmic challenges of life. We are warned in the scriptures against praying for things which are "not expedient" (D&C 88:65), but I have learned that expedient doesn't always mean only the great and grand things. Here is a wonderful example of that:

> When I was still a young mother, we moved into a ward that had only one organist. When he moved out of the ward, I was called to be the new organist. I had never played the organ, but I did play the piano, so I accepted the challenge, knowing there was no one else who could play. I struggled but enjoyed the challenge.
>
> About eight months later, I learned that an older couple, whom I'll call the Johnsons, was moving into our ward. Brother Johnson had a master's degree from Harvard University in organ performance. I was sure the bishop would immediately release me and put this man in as the ward organist.
>
> The chapel where we met was very old and didn't have a raised platform for the speakers. So directly in front of where I played the organ were benches where the congregation sat.

As if my level of intimidation wasn't high enough already, Brother and Sister Johnson, on their very first Sunday in our ward, sat on the bench just three feet from where I was playing the organ. They continued to do so every Sunday thereafter. I died every Sunday, imagining the torture I was putting Brother Johnson through as he was forced to listen to my abominable playing. (I must add that Brother Johnson is a kind man who never once made any kind of critical remark about my playing.)

About a month after the Johnsons had arrived, I approached the bishop. "Did you know that Brother Johnson is a concert organist?" I asked.

"Yes, I did," he said with a wise twinkle in his eye.

"Well," I persisted, "aren't you going to put him in as the ward organist?"

"No, I have something else in mind for him."

I was flabbergasted. My self-doubt and feelings of inadequacy grew exponentially every week that Brother Johnson sat on the pew in front of the organ.

One Sunday, I botched a verse in the sacrament hymn and began to cry. Tears were streaming down my cheeks, and my nose started running. I couldn't read the music through my tears, which only made my playing deteriorate further. I finished in disgrace—wiping at my eyes, wiping at my nose. I felt like every eye in the congregation was on me. Tears continued to pour down my face. In my mind, I cried out, "Why do I have to do this?"

I will never forget the most tender voice that came into my mind. It called me by my first name, then said, "Are you playing for them, or are you playing for me?"

The thought took me by surprise. I was forced to evaluate

where my focus was, and then I knew who I *wanted* to be playing for.

"I'm playing for you, Lord," I said in my mind.

Then came His loving response, "Then keep playing. It is good enough for me."[10]

## The Gentle Nudge

In my experience, there is another way the Lord extends His hand to us. I call it the "gentle nudge."

I believe there are times when it is better for us to learn through more subtle means, when we are left to wonder whether that was God's hand or not. In those cases, the Lord's help might come as a fleeting thought, a quiet impression, or even a vague feeling that something is wrong. Sometimes it comes as the Lord influences things around us—someone says something, or we run across something "by accident" that is exactly what we need, or a choice opportunity pops up unexpectedly.

As I reflect back over my life and look for times when the Lord's hand was present, I find many instances where the answers and blessings were direct, sweet, and clearly discernable. But I also see other times when the help came so unobtrusively that it was only much later that I recognized the Lord's hand in it at all. At the time, I thought it was just me making a wise or a lucky choice or a lucky break. Or I didn't notice it at all. Now I know better. Some years ago, as part of a lecture I wrote these words:

There are times in one's life that may seem trivial or only marginally important at the moment they happen, but as the years roll on, they prove to have been like the switch points on a railway line. In a fast-moving train, one is hardly aware of passing over those points where two lines are joined, separated by no more than an inch or two of space. Yet, depending on how the switch is thrown, one can end up in destinations as divergent as New York and Los Angeles.[11]

Here is one example of an unrecognized switch point that still makes me smile when I think about it. I'm often asked how I got started writing novels. I wish I could say it came as a direct answer to prayer or that one day I was swept away by a grand impulse to write fiction. Here's how it actually happened. It may not be an "inspiring" answer, but it was an important moment.

One night as my wife and I were preparing for bed, she said, "Our oldest daughter will be going to college next fall. Just how did you plan to pay for that?"

I thought for a moment, then replied, "Lately, I've been thinking about trying my hand at fiction, but I need a really strong concept. If I could find one, then I'd like to write a novel."

Without a moment's hesitation, she said, "You love Israel. Why don't you write a novel set in Israel?"

That did it. One year later my first novel, *One in Thine Hand*, was sent to the publisher and was on bookshelves a short time later.

Though seemingly trivial at the time, that conversation proved to be a significant turning point in my writing career.

As I ponder on these kinds of experiences, I realize that if it were not for the gentle nudges along the way, I would not have gone on a mission. I would not have gone to college—at least, not at first. I would not have married the woman I did. I would never have become a religion teacher. I don't believe I would ever have been privileged to serve as a General Authority. And I very likely would not be writing this book either.

Sometimes the nudge pulls us up short and makes us reconsider our circumstances. Other times it may be a quick—even hard—shove to get us out of the way of danger. Often it's more like a lift, given as some form of personal revelation, which keeps us going in tough times.

One example of that kind of lift is found in the life of Elizabeth Horrocks Jackson, who lost her husband in the middle of the night near Red Buttes, Wyoming (see chapter 1). Her hope in the resurrection gave her the strength to cope with her loss, but her situation was still extremely critical. Because the weather had turned bitter cold, the weakened men were unable to put up the tents. There was no choice but to stay out in the open in temperatures that hovered near zero degrees Fahrenheit. That in and of itself was a life-threatening situation. She had three young children. Were they to be taken too? Or would they be left as orphans for someone else to take to Zion? We can only wonder at the sense of hopelessness that must have swept over her at that moment.

Here is the conclusion of her story:

> I sat down on a rock with one child in my lap and one on each side of me. In that condition I remained until morning. . . .
>
> It will be readily perceived that under such adverse circumstances I had become despondent. [How's that for an understatement!] I was six or seven thousand miles from my native land, in a wild, rocky, mountain country, in a destitute condition, the ground covered with snow, the waters covered with ice, and I with three fatherless children with scarcely nothing to protect them from the merciless storms. When I retired to my bed that night, being the 27th of Oct., *I had a stunning revelation.* In my dream, my husband stood by me and said—"Cheer up, Elizabeth, deliverance is at hand."[12]

The *very next day,* three men from the rescue party coming from Salt Lake galloped into camp and announced that wagons filled with food, clothing, and warm bedding were waiting a few miles from where the handcart company was camped.

Many years later, Elizabeth wrote this introductory paragraph to the account she left for her posterity:

> I have a desire to leave a record of those scenes and events, thru which I have passed, that my children, down to my latest posterity may read what their ancestors were willing to suffer, and did suffer, . . . for the Gospel's sake. . . . I also desire them to know that it was in obedience to the commandments of the true and living God, and with the assurance of an eternal reward—an exaltation to eternal life in His kingdom—that we suffered these things.[13]

What a powerful example of how having the proper perspective and seeing the hand of the Lord in our lives can profoundly change our hope and faith. We have seen how His hand is manifest in personal blessings given as tender mercies to us. We have seen how at other times, His hand gives us a gentle nudge or a needed lift to get us moving or to help us change directions.

Let us now turn to two other ways the hand of the Lord is manifest in our lives and see how they too can strengthen our hope.

## When the Hand of God Is Withheld

A third way that God's hand operates in our lives has a touch of irony to it. The hand of God is always there, but sometimes He chooses *not* to extend that hand in our behalf. There are times when He stands back and lets things play out without directly intervening. One of the most dramatic examples of that is when the Father withdrew His presence at the hour of Christ's most agonizing suffering, causing the Savior to cry out, "My God, my God, why hast thou forsaken me?" (Matthew 27:46).

There are other examples. When Alma was converted by the words of Abinadi and took his small band of believers into the wilderness, the Lord helped them safely escape into the wilderness (see Mosiah 23:2). Yet a short time later, their enemies accidentally stumbled across Alma's little colony and put them into bondage (see Mosiah 23:35). Why didn't the Lord turn them aside and protect Alma and his people? Or warn Alma to flee? Mormon explained it this way: "The Lord seeth fit to chasten his people; yea, he trieth their patience and their faith" (Alma 23:21). Eventually the intervention came, but not until after Alma and his people had suffered a great deal.

The history of the Church is filled with examples of the Lord standing back—watching over His people, but withholding His help, and not delivering them from oppression or deflecting the fury of the mobs. Seventeen people were murdered at Haun's Mill. During the fall of Far West, the mobs raped, pillaged, and murdered. Wicked men drove women and children out of Nauvoo in the dead of winter.

Or consider the handcart companies of 1856. The winter storm that swept out of the north in mid-October was said by those who knew the area well to be the worst they had ever seen. The suffering of the pioneers was beyond description. We can see why the Lord might not give them balmy weather all the way to Salt Lake City, but the worst storm *ever*? This is the Master who stilled the storm on the Sea of Galilee. Why not quell a blizzard on the plains of Wyoming?

There are many answers to such questions. Sometimes it is our own stubborn disobedience that brings trials into our lives (see D&C 101:2–8). It is not that He has withdrawn from us; it is because we have withdrawn from Him (see, for example, Helaman 4:11–13,

20–26). It may be because we have grown too comfortable in times of prosperity and ease (see Helaman 12:2).

But other times it is not because of our failures or because we need to be punished. There may be a lesson we need to learn or an opportunity for growth we need to experience. There may even been other purposes we do not see.

In some cases, it could be because others must be blessed or given their agency. Think of the testimonies that have been strengthened and fortified by the example of the handcart pioneers. Youth from all over the Church undertake similar handcart treks so they can get a glimpse of what it means to be truly converted. The faith and sacrifice of those early pioneers is still influencing lives more than 150 years later. Surely that had to be part of the Lord's purposes too.

Just because we can't see or understand why He seems to have abandoned us doesn't mean that He is not there. This too is part of life. He who whispers comfort to a woman playing the organ may choose not to intervene as our financial circumstances disintegrate. For some, He blesses them with employment within a day or two of losing a job. Others go months without an answer. The same child who found a lost kitten may plead with the Lord that his or her parents not divorce, and that prayer is not granted.

Elder D. Todd Christofferson shared a personal experience which illustrates this aspect of God's will for us so well:

> Some time before I was called as a General Authority, I faced a personal economic challenge that persisted for several years. It did not come about as a consequence of anyone's wrongdoing or ill will; it was just one of those things that sometimes come into our lives. It ebbed and flowed in seriousness and urgency, but it never went away completely. At times this challenge threatened the welfare of my family and

me, and I thought we might be facing financial ruin. I prayed for some miraculous intervention to deliver us. Although I offered that prayer many times with great sincerity and earnest desire, the answer in the end was "No." Finally I learned to pray as the Savior did: "Nevertheless not my will, but thine, be done" (Luke 22:42). I sought the Lord's help with each tiny step along the way to a final resolution.

There were times when I had exhausted all my resources, when I had nowhere or no one to turn to at that moment, when there was simply no other human being I could call on to help meet the exigency before me. With no other recourse, more than once I fell down before my Heavenly Father begging in tears for His help. And He did help. Sometimes it was nothing more than a sense of peace, a feeling of assurance that things would work out. . . .

Though I suffered then, as I look back now, I am grateful that there was not a quick solution to my problem. The fact that I was forced to turn to God for help almost daily over an extended period of years taught me truly how to pray and get answers to prayer and taught me in a very practical way to have faith in God. I came to know my Savior and my Heavenly Father in a way and to a degree that might not have happened otherwise or that might have taken me much longer to achieve. . . . I learned to trust in the Lord with all my heart. I learned to walk with Him day by day.[14]

What a wonderful example of how having a broader perspective of our Father's plan and purposes can strengthen us in times of adversity. Without that perspective we may falter, or even fall. A warning, however. Just because we "see" what the Lord is doing doesn't make enduring it easy. And sometimes we can't see it. Joseph F. Smith said that the hand of the Lord may not be visible to all of us, or that we cannot discern the workings of His will.[15] Yet it is still there, whether we see it or not.

In the last few years, a short allegory has become popular among the Christian community. It comes from a poem credited to various authors and is entitled "Footprints." The idea of the poem is that there are times when we see two sets of footprints walking parallel in the sand, representing the times when Jesus is walking with us. Other times there is only one set. This is, according to the poem, because Jesus picked us up and carried us for a time.

It is a lovely thought, and I suppose there are times when it may be true, but in my experience, we are often left to walk alone. That shouldn't be too difficult for us to understand. When a child is learning to walk and stumbles, the answer is not to carry them. Sometimes we do have to walk alone. That doesn't mean He isn't there, but I think it is only rarely that He "picks us up" and carries us along.

## God Is at the Helm

When the hand of the Lord is manifested in our personal lives, it becomes a great source of faith, hope, trust, courage, patience, and endurance. But the hand of the Lord works on a macro as well as a micro scale. Keeping that perspective in mind can also be a tremendous source of hope and comfort in the "perilous" days in which we live.

In chapter 4, we discussed the prophetic view of the future, which is, in many ways, grim and deeply disturbing. The world grows more wicked; the future seems darker; violence spreads like a terrible disease; financial situations look more and more bleak. The world seems to be spinning out of control, and it appears that we can do nothing to stop it. More and more often we hear expressions of pessimism and gloom. Concern for the future is discussed in gloomy conversations around the dinner table, at work, in family gatherings, at church, and other places.

In the Church Administration Building in Salt Lake City, Utah, there is a small cafeteria reserved for the use of General Authorities and their invited guests. This allows the Brethren to have lunch without being constantly interrupted as people come up to greet them or ask them questions. The cafeteria has open seating, and often members of the Seventy end up with members of the Twelve or the First Presidency at their tables.

One day at lunch, several of us who were Seventies were seated around a table having one of those gloomy conversations. This was in the fall of 2008, not long after a substantial financial crash. Major panic had erupted in the banking, housing, and investment markets. In a matter of weeks, the United States was in a deep recession. Stocks plummeted, housing prices took a nosedive, and financial institutions began to unravel so disastrously that the government stepped in with massive infusions of funds. It would prove to be the worst financial crisis—both nationally and globally—since the Great Depression of the 1930s. We were discussing it all.

About then, one of the Twelve joined us. As he began to eat, we resumed our conversation. Someone noted that in the newspaper there had been reports of several European nations being on the verge of bankruptcy. Our conversation turned to the level of debt in the United States and what that meant for the future. We speculated on what would happen if the United States government collapsed.

That was when the member of the Twelve broke in. He said something like this. "The United States is home to the headquarters of the Church. Members in the United States contribute a major proportion of the funds needed to run the kingdom. If our country were to completely collapse, the work of the Church would be severely hampered. Do you think the Lord will let that happen?"

I can't speak for the others, but I was pulled up short by his words.

He went on. "I don't know what will happen. Surely there are difficult times coming. And we may face some severe crises, but remember, brethren, God is at the helm. The kingdom is not headed for a shipwreck. There is still much that must be done, and we must not lose hope."

What a great reminder. What a significant teaching moment. God *is* at the helm. That perspective can be a significant source of hope in these dreary days. Things may be spiraling out of *man's* control, but they are not beyond God's control. Things are not hopeless, despite how hopeless they may look. Here are some scriptural validations of that concept:

- "God hath not given us the spirit of fear; but of power, and of love, and of a sound mind" (2 Timothy 1:7).
- God is the "Lord God Almighty" (1 Nephi 1:14), "the Lord God omnipotent" (Revelation 19:6), and there is none "who can stay his hand" (D&C 76:3).
- "He will not suffer that the wicked shall destroy the righteous. Wherefore, he will preserve the righteous by his power. . . . Wherefore, the righteous need not fear. . . . The Lord will surely prepare a way for his people" (1 Nephi 22:16–17, 22).
- "The works, and the designs, and the purposes of God cannot be frustrated, neither can they come to naught" (D&C 3:1).
- "My wisdom is greater than the cunning of the devil" (D&C 10:43).

- "Go thy way and do as I have told you, and fear not thine enemies; for they shall not have power to stop my work" (D&C 136:17).

Modern prophets frequently give a similar message:

*Joseph Smith. No unhallowed hand can stop the work from progressing;* persecutions may rage, mobs may combine, armies may assemble, calumny may defame, but the truth of God will go forth boldly, nobly, and independent, till it has penetrated every continent, visited every clime, swept every country, and sounded in every ear, till *the purposes of God shall be accomplished,* and the Great Jehovah shall say the work is done.[16]

*President Joseph F. Smith.* You do not need to worry in the least, the Lord will take care of you and bless you, he will also take care of his servants, and will bless them and help them to accomplish his purposes; and *all the powers of darkness combined on earth and in hell cannot prevent it.* . . . He has stretched forth his hand to accomplish his purposes, and the arm of flesh cannot stay it. He will cut his work short in righteousness, and will hasten his purposes in his own time.[17]

*President Howard W. Hunter.* I promise you . . . in the name of the Lord whose servant I am that *God will always protect and care for his people.* We will have our difficulties the way every generation and people have had difficulties. . . . *The Lord has power over his Saints and will always prepare places of peace, defense, and safety for his people.* When we have faith in God we can *hope for a better world*—for us personally and for all mankind. . . .

Disciples of Christ in every generation are invited, indeed *commanded, to be filled with a perfect brightness of hope.*[18]

Thanks be to God, who knows all things, and loves His children, and *wants us to be happy and joyful. He has not left us alone. He is there. He extends His hand to steady and to lift and to strengthen us.*

## A Time for Hope

We have frequently cited this statement by President Dieter F. Uchtdorf: "Hope is not knowledge, but rather *the abiding trust that the Lord will fulfill His promises to us.* It is confidence that if we live according to God's laws and the words of His prophets now, we will receive desired blessings in the future."[19] I would add, *even if that future is dark and gloomy.*

Let us not forget the grand promises as well as the personal ones. Let us not overlook God's hand in the affairs of nations as well as His blessings in the lives of His children. It is in these latter days that we need to see with eyes of faith, for in these perilous times, situations, and circumstances test us rigorously. This is where perspective makes a great deal of difference. All around us, even in the lives of the most faithful, we see adversity, tragedy, and tribulation, and these things are always intensely personal and intensely painful. It takes a great deal of faith and trust to see that we must pass through the fire, because, as Elder Neal A. Maxwell points out, God is in the process of making "soul-steel."[20] The refining process will often cause us to wonder what is happening and why. We know God is there, so the question is not always "Why *can't* God do something?" but often "Why *isn't* He doing something?"

Whether our fears and despair come from what is happening in the world around us, or from our own personal and family challenges, having this broader perspective strengthens us for the test.

God has assured us that He is still in control of things. He will not let His work career off the track like a runaway train. Nor will He abandon us, if we will but turn to Him. As the Savior promised the Twelve on the night before He died, "I will not leave you comfortless: I will come to you" (John 14:18).

He may not pick us up and carry us, but He is there to guide, direct, comfort, sustain, strengthen, and fortify us. He extends the gifts of the Spirit, takes our burdens upon Himself, pays for our mistakes and puts all things right through His Atonement. I find this perspective brings a great calming influence in my life. Life is not hopeless. *God is at the helm.* He has shown us how to draw down the powers of heaven in our behalf so we can work our way successfully through mortality in much the same way that we use a GPS device to find out where we are and how to get to where we are going. His hand is always extended in our behalf, even when we cannot see it. His work will not fail. We worship a God who can move "popcorn day" back twenty-four hours and, at the same time, sweep His hand over national or global events and alter the flow of history.

Let us close with this reminder from President Gordon B. Hinckley, who maintained this perspective with such optimism and hope:

> This is a season to be strong. It is a time to move forward without hesitation, knowing well the meaning, the breadth, and the importance of our mission. It is a time to do what is right regardless of the consequences that might follow. . . .
>
> We have nothing to fear. God is at the helm. He will overrule for the good of this work. . . .
>
> The little stone which was cut out of the mountain without hands as seen in Daniel's vision is rolling forth to fill the whole earth (see Dan. 2:44–45). No force under the heavens can stop it if we will walk in righteousness and be faithful and true.[21]

## Notes

*Part III Epigraph. The Neal A. Maxwell Quote Book,* ed. Cory H. Maxwell (Salt Lake City: Bookcraft, 1997), 248.

1. *The Random House Dictionary of the English Language,* 2d ed. (New York: Random House, 1987), s.v. "perspective," 1446.

2. Harold B. Lee, *Decisions for Successful Living* (Salt Lake City: Deseret Book, 1973), 220.

3. Joseph F. Smith, *Gospel Doctrine* (Salt Lake City: Deseret Book, 1986), 52.

4. Gordon B. Hinckley, Regional Representatives' seminar, 6 April 1984; as cited by Mack M. Lawrence, "Conversion and Commitment," *Ensign,* May 1996, 75.

5. See Dieter F. Uchtdorf, "The Infinite Power of Hope," *Ensign,* November 2008, 22.

6. Gerald N. Lund, *Divine Signatures: The Confirming Hand of God* (Salt Lake City: Deseret Book, 2010), 20–21.

7. In Andrew D. Olsen, *The Price We Paid: The Extraordinary Story of the Willie and Martin Handcart Pioneers* (Salt Lake City: Deseret Book, 2006), 310.

8. In Olsen, *Price We Paid,* 310.

9. Janice Kapp Perry, "A Child's Prayer," in *Children's Songbook* (Salt Lake City: The Church of Jesus Christ of Latter-day Saints, 1989), 12.

10. Personal account in possession of the author. Used by permission. This person preferred to remain unnamed.

11. Gerald N. Lund, *Selected Writings of Gerald N. Lund* (Salt Lake City: Deseret Book, 1999), 262.

12. *Leaves from the Life of Elizabeth Horrocks Jackson Kingsford* (Ogden, Utah: n.p., December 1908), 8.

13. Ibid., 1.

14. D. Todd Christofferson, "Give Us This Day Our Daily Bread," CES Fireside for Young Adults, 9 January 2011, 2–3.

15. Smith, *Gospel Doctrine,* 52.

16. Joseph Smith, *History of The Church of Jesus Christ of Latter-day Saints,* 7 vols., ed. B. H. Roberts (Salt Lake City: The Church of Jesus Christ of Latter-day Saints, 1932–51), 4:540.

17. Smith, *Gospel Doctrine,* 78.

18. Howard W. Hunter, *The Teachings of Howard W. Hunter,* ed. Clyde J. Williams (Salt Lake City: Bookcraft 1997), 201.

19. Uchtdorf, "The Infinite Power of Hope," 22.

20. Neal A. Maxwell, *All These Things Shall Give Thee Experience* (Salt Lake City: Deseret Book, 1979), 46.

21. Gordon B. Hinckley, "This Is the Work of the Master," *Ensign,* May 1995, 71.

# "Be Still and Know That I Am God"

Here are two examples of how the Lord's hand can be found in our lives and generate hope and testimony. The first is an experience my wife and I had many years ago. The second comes from the history of the Church.

## "You've Had a Little Miracle Here"

It wasn't a great and grand miracle—not like dividing the Red Sea or healing a leper. It happened quietly, unnoticed by any outside of the circle of family.

Julie, our second daughter, was thirteen months old at the time. Off the corner of our kitchen was a shallow stairwell—two steps down, then a landing that led outside. We had been wise enough to block it off with a board about two feet wide—chest high for Julie at that time. We assumed that would be sufficient.

But one day there was a loud crash, and then a piercing scream. Somehow she had gone up and over the top and fallen into the stairwell. In an instant we were both to her. Her mouth was filled with blood, and as I looked to see where she was hurt, I saw two tiny white teeth sitting on her tongue. Then she gasped for breath and swallowed, and they were gone.

Fortunately, there was no other serious damage. We took her to a dentist the next morning. Without the teeth to examine, he couldn't tell if she had broken them off or knocked them out, roots and all. He recommended a children's orthodontist who could take X-rays to show whether the root buds had been destroyed. "And if they were?" I asked. He shook his head. A person's baby teeth and permanent teeth are both present deep within the jaws at birth, in small swellings called buds. If the buds were not damaged, then at six she would get her permanent teeth. If the buds had been lost, then Julie would never have her own front teeth. He explained what that would mean. Without her bottom teeth, she would use a reverse tongue thrust to stop from drooling through the gap in her mouth. This would create a "bucktooth" effect. She would need braces early and for an extended period to correct that. She would also require a dental bridge in her mouth for the rest of her life.

Sick at heart, we made an appointment and began to pray as he took Julie in to X-ray her teeth. The orthodontist brought in the X-rays, shaking his head gravely. The damage was total. Nothing was left of the tiny buds. He told us to return in about five years so that he could begin the long process of correction.

Knowing how cruel some children can be to those who are "different," my wife and I decided to turn to the Lord with even greater fervency and ask for His help. Our prayers intensified. We added fasting to our pleadings that perhaps the X-rays hadn't shown the whole picture, that perhaps at age six her permanent teeth would appear after all.

It was several months later. The baby was laughing up at her mother. "Come here!" my wife called. When I knelt down beside them, she pointed, tears in her eyes. "Look!" And there they were—the first edge of two new little baby teeth just poking through the bottom gum.

The next day, that same orthodontist once again shook his head, only this time in astonishment. "If this were five years from now and you showed me she was getting permanent teeth, I would be amazed. But to get a second set of baby teeth? And when there was not even the hint of any root buds left? I don't understand it. I can't explain it. But you've had a little miracle here."[1]

## In-Service Training

The late summer and fall of 1838 saw some of the darkest days in the history of The Church of Jesus Christ of Latter-day Saints. The Saints—including much of the leadership of the Church—had been driven from Kirtland following widespread apostasy. Joining the Saints who had previously been driven from Jackson County, these refugees quickly swelled the population of Mormons in Northern Missouri. And with that increase in population, previous animosities and opposition began to rise again. As Elder Parley P. Pratt described it:

> War clouds began again to lower, with dark and threatening aspect. Those who had combined against the laws in the adjoining counties, had long watched our increasing power and prosperity with jealousy, and with greedy and avaricious eyes. It was a common boast that, as soon as we had completed our extensive improvements, and made a plentiful

crop, they would drive us from the state, and once more enrich themselves with the spoils.[2]

Things quickly deteriorated. When a mob kidnapped several Latter-day Saints, the Mormon militia gave chase and caught the Missourians at a ford of the Crooked River. A brief but intense battle erupted, and men on both sides were killed. Wild reports of a Mormon uprising followed, and Governor Lilburn W. Boggs issued his infamous "extermination order." Three days later, about two hundred armed men rode into the little hamlet of Haun's Mill and killed at least seventeen men and boys.

In those tense and dangerous times, apostasy within the Church increased. Many people defected because of the danger. Others turned against Joseph, blaming him for getting them into this situation. Thomas B. Marsh, a senior apostle, defected and actually swore out statements against Joseph that directly inflamed tensions even more. Colonel George Hinckle, commanding officer of the Mormon militia, betrayed all three members of the First Presidency and other leaders into the hands of the Missourians and helped disarm his own people. When the troops were turned loose on Far West, the soldiers looted, pillaged, raped, and murdered.

The Missourians decided they could destroy the Church once and for all by decapitating the leadership. They already had the First Presidency and a few others, but they wanted to eliminate any others who could lead the Saints through the crisis. The Missourians paid some of the apostates and promised them they wouldn't be harmed if they would make a list of other prominent men in the Church. They did so, and fifty-six more men were arrested and marched away to prison.[3]

However, there were two important names left off that list. One was Brigham Young, who had replaced Thomas B. Marsh as the president of the Quorum of the Twelve. The other was Heber C. Kimball, who was next in seniority in the Quorum of the Twelve. Considering the importance of both of these men, that was an astonishing oversight. How could the next two men in the leadership line have possibly been overlooked? Elder Kimball explained:

> I have no doubt that I would also have been taken a prisoner, for every means was adopted by Hinckle to have me taken, *but he could not remember me.* The mob had not become acquainted with Brother Brigham, as he lived three or four miles from the city on Mill Creek; and I had not been there over three weeks [from his mission to England] when the mobbing commenced, and was only known by the brethren, and many of them I had not seen since my arrival.[4]

For the next six months, while Joseph and the others endured the miseries of Liberty Jail, the leadership of the Church fell on the shoulders of Brigham Young and Heber C. Kimball. They were the ones who led the exodus from Missouri in the midst of a bitter winter. They were the ones who organized the priesthood and put the Saints under this covenant: "We this day enter into a covenant to stand by and assist each other to the utmost of our abilities in removing from this state, and that we will never desert the poor who are worthy, till they shall be out of the reach of the exterminating order."[5]

About eight years later, in February 1846, Brigham Young and Heber C. Kimball led the exodus from Nauvoo to the Great Salt Lake Valley, an exodus that would eventually bring more than 70,000 Saints across the plains in one of the greatest western migrations in the history of the United States of America.

Some people might call leaving the names of Brigham Young and Heber C. Kimball off a list a fortunate coincidence. I prefer Elder Neal A. Maxwell's explanation: "When we say God has a plan, he truly has a plan—not simply on a grand scale, but for each of us as individuals, allocating some special talent to this dispensation and some to another. I regard God *as the perfect personnel manager,* even though he must work with and through all of us who are so imperfect."[6]

## Notes

1. Gerald N. Lund, in *Why I Believe* (Salt Lake City: Bookcraft, 2002), 201–2.

2. "A History of the Persecutions of The Church of Jesus Christ of Latter-day Saints in Missouri," *Times and Seasons* 1, no. 5 (March 1840): 81–82.

3. See *Church History in the Fulness of Times* (Salt Lake City: The Church of Jesus Christ of Latter-day Saints, 1989), 193–209 for a summary of this time in Church history. It is Heber C. Kimball who tells us that the apostates were paid money to inform on their brethren and identify key leaders (see Heber C. Kimball, in Orson F. Whitney, *Life of Heber C. Kimball* [Salt Lake City: Bookcraft, 1945], 223).

4. Kimball, in Orson F. Whitney, *Life of Heber C. Kimball,* 222.

5. Joseph Smith, *History of The Church of Jesus Christ of Latter-day Saints,* 7 vols., ed. B. H. Roberts (Salt Lake City: The Church of Jesus Christ of Latter-day Saints, 1932–51), 3:250.

6. Neal A. Maxwell, *Deposition of a Disciple* (Salt Lake City: Deseret Book, 1976), 45.

*I speak, not to the slackers in the Kingdom, but
to those who carry their own load and more;
not to those lulled into false security, but to those
buffeted by false insecurity, who, though laboring
devotedly in the Kingdom, have recurring
feelings of falling forever short. . . .*

*The first thing to be said of this feeling of
inadequacy is that it is normal. There is no way
the Church can honestly describe where we must yet
go and what we must yet do without creating
a sense of immense distance.*

NEAL A. MAXWELL

CHAPTER THIRTEEN

# REMEMBER, PERFECTION DOESN'T COME IN THIS LIFE

———— ❧❖❧ ————

## Remembering

REMEMBERING CAN BE another way of changing our perspective. President Spencer W. Kimball once said, "When you look in the dictionary for the most important word, do you know what it is? It could be 'remember.' Because all of [us] have made covenants . . . our greatest need is to remember. . . . 'Remember' is the word."[1] One of the clearest charges to remember is in the sacrament prayers where we covenant to "always remember" the Savior (D&C 20:77, 79).

In the scriptures, we are also told to remember other things, including remembering His words, keeping the commandments, and remembering what He has done for us. There are two practical "remembers" that are particularly helpful when we start feeling discouraged or disheartened. I believe that simply remembering certain things can make a big difference in the strength and quality of our hope.

Since remembering is a mental, emotional, and spiritual exercise, it can have a direct influence on our hope, which is a mental, emotional, and spiritual attribute. These "remembers" have a way of pulling us up when we start wondering if we are going to be able to see something through, or, more commonly, when we slip into one of our "poor me" moments. These "remembers" soften the heart, and that, in turn, brings the comforting influence of the Holy Spirit, which then bolsters our hope and faith. To sum up: Remembrance can change our perspective, and the proper perspective can increase our hope.

## Knowing and Doing

Our first "remember" is a simple one. We need to remember that while perfection is our ultimate goal, it is not going to happen in this life.

Let's begin by sharing three statements that have come to my attention over the years. I heard the first statement in a college philosophy class from a teacher I highly respected. He said, *"The terrible predicament of most people is that they know what is right, but they want what is wrong."*

The second statement was made by a boy about eight years old. Just as his family was preparing to go to sacrament meeting, he announced that he didn't want to go to church anymore. His mother tried to reason with him by telling him how important attending church was.

"Why do we have to go?" he asked stubbornly.

Fighting to be patient, his mother explained, "Well, first of all, we go to partake of the sacrament. Secondly, we go to learn more about the gospel."

To which this young boy said, *"Don't we already know more than we do?"*

The third statement is a little rhyme I picked up somewhere many years ago. It's not wonderful poetry, but it does reflect life.

> *I want to be good,*
> *And do what I should.*
> *But I can't seem to do it*
> *As much as I would.*

When I first heard the philosophy professor make his statement, I thought he had accurately described the hearts of most people. Now I believe that it is an accurate assessment of the hearts of *some* individuals, *but not all.* The longer I live and the more I meet the good people of the world, the more I am convinced that the little poem better describes the hearts of many people than the professor's statement. And I believe the statement of the eight-year-old boy catches the essence of the struggle. We do know more than we live, but often that is not for lack of trying.

I would amend the professor's statement to something more like this: "The terrible predicament of many people is that they know what is right, *and they want what is right,* but they just can't seem to always *do* what is right." How many times do we find ourselves saying, "I hate it when I do that" or "I'd give anything if I could break this habit"?

I remember talking to a frustrated young mother who had six young children, including four-year-old twin boys. One day she said to me, "Before I was married and had children, I never raised my voice or got angry. Now I find myself getting so frustrated and angry that I yell at my children all the time." She paused for a moment, then added, "Here's what I don't understand. At the very moment when I am yelling at them, there is a voice in my head crying out to me, saying, 'Listen to yourself! Stop it! Get a grip.'" She looked away. "But I can't. I just can't seem to stop."

That is a different kind of despair. One that doesn't come from the challenges and setbacks of life or because we have committed some terrible sin. Here our feelings come from a keen awareness of our failings. As Elder Neal A. Maxwell said, we are always being "buffeted by false insecurity" and having "recurring feelings of falling forever short,"[2] even when we are doing good things and making a determined effort to be good.

### "Be Ye Therefore Perfect"

The Savior taught the ultimate standard of discipleship when He said, "Therefore, I would that ye should be perfect even as I, or your Father who is in heaven is perfect" (3 Nephi 12:48; see also Matthew 5:48). There it is: simple, clear. *And overwhelming!* For those of us who really desire to live as God would have us live, the gap between where we are and where we are supposed to be really is an "immense distance." And this gap between our expectations and the discouraging reality can leave us feeling sad, deflated, and downhearted.

As we saw in chapter 6, Satan understands this about us and seeks to capitalize on our desire to be better. He whispers such things as "You're not doing enough," "You need to be better," "You need to try harder," and "How can you please the Lord when you're making so many mistakes?"

Someone (surely tongue in cheek) once made a list of what active Latter-day Saints are expected to do.[3] Look at any one of the items on this list and it is clear that each is a good thing, a desirable thing. But put them all together, and no wonder we feel overwhelmed.

### Checklist of Things to Do

Repent
Listen to the Holy Ghost
Love the Lord
Love one another
Walk in the Spirit
Lengthen your stride
Go to the temple
Do genealogy work
Get your year's supply
Rotate your year's supply regularly
Be a member missionary

Magnify your calling

Serve with commitment

Spend one-on-one time with each child

Hold personal interviews with each child

Sanctify your marriage

Support your spouse in righteousness

Pay your tithing

Double your fast offerings

Support Scouting

Have every son earn his Eagle Scout

Plant a garden

Plant trees and vines

Bottle fruit

Bake your own bread

Don't eat junk food

Lose weight

Get physically fit

Study the scriptures daily

Have family prayer twice daily

Read the Book of Mormon with your family

Do your visiting teaching

Do your home teaching

Stay out of debt

Make your own clothes

Get an education

Prepare sons and daughters for missions

Support missionary work

Go on a mission

Love your neighbor

Clean up your yard

Prepare nutritious meals

Eat lots of whole wheat

Listen to general conference

Read the *Ensign*

Read the *Church News*

Get a first-aid kit

Get 72-hour emergency kits

Don't swear

Don't lie

Make visual aids for class

Be anxiously engaged

Fill welfare assignment

Cease to be idle

Listen to good music

Read the best books

Read to your children

Be a good citizen

Understand the issues facing your community

Vote

Take meals in to others

Care for aging parents

Go the second mile

Turn the other cheek

Develop your talents

Write in your journal

Hug your kids each day

Pursue excellence

Date your spouse each week

Keep romance alive

Serve others

Prepare excellent family home evening lessons

Attend leadership meetings

Have a prayer in your heart

Love your enemies

Always say yes to callings

Have fun with the family

Hold family reunions

Sew clothes and do crafts

Quilt a quilt

Multiply and replenish the earth

Save 10 percent of your salary

Arise early

Serve your country

Overcome the world

Don't watch junk television

Fellowship the less active

Don't leave dirty dishes in the sink

Floss

Read priesthood or Relief Society lesson

Sing in the ward choir

Drive the neighborhood carpool

Cut the lawn

Shovel the snow

Teach a Sunday School class

Disinfect the house

BE YE PERFECT!

ENDURE TO THE END!

DO IT!

## Some Bad News

It's because of lists like these that we need to remind ourselves from time to time that we are not perfect, and neither is anyone else. The old adage that "nobody's perfect" is a two-edged sword. Sometimes we use it to justify inexcusable behavior. We know we've done wrong, or we've been stupid, and we sheepishly say, "Well, nobody's perfect." The other side of the sword is that we can be unrealistic in our expectations of ourselves and unnecessarily beat ourselves up emotionally. It is easy to do, because . . . well, let's just say there's bad news for all of us.

- One of the reasons we feel inadequate is because we are. In some ways.
- One of the reasons we feel inferior is because we are. In many ways.
- One of the reasons we often feel that we're failing is because we are. To some degree.
- One of the reasons we feel like sinners is because we are.
- And one of the reasons we feel we are imperfect is because we really and truly are.

No wonder we get down on ourselves. No wonder we feel as if we'll never measure up. No wonder our feelings of self-worth take a beating at times. And while we're dumping the bad news, here's something else to consider. It has been my observation over a lifetime of experience that there are four callings or responsibilities that we have in life where we will *never* come out feeling like we've done everything right and made no mistakes. They are being a *spouse,* being a *parent,* being a *teacher,* and being a *leader.* I know of no one who can say, "I did it right. I have absolutely no regrets, and if I had a chance to do it all over again, I wouldn't change a thing."

## Some Good News

Fortunately, there is good news too. And it far outweighs the bad.

Parenting is one of the deepest satisfactions we can have in this life, but at the same time it can bring some of the highest levels of frustration, challenge, and even sorrow. For those who are in the thick of it—lots of young children (or even one teen who can be more demanding than five or six young children)—the good news is that eventually the kids grow up. Many parents—in tones of wonder—are heard to say, "Now that my kids are adults, we've become more like friends than parent and child." Eventually we see some of the fruits of our efforts.

And as grandparents, we can stand back and watch our children dealing with their children and having all the same frustrations that they caused us. And we smile.

For example, one day I happened across a handwritten letter from our oldest daughter to my wife, written when she was about sixteen years old. I had forgotten that I had even saved it, but as I read it, I laughed right out loud.

> Mom—I'm *terribly* sorry, but I drank the pink lemonade for your party tomorrow. At work I was so thirsty I thought I'd die, so when I was off I bought me some grape Hi-C. I gulped down the whole can before I got home yet I was still thirsty. When I got home I had dinner & a whole bunch of milk, but after a while I was *still* so thirsty, so I put water in a qt. jar and drank it, but after a few minutes I was still dyin' so I looked in the freezer & saw the pink lemonade and so made it up. After I had drank ½ of it Julie told me it was for tomorrow. I feel so bad & I'll go down with my own money & buy another can. I really am sorry. Love, Cyndie. P.S. I'm not thirsty anymore.

Cyndie now has seven children of her own, ranging in age from kindergarten to college. I read the letter to her, and we had a good laugh together. Then a week or so later, she shared an experience with me that sparked another shared laugh.

When my wife and I stopped at her house, her voice was hoarse and croaky. I asked if she was sick. She said no, that she had just lost her voice a day or two earlier. She wasn't sure why. Then she chuckled. "It's ironic," she said. "The day before this all happened, I decided that this year I was going to stop shouting at the kids. I told them as much, and I promised I would try to do better."

She went hoarse the very next day. Her kids thought it was hilarious. Her thirteen-year-old daughter said to her, "Usually you go hoarse from shouting at us. Maybe this is the Lord's way of making sure you do as you promised." Lynn and I had a good laugh at that too.

### Some More Good News: A Keen Awareness of Our Failings Is Good

Have you ever considered that a keen awareness of our weaknesses is actually a positive sign? If you want a broader perspective on life and need some cheering up, look around at the world. For example, some of the rich and famous—those people our society idolizes most—go through a whole shopping list of sins and seem completely unfazed by the consequences of their actions. Millions of couples now choose to live together rather than marry. As near as I can tell, most of them shrug off any sense of wrongdoing or sin. In fact, they actually justify their actions by saying this is the best way to find out if a marriage will work. (Which incidentally is not true. Studies show just the opposite.[4]) There are people who become violently upset about animal cruelty (a worthy cause), but fully support the termination of human life in abortions. As Elder Neal A. Maxwell once noted:

> Reflect, for instance, on how inoperative the Ten Commandments are in many lives. Today, *killing, stealing,* and bearing *false witness* still carry some social stigma and legal sanction, but sanction is effectively gone regarding sexual

immorality, the Sabbath day, honoring fathers and mothers, and the taking of the name of the Lord in vain.[5]

Remember what Nephi said to Laman and Lemuel? "[The Lord] hath spoken unto you in a still small voice, but ye were *past feeling*" (1 Nephi 17:45; see also Moroni 9:20). The Apostle Paul used the same phrase to describe some people of his day "who being past feeling have given themselves over unto lasciviousness, to work all uncleanness with greediness" (Ephesians 4:19). He also said that some people have "their conscience seared with a hot iron" (1 Timothy 4:2).

So both my daughter and the young mother who feel terrible about yelling at their children can at least take heart in knowing that their feelings come from their goodness and their desire to be good. The "voice" the young mother hears in her head telling her to stop yelling is the Spirit. And if the Spirit is still striving with her, there is still hope.

## Even More Good News: God Does Not Expect Us to Be Perfect in This Life

Here is something else I find helpful. The Savior did give a very clear and specific commandment that we are to be perfect even as He is perfect. And so it is. We are expected to strive for perfection at all times. But that is only part of the picture. We also know that we will not obtain perfection in mortality and that part of the Father's plan was to prepare a way to make things right when we do fail. This teaching is not simply my interpretation; note what the prophets have said:

*Joseph Smith.* When you climb up a ladder, you must begin at the bottom, and ascend step by step, until you arrive at the top; and so it is with the principles of the Gospel. . . . It will be a great while *after you have passed through the veil* before you will have learned them. It is not all to be

271

comprehended in this world; it will be a great work to learn our salvation and exaltation even beyond the grave.[6]

*Elder James E. Talmage.* Our Lord's admonition to men to become perfect, even as the Father is perfect (Matt. 5:48) cannot rationally be construed otherwise than as implying the possibility of such achievement. Plainly, however, *man cannot become perfect in mortality* in the sense in which God is perfect as a supremely glorified Being.[7]

*Elder Bruce R. McConkie.* We don't need to get a complex or get a feeling that you have to be perfect to be saved. . . . There's only been one perfect person, and that's the Lord Jesus, but in order to be saved in the Kingdom of God and in order to pass the test of mortality, what you have to do is get on the straight and narrow path—thus charting a course leading to eternal life—and then, being on that path, pass out of this life in full fellowship. I'm not saying you don't have to keep the commandments. I'm saying you don't have to be perfect to be saved. . . . If you're on that path and pressing forward, and you die, you'll never get off the path. There is no such thing as falling off the straight and narrow path in the life to come, and the reason is that this life is the time that is given to men to prepare for eternity.[8]

These words underscore just how great Satan's lie is when he whispers to us, "You are not perfect, therefore you are failing." C. S. Lewis, the great Christian writer, shared this wonderful insight:

[While Christ] will, in the long run, be satisfied with nothing less than absolute perfection, [He] will also be delighted with the first feeble, stumbling effort you make tomorrow to do the simplest duty. As a great Christian writer (George MacDonald) pointed out, every father is pleased at the baby's first attempt to walk: [but] no father would be satisfied with anything less than a firm, free, manly walk in a grown-up son. In the same way, he said, *"God is easy to please, but hard to satisfy."*[9]

## And Even More Good News: We Are Judged for Our Desires

We are not judged solely on what we do. In His infinite wisdom, the Lord also takes into account whether *"the desires of their hearts were good"* (Alma 41:3; see also D&C 137:9). He takes into account our intentions, our hopes, our desires, our circumstances, our abilities, and our efforts, imperfect as they may be. (We discussed this idea at length in chapter 11.)

Remembering that truth provides an enormous boost to our hope. We can find hope in remembering that the Savior did the following:

- He told the Samaritan woman (who had been married and divorced five times, and was presently living with a man who was not her husband) that He had living water for her (see John 4:10, 18).
- He told the woman taken in adultery that He did not condemn her either, but to go and sin no more (see John 8:1–11).
- He accepted Saul after he held the coats of those who martyred Stephen and "made havock of the church in Jerusalem" (Acts 8:3; see also Acts 7:58; 22:4).
- He took Alma, who was described as "the very vilest of sinners" (Mosiah 28:4), and eventually made him the head of the Church in his time.

- He forgave King Lamoni, who was having his servants killed for not protecting his flocks from a band of violent thieves (see Alma 18:5–6).

### The Best News of All: Our Problem Is Fixable

The ultimate good news is that while nobody's perfect, imperfection is a condition that has a solution. The word *gospel* comes from the old English *godspell,* which literally means "God's word," and is the translation of a Greek word meaning "good news" or "glad tidings." These words are found about 420 times in the four standard works. That should tell us how important that concept is.

There are two eternal givens that contain no shade of compromise. The first is that "No unclean thing can inherit the kingdom of heaven" (Alma 11:37; see also Moses 6:57). The second is that "I the Lord cannot look upon sin with the least degree of allowance" (D&C 1:31). I note these scriptures so that we make no mistake. We're not downplaying the seriousness of sin and transgression. Any violation of God's law brings sorrow and jeopardizes our eternal happiness. Those who think they can "sow their wild oats" and then come back and do a "quick fix" by confessing to their bishop do not understand the full consequences of sin.

But God knew what we would face in this life. He knew our bodies would not be perfect. That when we don't get enough sleep, we become irritable or make mistakes. That when we are hungry, we become snappish. That the physical attraction between a man and a woman is powerful enough to tempt even the faithful to break the law of chastity. We have a great emotional need to love and be loved, and seeking either or both of those sometimes leads us into error. Boredom can become a catalyst for stupidity. The fact that we look at ourselves in the mirror every day can lead us to vanity or depression.

That's how we are. If this were not one of the realities of life, there would have been no need for an atonement. Christ went to the cross *precisely because* we are not perfect. That was the whole focus of chapter 4. If you are still struggling to understand this teaching, I would suggest you study that chapter carefully. The teachings of Christ are clear.

Remember: Our mistakes and imperfections are not fatal. They're fixable.

The solution lies in the Atonement of Jesus Christ and in the love of the Father and the Son. It flows from their grace and mercy. By extending the gifts of the Spirit to us, they energize and empower our efforts. Faith, hope, and charity—which are all gifts of the Spirit—are what enable us to endure with patience, learn by faith, and experience true conversion. This truth helps us better understand why Nephi said, "Believe in Christ, and . . . be reconciled to God; for we know that it is by grace we are saved, after all we can do" (2 Nephi 25:23).

---

## Notes

*Epigraph.* Neal A. Maxwell, "Notwithstanding My Weakness," *Ensign,* November 1976, 12.

1. Spencer W. Kimball, "Circles of Exaltation," Address to religious educators, Brigham Young University, 28 June 1968, 8.

2. Maxwell, "Notwithstanding My Weakness," 12.

3. List in possession of author. No author is listed. Some minor changes were made to the list to eliminate outdated programs.

4. See Craig Alan Myers, "On Living Together Before Marriage"; http://www.brfwitness.org/?p=652.

5. *The Neal A. Maxwell Quote Book,* ed. Cory H. Maxwell (Salt Lake City: Bookcraft, 1997), 279; emphasis in original.

6. Joseph Smith, *Teachings of the Prophet Joseph Smith,* comp. Joseph Fielding Smith (Salt Lake City: Deseret Book, 1977), 348.

7. James E. Talmage, *Jesus the Christ* (Salt Lake City: Deseret Book, 1982), 232.

8. Bruce R. McConkie, "The Probationary Test of Mortality," address given at University of Utah Institute of Religion, 10 January 1982, 12.

9. C.S. Lewis, *The Complete C. S. Lewis Signature Classics* (New York: HarperSanFrancisco, 2002), 107–8; emphasis in original.

*No Latter-day Saint should be content
to stand day after day in the
same place on the way to eternal life.*

MARION G. ROMNEY

CHAPTER FOURTEEN

# REMEMBER HOW WE LEARN AND GROW

———— ❧ ————

I WROTE ON this subject briefly in my book *Hearing the Voice of the Lord*,[1] and introduced some of these same concepts. Here they are treated in more detail and applied particularly to how we can increase our hope.

## Learning

One aspect of having grandchildren that I have particularly enjoyed is watching them grow from infancy to fully functioning children.

One day, my wife and I were tending some of our grandchildren, including a grandson who was only a few months old. His mother laid him on his back in a playpen and attached a child's mobile to one side. When his mother adjusted the toy so that it was easily within reach of my grandson, the brightly colored objects swaying back and forth above him immediately caught his eye.

For the next quarter of an hour I sat beside him, fascinated by what was happening. Though he was barely cooing yet, I could see intelligence in his eyes. I could see that his brain was registering the visual image that was before him. I could tell he wanted the toy very much, but when he tried to reach for it, his movements were almost spastic. He was trying so hard, but he missed it again and again. Then he accidently connected. His little fist instantly closed around part of the toy and, for a moment, he had it. Then it slipped out of his grasp. He went after it again. I could see the determination in his eyes. He was going to do this. He tried again. The same thing happened—random groping, accidental connection, gripping it tightly for a few moments before losing it again. But I noticed that his movements were gradually becoming less random and more controlled. He was hitting the target more consistently and holding it longer.

After about five or six minutes, he had mastered his task. I felt like standing up and cheering because I knew it had been such a tremendous effort on his part. And it tickled me to see in his eyes how utterly pleased he was with himself.

## To Gain Experience

One of the major reasons we have come to earth is to gain experience. What exactly does that mean? When I was younger, I assumed it meant learning the difference between good and evil. Now I realize it is so much more than that.

Some comments from modern prophets are very instructive here. The first comes from President Boyd K. Packer: "*Your body becomes an instrument of your mind* and the foundation of your character. Through life in a mortal body you can *learn to control matter,* and that will be very important to you through all eternity."[2] How important? Note this declaration in the Doctrine and Covenants: "For man is spirit. The elements [i.e., the physical aspects of our bodies] are eternal, and *spirit and element, inseparably connected, receive a fulness of joy;* and when separated, man cannot receive a fulness of joy" (D&C 93:33–34).

Elder Bruce R. McConkie expanded on that idea in this way:

There are some things that can only be understood by experience. . . . We get a mortal state where we will experience disease, pain, afflictions, and sorrow. If we didn't experience these, they would never become part of us and be engraven in our souls in the manner in which they will be. . . .

. . . We're here to get the kind of experience that *could not have been gained in any other way.*[3]

And finally, this from Elder M. Russell Ballard:

In the premortal world before we left the presence of Heavenly Father, He warned and cautioned us about new experiences we would have in mortality. We knew that we would have a physical body of flesh and bone. . . . He charged us to *control our mortal bodies and to make them subject to our spirits.*[4]

That was what I watched that day with my grandson. I could see there was an adult intelligence inside him "operating" his tiny body. His failure was not from lack of intelligence, it was because he hadn't yet learned how to make his body obey his mind. Operating it is one thing, *controlling* it is something else again.

So what has all of this got to do with remembering and hope? It is a fascinating topic in and of itself, but it has particular relevance for our discussion on hope. It is another way we can gain the perspective necessary to help us better endure times of stress and difficulty. When tragedy strikes, or tribulation and adversity become our lot, we may want to be patient and courageous so we can endure to the end. We may even desire it with all our hearts. But, like my grandson, we have to learn how to make our bodies and minds and hearts *obey our spirits.* Just wanting to do something is not enough.

## Exaltation Requires Both Knowledge and Skills

Elder Bruce C. Hafen, an emeritus member of the Seventy, taught this principle clearly. Since it is critical to our understanding of how we learn in this life, I shall draw extensively on his words:

> There are two different kinds of knowledge. One involves such *rational processes* as gathering information and memorizing. The other kind of knowledge I would call *skill development*—learning how to play the piano or swim or take a car engine apart; learning to sing or dance or think. *The process of developing toward a Christlike capacity is a matter of acquiring skills more than a matter of learning facts and figures.* And there is something about the nature of developing those divine skills that makes it *impossible even for God to teach us those things unless we participate in the process.* . . .
>
> Imagine an innovative music school with a revolutionary approach, in which the piano students did not have to practice. The school would teach in a purely theoretical way all the rudiments; describe in detail how to move one's fingers; go deeply into music theory and history; teach thoroughly how to read music. The students would memorize all the best books that have ever been written on how to play the piano. The course could last for four years. The students would each have a project, such as memorizing the score of a major piano concerto. They would be able to close their eyes and see the manuscript for both piano and orchestra flow through their minds—they could tell you everything about it.
>
> Then, when the first graduate of the "Do It without Practice Piano Course" walks onto the stage of Carnegie Hall to perform his debut with the orchestra, what do you suppose will happen?

Not much. Why?

Even though "thinking" is an essential element in any form of learning, *some things can be learned only by practice.*[5]

Ponder for a moment the significance of that concept. Some things in life we can learn by study or through listening to others. But many things we can learn only by *doing.* Elder Hafen calls this "skills development."[6] Another way of saying it could be "experiential knowledge," meaning knowledge we gain through experience or doing. There are two kinds of knowledge—cognitive (what we learn and know in the mind) and experiential (what we learn by doing).

Remember the question the eight-year-old boy asked his mother about why they needed to go to church? "Don't we already *know* more than we *do?"* Indeed we do, and one of the reasons is because it is usually easier to acquire knowledge than it is to acquire skills.

Let's go back to the example of the young, frustrated mother who hates herself for yelling at her children. She knows what is right. And she *wants* what is right. But she hasn't yet managed to actually make it happen. In her own way, she's like my grandson, wanting something intensely, grasping at what she wants, but often missing it. Remembering how we learn and develop both knowledge and skills in the physical world can serve as a model for how we learn and develop spiritual knowledge and skills. And this understanding is a perspective of great value to us as we strive to maintain hope.

## How We Learn to Control Our Bodies and Minds

Acquiring any skill or activity requires three things.

First, we have to *want* that skill or ability. But, remember, wanting alone does little for us.

Second, we have to *know* how to do certain things. But knowing how to do something is not sufficient either; it is not just the *mind* that must be trained, it is the *physical body* as well. The bones, muscles, sinews, tendons, ligaments, and nerves must "learn" how to perform the multiple combined movements before the mind can have them carry out its will.

Third, we have to remember that physical mastery of any skill comes step by step, and it almost always begins with the simple before moving to the complex.

My grandson's triumph in the playpen that day was one tiny step in an incredibly complex and prolonged process of learning. His learning progressed in tiny increments, one little skill acquired after another. Over the next few months, after I observed him in the playpen, he learned to raise himself up with his arms, then roll over, then sit up by himself. Scooting turned into crawling, crawling was followed by pulling himself up to the furniture. His first tentative steps (accompanied by many falls and a few bumps on the nose) were followed by toddling, then walking, running, hopping, skipping, jumping, playing soccer, skating, throwing a Frisbee, and dancing. No one expects a child to leave his parent's steadying hands and skip across the room. It simply doesn't happen that way.

This learning process so permeates every aspect of our life, and we are so used to it, that no one thinks of it as unfair or unrealistically harsh. To suggest that we can circumvent it somehow, or speed it up by skipping some of the steps, is ridiculous. Wouldn't it be nice if once we decided to become physically fit, we could stop off at the gym, put in a vigorous hour or two of exercise, and go home in great shape? Nice or not, that's not how it works.

So why is it we have such unrealistic expectations when it comes to getting ourselves spiritually fit? Why do we think we can decide to be better and it will just happen, or that we will undergo a drastic change overnight? There are a few examples of that happening, but they are the rare exception. How much "practice" does it take to control frustration? Fight back despair? Clean up our language? Triumph over pornography? What kind of piano teacher rejects a student because he hasn't mastered the scales in a week? *In spiritual things, we also have to learn how to make our bodies and minds obey our will, and that knowledge comes step by incremental step over a process of time.*

## Strength, Stamina, and Endurance

Mastery in any human endeavor is defined as the ability to perform at high levels of excellence when one wishes to do so. In a way, this principle could be thought of as a form of personal freedom—freedom being defined as the ability to choose to do something, and then actually be able to do it.

A marathon is one of the most challenging physical tasks a person can undertake. A marathon race is officially 26.2 miles (or 26 miles and 385 yards). I'm not a marathon runner (and I don't lose a lot of sleep over that), but I can see where there would be tremendous satisfaction in accomplishing such a demanding task. So, let's say that one day I decide I want to do it. (I have the desire.) I study what the experts have said about running marathons, and I interview dozens of marathon runners. (I acquire knowledge.) I practice running properly with a coach until he is satisfied that I know how to run. (I have the skills.) I've now met the three basic requirements for learning.

So, at 5:30 A.M. on the day of the race, I line up with all the other runners. As the starting gun is raised, I say to my body, "All right, here we go. I know, I know. It's going to be tough, but I really want to do this, so we're going the distance." I can tell you right now, my body would roll on the ground laughing hysterically. Just because I want to be a marathon runner, and just because I know how to run a marathon, and just because I can run properly, doesn't mean I can choose to run a marathon. Something else is required—strength, stamina, and endurance. Without that, I am not free to do what I want. I'm not free to climb Mount Everest or play a piano concerto, even though I would very much like to do both of those things.

I was talking to a former colleague of mine in the Church Educational System and in the course of our conversation he mentioned that he had recently completed a marathon and placed fourth in his division. Curious, I asked how long he had been running marathons. He said ten years. Then I asked him to describe his experience in his first marathon. He chuckled ruefully, and, somewhat tongue-in-cheek, said, "By the time I ran the first thirteen miles, I was exhausted. So I walked the next twelve miles, crawled another mile, then was dragged across the finish line by my wife." And yet, ten years later he came in fourth in his division. I think we can safely conclude that during those ten years he didn't spend a lot of time in bed contemplating how to run a marathon.

There is a great lesson in that example for us. In the physical and intellectual world, we achieve mastery by constantly pushing against the limits of our previous performance, always striving to improve, and we do that countless times, usually over a period of years. There are many motivational imperatives used in sports to describe how mastery is achieved—we say we must "raise the bar," "do the drills," "run the laps," "push the limit," "go the distance." That's how it's done.

Is it any different in the spiritual realm? When we achieve one level of obedience—say in mastering the temptation to yell at our children—have we won the race? No, we have just crossed the first hurdle, and one of the lower ones at that. Why should it surprise us then when the Lord—like any good track coach would do—raises the hurdles? The scriptures also have imperatives for achieving mastery—"be patient," "hold fast," "feast upon the word," "endure to the end," "put your hand to the plow," "humble yourself," "soften your heart," "ask, seek, knock."

## Start from Where You Are

Picture the path to exaltation as an inclined plane with a dot marking the position of every individual and an arrow beside each dot showing which way he or she is moving. There would be dots all along the line, and arrows showing how people are either moving up or down, or standing still. Some dots would be high up and moving even higher. A few might be high but moving downward. Some dots at the very bottom, representing people who we might have once written off as hopeless, could actually be moving in an upward direction.

None of us are in exactly the same place. Fortunately, the Lord has made it clear that He is concerned not just with *position,* but also *direction.* He tells us that He stands ready to help us, no matter where we may be on that path.

Let's return to the analogy of running a race. Suppose that all we had to do to be exalted was run a six-minute mile. (Actually, the ultimate would be a four-minute mile, but since very few people in the world have ever achieved that, we'll lower the bar a little.) There would be no other requirement. As soon as we could run a mile in six minutes, we would be saved.

How would we go about achieving that goal? Where would we start? Obviously, that would differ for every one of us, wouldn't it?

Some of you could go out and run a six-minute mile today and gain exaltation.

Some of you could run an eight-minute or a ten-minute mile. In that case, you could go to the track and start running laps, knowing your goal is close.

Some of you would find it a challenge to complete a mile in fifteen minutes. You would have to walk around the track to begin with, increasing your pace each day, one step at a time. Eventually, you would be able to alternate between walking a lap, then jogging a lap.

And some (names withheld by request) would walk a lap—then call a cab to finish the mile.

Whatever the situation, we need to assess our current abilities and physical condition, and then start there and go to work. However, there are some warnings we need to keep in mind.

## Warning #1: Practice Is Essential

In many cases we may start our spiritual quest with the highest of hopes, only to find ourselves in what seems like a maddeningly slow crawl. Many times we will find that we can't make it all the way around the track on our own. We may need someone we trust and who loves us to prod us onward (maybe even drag us a little closer to the finish line). But if we don't give up, if we keep pressing forward, recognizing that while we are nowhere close to where we want to be, we are still making progress. And progress is pleasing to the Lord. Then, when we do finally cross the finish line, we will have achieved enough strength and power and endurance to undertake the next race. Which, of course, almost always involves a higher level of performance.

The concluding verse of Doctrine and Covenants 46—which is the section discussing the gifts of the Spirit—has this interesting exhortation: "Ye must *practise* virtue and holiness before me continually" (D&C 46:33).

The word "practice" (or "practise," which is the British spelling) has two primary meanings in everyday usage. One meaning is to engage in a pattern of action or behavior in a repetitive fashion to enhance or acquire a skill (e.g., he *practiced* hitting the ball). But practice can also mean a way of life or a profession (e.g., the doctor's *practice* is thriving, or he is a *practicing* attorney). We use the word in its second sense when we say, "It is his practice to be scrupulously honest." Which of those two meanings do you suppose is intended in this verse? I think it is most likely both. We need the daily repetition to achieve mastery so that it becomes our way of life. We have to practice virtue. We have to practice being good. We have to practice holding our tongue, and reading our scriptures, and saying meaningful prayers.

### Warning #2: Don't Lose Heart

When we get out on that track, we need to remember that running will come more naturally and more easily to some than to others. So when others go whizzing by us, or start from the same place we do and yet quickly outdistance us, we have to be careful not to lose heart. We cannot assume that this difference somehow defines us as superior or inferior to others.

This is true of our spiritual natures as well. There are many factors that must be considered in our spiritual progress, including faith and obedience. But even faith and obedience may be enhanced by spiritual gifts that all do not have. I know a woman who is gifted with a natural spirituality, but I wonder how much of that spirituality comes from her efforts, how much she brought with her from the premortal existence, and how much is a gift from God. I can't tell. I envy her that gift, but I'm not sure I should be wishing I were her. Remember, they are called *gifts*. That means that while we may have developed the gift, originally it was given to us.

One other thing. When we look around and see others doing so much better than we are, it doesn't help to whine about how much harder it is for us than for them. Each of us has to run the race with our abilities and gifts. If that is discouraging, remember the promise which is extended to all:

> If men come unto me I will show unto them their weakness. I give unto men weakness that they may be humble; and my grace is sufficient for all men that humble themselves

before me; for if they humble themselves before me, and have
faith in me, then will I make weak things become strong
unto them. (Ether 12:27)

### Warning #3: Don't Forget the Enabling Power of Christ

King Benjamin said this: "See that all these things are done in
wisdom and order; for it is *not requisite that a man should run faster
than he has strength.* And again, it is expedient that he should be diligent, that thereby he might win the prize; therefore, all things must
be done in order" (Mosiah 4:27). Wisdom, order, and diligence. That
is great counsel to remember as we undertake our quest for spiritual
mastery.

Elder Dean L. Larsen, who was then in the Presidency of the
Seventy, shared this counsel about order and priorities:

> Some of us create such a complexity of expectations for
> ourselves that it is difficult to cope with the magnitude of
> them. Sometimes we establish so many particulars by which
> to evaluate and rate ourselves that it *becomes difficult for us
> to feel successful and worthy to any degree at any time.* We can
> drive ourselves unmercifully toward perfection on such a
> broad plane. When this compulsion is intensified by sources
> outside ourselves, the problem is compounded. *Confronting
> these demands can bring mental and emotional despair.* . . .
>
> . . . The recognition of our frailties need not propel us to
> try to achieve perfection in one dramatic commitment of ef-
> fort. The best progress sometimes comes when we are not un-
> der intense duress. Overzealousness is at least as much to be
> feared as apathy. *Trying to measure up to too many particular*

*expectations without some sense of self-tolerance can cause spiritual and emotional "burn-out."*[7]

While Elder Larsen describes a *symptom* found in many of those striving to be faithful disciples, Elder David A. Bednar gives the *treatment*: the "enabling power of the atonement." We made this point in chapter 4, but I shall repeat it here because of its relevance to this discussion.

I think most of us know that when we do things wrong, when we need help to overcome the effects of sin in our lives, the Savior has paid the price and made it possible for us to be made clean through His redeeming power. Most of us clearly understand that the Atonement is for sinners. I am not so sure, however, that we know and understand that the Atonement is also for saints—for good men and women who are obedient and worthy and conscientious and who are striving to become better and serve more faithfully. I frankly do not think many of us "get it" concerning this enabling and strengthening aspect of the Atonement, and I wonder if *we mistakenly believe we must make the journey from good to better and become a saint all by ourselves through sheer grit, willpower, and discipline,* and with our obviously limited capacities.[8]

That last sentence resonates deeply with me. We often find ourselves with a great desire to do more, to try harder, to push forward with greater effort. We say to ourselves, "I just need more willpower, more self-discipline, more teeth-clenching 'sheer grit,' to overcome my weaknesses and failures." But when that doesn't work, we start beating ourselves up. "What is wrong with me? Why can't I do better? Why can't I *be* better?"

What Elder Bednar suggested we need, in addition to our

willpower, self-discipline, and grit, is the enabling power of Christ. Consider that for a moment. Who in all the world is more eager to see us change for the better, to improve our behavior, to move closer to perfection than our Father in Heaven and His Beloved Son? After all, *we* are Their work. *We* are Their glory. This is why Christ came to earth, so that our falling short could "be perfected *in Him*" (Moroni 10:32). They want us to try harder. They want us to do better and to be better. But They don't ask that we do it alone. They are there to help.

## Spiritual Mastery

Let's apply the "start from where you are" philosophy to our young mother who was so discouraged because she yelled at her children. In her frustration she fervently said to me, "I was so disgusted with myself the last time it happened, that I vowed I would *never* yell at them again." Translated, that means, "I'm going out and running a marathon tomorrow."

We talked briefly about the principles we've been discussing here, and the importance of starting from where we are, and then increasing our abilities in small increments. "Why don't you give that some thought," I suggested, "then set some more realistic goals."

About a month later, we talked again, and I asked her how it was going. She told me that, after careful consideration, she had set three goals for herself.

First, she would not allow herself to yell at the children *before* 8 A.M. I had to suppress a smile, but she was very serious about it. "Getting them ready for school is always the worst time for me. So I vowed I would hold my tongue until they were out the door." She grinned. "I found myself glancing up at the clock and thinking, 'Hang on. Only four more minutes.'"

Second, she decided she needed an alternative outlet for her frustration. It was unrealistic to think she could hold it all in. It had to come out, but in a more positive way. So she developed a series of consequences for the children. "If you are late for the bus and I have to drive you to school, you have to wash the dishes by yourself tonight." Or, "If you don't get up when I wake you up, you will have no playtime with your friends the rest of the day." She said that goal really helped her because now there was a constructive way to deal with the situation.

Third, she vowed that each time she felt her anger start to rise, she would offer a quick, silent prayer for patience and control.

"I can't believe the difference it's made," she said. "I'm actually doing better, and I don't hate myself anymore."

Elder D. Todd Christofferson shared a similar lesson his mother had learned from her mother:

> In the 1950s my mother survived radical cancer surgery, but difficult as that was, the surgery was followed by dozens of painful radiation treatments in what would now be considered rather primitive medical conditions. She recalls that her mother taught her something during that time that has helped her ever since: "I was so sick and weak, and I said to her one day, 'Oh, Mother, I can't stand having 16 more of those treatments.' She said, 'Can you go today?' 'Yes.' 'Well, honey, that's all you have to do today.' It has helped me many times when I remember to take one day or one thing at a time."[9]

Remember:

- We can't run spiritual six-minute miles until we've made hundreds of laps around the track.

- We can't work spiritual calculus until we master the spiritual multiplication tables.
- We can't write spiritual symphonies until we master the spiritual musical scales.

---

## Notes

*Epigraph.* Marion G. Romney, in Conference Report, October 1956, 16.

1. See Gerald N. Lund, *Hearing the Voice of the Lord* (Salt Lake City: Deseret Book, 2007), 155–59.

2. Boyd K. Packer, *"That All May Be Edified"* (Salt Lake City: Bookcraft, 1982), 17.

3. Bruce R. McConkie, "The Probationary Test of Mortality," address given at University of Utah Institute of Religion, 10 January 1982, 6–7.

4. M. Russell Ballard, "Keeping Covenants," *Ensign,* May 1993, 6.

5. Bruce C. Hafen, *The Believing Heart: Nourishing the Seed of Faith,* 2d ed. (Salt Lake City: Deseret Book, 1990), 43–44.

6. Hafen, *Believing Heart,* 43.

7. Dean L. Larsen, "The Peaceable Things of the Kingdom," *New Era,* February 1986, 6.

8. David A. Bednar, "In the Strength of the Lord," BYU Speeches, 23 October 2001; emphasis in original; http://speeches.byu.edu/reader/reader.php?id=789.

9. D. Todd Christofferson, "Give Us This Day Our Daily Bread," CES Fireside for Young Adults, 9 January 2011, 3.

# Developing Spiritual Mastery

❧❦☙

ERE ARE FOUR real-life examples of how understanding how we learn and grow can directly support and maintain our hope in difficult times. Three examples are drawn from my own life. The final one comes from close friends.

### Pleading for Power

I have a problem. Actually, it's my body's problem. My body hates to get up when it wakes up. It doesn't matter when I wake up in the morning, I love to lie in bed for a few minutes and gradually make the transition from sleep back to wakefulness. I've never been one of those types who leap out of bed and is showered and shaved and ready for life in a couple of minutes.

Even in the mission field, I set my alarm for ten minutes earlier than we were required to get up so that I could lie there. One companion thought I was crazy. He was one of those types who could be up and ready in minutes. It really frustrated him that I didn't do that. "Set your alarm for when we need to get up," he would say, "and then you'll get more sleep and won't find it so hard to get out of bed." Uh-uh. It doesn't work like that for me.

I mention this habit because during the years when our family was young, it created a challenge. The only time I could consistently have uninterrupted, personal scripture study and prayer time was in the early morning hours before my family woke up. So each night I would set my alarm and vow to get up early.

But when my alarm went off, I would lie there and think, *I'll just take a minute. I won't go back to sleep. I'll just lie here for a moment.* The next thing I'd know, my wife would be shaking me and telling me I was going to be late for work.

I felt terrible. I really wanted to spend my mornings in study and prayer—I knew it was important to my spiritual health—but I couldn't make it happen. I thought about praying about it, but the idea of asking God to help me wake up seemed too humiliating, so I made up my mind to just try harder.

I tried in many ways to overcome this weakness. Sometimes I was successful, but most times I fell into the same old pattern. One day I even put my alarm clock out in the hall, thinking that if I had to go that far, I definitely wouldn't go back to sleep. But after I shut off the alarm, I returned and sat on the edge of the bed, thinking, *I won't lie down; I'll only sit here for a minute.* Next thing I knew, it was an hour later.

I reached the point where I felt real despair about it. I was frustrated that my willpower was so weak. One night, as I said my personal prayer, I said something like this: "Heavenly Father, I can't do it. I've proved that to myself. I've proved that to Thee. Help me, Father. Help me to get up in the morning and have my personal time with Thee."

What happened that next morning was quite remarkable. One minute before my alarm went off, I was wide awake and totally alert. I could scarcely believe it. Could it really have come from a single prayer? I suppose there are some who might suggest that I "psyched" myself into it. No way! I had tried psyching myself into waking up early dozens of times before and it didn't work.

I wish I could tell you I never slipped again, that from that time on I had my personal time with the Lord every morning. I didn't. But where before I was getting up maybe once or twice a week, now it was four or five times. Then gradually, with His continuing help, it became a habit. In about six months, I was no longer even turning on my alarm.

I had won the victory, but I hadn't done it alone.

## Six More Ridges

I grew up for most of my life in Murray, Utah, a suburb five or six miles south of Salt Lake City. Directly east of our home was Mount Olympus, though I didn't know that was its official name until I was in my teens. From where I lived, the mountain formed two distinct and similar peaks, so to us they were always the "Twin Peaks." All through my growing-up years—summer or winter—I would often look up at the mountain and think what a great thing it would be to be on top and look down into the Salt Lake Valley.

One summer, when I was about fourteen, a couple of my buddies and I decided we would do just that. We were pretty naïve and knew nothing about vertical rise (the mountain is about 4,500 feet from the valley floor to the summit) or hiking trails (if there were any back then). We had no special equipment, just our well-worn tennis shoes. For food, we took lunches packed by our moms in flour sacks, and we filled our canteens with water.

We started out in the early morning and headed east. From our house to the base of the mountain was eight to ten miles, but we rode that far almost every day on our bikes so that was no deterrent.

By the time we arrived at the base, the sun was fully up and the temperature was climbing. I was excited. I had dreamed of climbing the mountain for years. Off we went. We didn't have a plan. We didn't scout out a route or look for a trail. We just headed up the mountainside, zigzagging back and forth up the steeper parts.

We hiked steadily for an hour or more before our excitement began to fade. We were hot and dusty and sweaty. We were drinking a lot of water, and our canteens were nearly empty. We were trekking through sagebrush, cheatgrass, and scrub oak wearing cheap tennis shoes. The hike wasn't turning out to be nearly as wonderful as I had expected.

Near the two-hour mark, not only were we running out of water, but also out of heart. We stopped at a semiclear spot to catch our breath. There was talk about going home. Then one of the guys cried out, "Hey, look! There's the top." Sure enough, two or three hundred yards above us there was nothing but blue skies through the scrub oak. Any thoughts of quitting were instantly gone. We took off again at an increased pace.

And finally we crested the top. What I saw nearly took my breath away, but in the way that being kicked in the stomach takes your breath away. We hadn't reached the top at all. We had merely come to the top of the first major ridge. There were at least six more ridges between us and the summit.

I couldn't believe it. It was one of the most deflating experiences of my early life. But as we stared up in dismay, something else happened. Someone behind me spoke in almost reverential awe. "Look!" We turned around.

Again there were gasps, but this time of amazement. There, spread out about a thousand feet below us, was the entire Salt Lake Valley. It was a stunning sight and for the next ten or fifteen minutes we just stood there, taking it all in. We excitedly pointed out landmarks that we could see and identify, including our own streets and neighborhoods.

I don't remember for sure what happened next. I think we realized that we weren't going to climb all the way to the top—at least not on this day—and we went back down. But I've never forgotten the exhilaration of that moment.

We were nowhere near the top, but we had surely come a long way up the hill.

## "You're Doing Better Than You Know"

The lessons in that experience are pretty much self-evident. So many times, life is like toiling up an endless mountain in the heat of the day. We're hot, sweaty, and thirsty, and our legs feel like rubber.

But seeing six more ridges between us and perfection can be pretty disheartening. It shouldn't surprise us if we find ourselves asking, "Is this really worth it?" But occasionally stopping to "look back" can help us regain our perspective and renew our hope.

I can remember one time very clearly when remembering my mountain experience helped me regain my focus.

My wife, Lynn, and I were living in Southern California. I was teaching at a nearby institute of religion. I was also working on a master's degree and going to school one night a week in Los Angeles. I was in the bishopric of our ward, and my wife taught the Laurels in the Young Women auxiliary. Between ward meetings, institute night classes, institute social activities, and graduate school, I was almost always gone four nights of the week and most of Sunday. In addition, to help make ends meet, once a month I would give Know Your Religion lectures for BYU Continuing Education all over the state of California.

We had five children at the time. Our oldest was eight, the youngest only a year. We had only one car, so my wife was often left without transportation or else had to catch rides with ward members.

To put it mildly, it was a grueling time for us.

With all of that going on, we were also trying to do what was expected of us. We had scripture study and family prayer in the morning—rather, to be precise, we *scheduled* study and prayer each morning. But many times things were so hectic, it just didn't happen. We tried to hold family home evening every Monday, but that was often hit-and-miss too. It was also during this time that I was struggling to get up early in the morning to have my own personal study time.

I remember one particularly bad week. In sacrament meeting, my wife had the children lined up on the bench with her, trying to maintain some semblance of order (while I watched helplessly from the stand). We had a couple in the ward who had made no secret of the fact that they didn't want children until they could "afford them," which meant first paying off their two cars and the mortgage on their house.

On this day, Lynn and the kids ended up in the row right behind this couple. During the sacrament, a couple of the children were poking at each other and giggling. My wife was trying to get them under control when the woman in front of her leaned over to her husband and said, loud enough for Lynn to hear, "Some people sure make it difficult to have the Spirit during the sacrament."

Fighting back tears, Lynn took the children out to the foyer and stayed there for the rest of the meeting. That night, she said she was never going back to church. She did, of course, but this gives you a sense of how life was for us at that time.

The next day, though it was packed with things I had to do, I decided to plan a really good family home evening lesson for that night. My previous preparation had been kind of hit-and-miss—you know, throw together enough of a lesson to get by—but I was determined to do better. I prepared what I thought was a brilliant lesson. I never got to give it. We didn't get through the opening prayer before the whole evening collapsed into disaster. We sent the children to their rooms, me yelling, them bawling. Then I turned to Lynn and said, "What's the use? Why even try?"

That weekend I had a Know Your Religion lecture in the Bay Area. Wracked with guilt for leaving Lynn alone to handle the family yet again, I left Friday afternoon and flew to Northern California. In addition to my guilt, I couldn't get it out of my mind that I wasn't making it spiritually. Our family home evenings were a farce. I was away from my family all the time. I was leaving my wife to cope with the load alone. I wasn't doing my scripture study. My prayers were intermittent. It felt like instead of moving forward, I was actually regressing. Those discouraging thoughts weighed me down the whole weekend.

Early Sunday morning, I was sitting in one of the San Francisco International Airport concourses with an hour or more before my flight would depart. I was weary and still feeling discouraged. And that's when it happened.

I saw four young people—two males, two females. One held a hand-lettered, cardboard sign that read HUNGRY! PLEASE HELP! They were panhandlers who looked like they were not yet old enough to be out of high school. They were thin and haggard. Their clothes were tattered and worn. Their hair, makeup, dress, and jewelry represented extreme styles. There was a desperate urgency about them.

Seeing them made me remember a television report I had seen a few days earlier about California's "throw-away" teens. They weren't teens who had run away from home, they were kids who had been thrown out by their parents, told they weren't wanted, and ordered not to come back. The report said there were thousands of teens in California who had been "thrown away." Most of them were homeless, roaming the streets and stealing in order to live. Girls as young as thirteen and fourteen ended up in prostitution in order to survive.

Had these teenagers been "thrown away"? I had no way of knowing, but it appeared to be so.

As I watched the teens begging for help, I felt a great sadness for them. I wondered where they would go when they left the airport. Where would they sleep? What kind of food would they buy? Or would they buy drugs?

I thought of their parents and felt a deep sense of horror at what they had done.

I started thinking about our children and the good times we had enjoyed together. Family vacations and trips. Wrestling on the floor. "Monster chases" up and down the halls. Christmases at Grandma's house. I realized that my children were happy and felt safe.

And it was then that my experience climbing Twin Peaks came back to me. It was like a flood of light. Suddenly, a disastrous family home evening didn't seem nearly as catastrophic as it had before. Maybe we were missing family scripture study on some days, but we *were* trying. How many people in the airport that Sunday morning ever even considered going to church? How many people out there even had a Bible in the home, let alone worried about reading it?

I realized that yes, it was tough coming up the mountain, especially right now. Yes, the legs were hurting, and yes, there were still six more ridges looming above me. But when I turned around and looked back, a great sense of hope came over me. We weren't doing everything right. But we were doing many things. We were diligently trying. And we were coming slowly up the hill.

Elder Neal A. Maxwell once said, "We will never see the spiritual scenery beyond the next ridge unless we press forward on the strait and narrow path."[1] On another occasion, he used a similar metaphor: "We [should] distinguish more clearly between divine discontent and the devil's dissonance, between dissatisfaction with self and disdain for self. We need the first and must shun the second, remembering that when conscience calls to us from the next ridge, it is not solely to scold but also to beckon."[2]

Hugh B. Brown of the First Presidency added a similar thought: "The evil of tomorrow loses much of its size as we approach it. Our eyes are not fitted with telescopic lenses so we must await a close-up for a proper focus, and then we shall find ourselves equal to the task. Persistent climbing levels the hills and gives added strength to travel on."[3]

My wife and I have now put another thirty years or so into climbing the mountain. There are still a couple of ridges above us, but we've mostly survived the heat of the day and can feel the cool of the evening coming on. So for you who may still be on that first ridge and are feeling overwhelmed with the demands of your young families or the hectic schedules which define your lives, I hope you can take some comfort from our experience. Our "look back" is now more satisfying than ever. The children that I sent to bed that night now have children of their own. I watch my children and my grand-children climbing their own mountains and making their own mistakes. I know they are feeling like they are forever falling short—and yet, they are doing many things that are deeply pleasing to the Lord. And from time to time I remind them, "Be sure you take time now and then to turn around and see how far you've come."

### Hope Is an Active and Powerful Verb

The following story is from Shawn and Jeff Stringham of Bountiful, Utah. You may think at first that the primary lesson to be drawn from this is about hope—and there is a lesson there—but there are also lessons on perspective and on how we grow spiritually.

When our active, healthy, twenty-five-year-old son was diagnosed with idiopathic cardiomyopathy, my husband and

I were stunned. Neither of us had heart problems, nor anyone in our family as far back as we could trace. So the call that told us our son was in the hospital with his heart enlarged and struggling to beat at only 8 percent of its normal strength was a shock. In the very difficult times that followed we became familiar with despair, but we also became very familiar with the word "hope."

Those who have been through unexpected challenges know that the situation changes many times during the process. "He is young and healthy; I see no reason why his heart cannot recover." "He is not handling the medications as well as he needs to." "The heart isn't recovering. We need to implant a device to help the heart pump in a more synchronized manner." And finally, "His condition is so grave, we have to consider a heart transplant."

My husband and I had just finished that last, long hard conversation with the doctor and were trying to adapt our hope once again to the situation, when I went to the temple in the town where he lived. It seemed like every time we began to hope that things were working, things changed and our hope had to be readjusted. It was hard, but it didn't discourage us because along with the adjustments came such an outpouring of the Lord's love and care for us, that, along with accompanying blessings, we never lost hope altogether.

That day in the temple was a special one. I felt that the person for whom I was a proxy was with me throughout the entire initiatory work. I felt her joy as each blessing and promise was pronounced. As I returned the names to the temple worker, by now a dear friend, she asked how our son was. I started to give my standard answer of "We're hoping for the best," when instead, I found myself saying, "He will be fine."

*He will be fine?* Where did that come from? And yet, I knew it was true. Upon leaving the dressing room, I met another temple worker who also asked about Chris. This time I was not surprised when I said, "He will be just fine." And there it was. Even though the latest news we had was alarming, I had been given a higher understanding that our son would be fine. Within a week, the doctor called us again to say that Chris had scored too well on the heart pressure test to be considered for a transplant at this time.

For us, hope went from being a rather anemic whisper of a wish to something we could lean on, gain strength and understanding from. And because of it, we received heavenly guidance and assurance. Hope became a very active and powerful verb for us. And it still is. Chris is a long way from being recovered, but we, as his parents, have added "hope" to our list of heavenly tools the Lord has given us to help us through the trials we are experiencing and will yet experience. Fortunately, we have discovered that another synonym for hope is "comfort," and we have been receiving much of that.

About three months after Shawn and Jeff shared their story with me, Shawn added this perspective:

As the days, weeks, and now months have passed since our "tutorial" with the Lord on hope and faith, we are learning another great lesson. The Lord will never leave us alone, but as we use the tools He has given us, He gently pulls His special ministering angels away from us. It's like He wants to let us stand on our own with the added knowledge and understanding He has given us. Much like new parents hovering over a child taking his first steps, I feel like heavenly helpers are close by. But as their little one starts to be more sure of himself, the parents give him more and more room until the child is secure on his own.

At first, I must admit, I missed that special, warm, protective feeling. It truly sustained me and my family during an experience I know I could not have handled alone. But I am not the same person I was before our son's heart failure. Through the Holy Ghost, I know I have been given special insights—and power and understanding—from heavenly principles that put me in a different place. That knowledge truly sprang from the seeds of hope that were planted many months ago. Now we are more firmly anchored and better prepared to face life's trials and tests.[4]

---

### Notes

1. Neal A. Maxwell, *"Not My Will, But Thine"* (Salt Lake City: Deseret Book, 1988), 121.

2. *The Neal A. Maxwell Quote Book,* ed. Cory H. Maxwell (Salt Lake City: Bookcraft, 1997), 307.

3. Hugh B. Brown, *The Abundant Life* (Salt Lake City: Deseret Book, 1965), 136.

4. Material in possession of the author. Used by permission.

IV

# FULFILLMENT

*Seeing life from an eternal perspective
helps us focus our limited mortal energies
on the things that matter most.*

JOSEPH B. WIRTHLIN

*And now, as the preaching of the word
had a great tendency to lead the people to do
that which was just—yea, it had had more
powerful effect upon the minds of the people than
the sword, or anything else, which had happened
unto them—therefore Alma thought it was expedient
that they should try the virtue of the word of God.*

ALMA 31:5

# CHAPTER FIFTEEN

# "By Small and Simple Things" —Part One

———— ❧✦❧ ————

## Practical Steps for Gaining Hope in Times of Hopelessness

IN CHAPTER 7 we quoted Thomas Jefferson, who, speaking of George Washington and Benjamin Franklin, said, "They laid their shoulders to the great points, knowing that the little ones would follow of themselves."[1] We are trying to follow that counsel in this book. It's not that the "little things" are unimportant, but when things of greatest worth are put into place, the other things often follow naturally.

We have spent considerable time looking at three of these great points: The importance of hope (part 1), the need for alignment (part 2), and the value of perspective (part 3). All of these were discussed in the context of trying to develop a deeper and more resilient hope.

Sometimes, however, what appears at first to be less important— what Alma called "small and simple things"—may actually be of great importance. It is because they only look to be small and simple, but in reality, "by small and simple things are *great things* brought to pass" (Alma 37:6).

In this chapter and the next, we shall examine two such small and simple things:

- The power of the word
- The prayer of faith

Though simple in concept and small in scope of action, the power of the word (or what we frequently call scripture study*) and meaningful prayer have a pivotal effect on our ability to

- Know and understand the doctrine
- Have spiritual experiences that lead to true conversion
- Resist the enticements, deceptions, and temptations of the devil
- Put our hearts into alignment with God
- Maintain patience and courage in times of adversity
- Perceive things as they really are and as they ought to be

That's a pretty significant sweep of influence for two things we may consider to be small and simple.

As this book was nearing completion, I received a note from my oldest daughter, Cynthia.

> I think if you're focusing on the great points of aligning our lives with God, the most fundamental things with the greatest potential to generate faith and hope are prayer and scripture study. For me, these things are even ahead of temple attendance because, as important as that is, I am not able to

---

* For convenience, I will frequently use the phrase "scripture study," but I include in that concept the words of those we sustain as prophets, seers, and revelators. By the definition given in Doctrine and Covenants 68:3–4, this too can be considered as scripture.

do that on a daily basis. When I'm discouraged and over-whelmed (not to mention grumpy), then I know I have been neglecting my gospel study and prayer. *Even a small amount of time in the scriptures and on my knees restores hope, increases faith, and gives me the spiritual power I need to press forward.*[2]

I couldn't agree more. We need to realize just how central these two simple principles and practices are, how much power they can unlock, how much faith they can generate, and how much hope they can sustain. Small and simple they may be, but I see them as a key (another small and simple thing) that opens the door to a room full of light. That is why I also rank them as "great points."

The Lord certainly sees them that way. Some form of the word *prayer* is found nearly eight hundred times in the scriptures. When you add passages that talk about prayer without using the word (e.g., ask, seek, knock), that number increases significantly. If we look for references to the scriptures and include phrases like "the word," "the word of God," "the word of the Lord," "my word," or "thy word," the number of references are about the same. That means we can hardly read a page of scripture without running across at least one of those concepts.

When I was a teenager, I learned that when my dad emphasized something over and over, it was important to him, and that it was to my benefit to pay attention to what he was saying. I think we can safely say the same principle applies here with our Heavenly Father.

Rather than offering a complete or extensive treatment on those two principles, however, we shall focus here on how scripture study and prayer directly relate to increasing our hope. We shall especially look for specific—and *practical*—suggestions for doing so. We shall begin with studying the scriptures.

## A Question of Priorities

If we were being honest, many of us would have to admit that we don't study the scriptures as much as we know we should. There are a lot of reasons for why that is so, but the two most common ones we hear are "I don't have enough time" and "They're too hard to understand." (That last is often expressed by youth in one word: "BORING!")

There is some validity to both answers. We are all busy, and our lives are filled with pressing demands and obligations. And the scriptures are a unique and more challenging form of literature. Let us address both of those questions. First: "I'm too busy."

I remember one day in a quorum meeting, the teacher asked, "Why don't we study the scriptures more than we do?" A quorum member raised his hand. "I know I should, but I'm just too busy. I can't seem to find the time." Yet just before quorum meeting started, that man had told me that the day before, he had gone to a college football game. He had left his home at about 10:00 A.M. and hadn't gotten back until after 6:00 P.M. Nothing wrong with that, of course, but it did seem to deflate his argument significantly.

Don't we all have the same allotment of time? Then why is it that some of us are too busy for scripture study while others make time? (It's been my experience that you rarely *find* time for scripture study. You have to *make* time.) Some of the busiest people I know make studying the scriptures every day a top priority in their lives. Why? Because they hold a deep conviction that the effort brings great benefits.

So, when it comes right down to it, I don't think it's a matter of time at all. I think it's a matter of priorities. I think that what we are saying when we say we're too busy is "I don't see sufficient personal benefit in scripture study to give it a higher priority in my life."

The late Elder Carlos E. Asay, then in the Presidency of the

Seventy, made this pertinent—and somewhat painful—observation about scripture study:

> I fear that many of us rush about from day to day taking for granted the holy scriptures. We scramble to honor appointments with physicians, lawyers, and businessmen. *Yet we think nothing of postponing interviews with Deity—postponing scripture study.* Little wonder we develop anemic souls and lose our direction in living. How much better it would be if we planned and held sacred fifteen or twenty minutes a day for reading the scriptures. Such interviews with Deity would help us recognize his voice and enable us to receive guidance in all of our affairs.[3]

Here's another observation, and it has to do with motivation. During my career with the Church Educational System, there was a time when I was responsible for teacher training throughout the world. As part of that assignment, I had a lot of opportunity to observe teachers actually teaching the scriptures to each other or in the classroom. I also became interested in seeing how we approach scripture study in our homes and at church.

We talk a lot about the scriptures and the importance of studying them. And studying the scriptures consistently has a lot to do with motivation. We try to motivate ourselves, our children, and others to read and study them.

Our priorities are driven by desire, or what motivates us. There's an old adage that says "If you want to know what a person really values, don't listen to what they say. Watch what they do." I have found that we typically use three different motivational approaches both for ourselves and for others to encourage scripture study. These are not necessarily wrong. Each has some positive aspects to it. I've used all three in different settings and had some success with them. I'm just not sure if they are the most effective way to motivate ourselves and others to study the scriptures regularly.

- *Guilt and shame.* Here we say things to ourselves or to others like "The scriptures are important." "We're commanded by God to read them." "You need to do more." "You should feel awful because you're not doing what you should." "You need to make the scriptures a higher priority in your life."

- *Bribes and punishment.* Here are two real-life examples of this I have witnessed: "My dad promised to buy me a bike if I would read the entire Book of Mormon." "If you won't join us for family scripture reading, you're grounded for the week." And here's one from a seminary teacher: "If the whole class finishes the reading assignment over the weekend, we'll have a pizza party on Monday."

- *The medicine approach.* Those of us who are older remember the times when our parents gave us cod-liver oil. It was awful. You had to gag it down, and then race for a glass of something to take away the taste. We'd protest vigorously, but the standard line from our parents was "I know it doesn't taste good, but it's good for you." We may not talk about scripture study quite that bluntly, but that's the approach. For example, a mission president in a zone conference once said, "I know that personal study time can be really boring, but if you just buckle down and make yourself do it, you'll be surprised how good you'll feel." And an early-morning seminary teacher said, "If you'll just stay with me for a few more minutes while we finish this chapter, then we'll do something fun."

## A Promises Approach to Scripture Study

Go to the Topical Guide and look under "Scriptures, Study of," and "Scriptures, Value of." A careful study of the references listed there reveals a different motivational approach used by the Lord. I call it a *promises approach* to scripture study. See for yourself. (I have tried to keep the lists of scriptures relatively short in this book, but in this case, I think it is important for us to see the sheer volume and richness of what the Lord offers to those who study and learn His word.)

These promises cover a wide range of blessings. Not all of the promises may seem directly related to hope at first. But keep in mind the definition of hope we have been discussing: *Hope is to trust in the promises of the Lord.* Well, here are some promises that will directly and significantly add to that hope:

- "This book of the law shall not depart out of thy mouth; but thou shalt meditate therein day and night, . . . for then thou shalt make thy way prosperous, and then thou shalt have good success" (Joshua 1:8).
- "The law of the Lord is perfect, converting the soul" (Psalm 19:7).
- "Thy word is a lamp unto my feet, and a light unto my path" (Psalm 119:105).
- "Through [the] patience and comfort of the scriptures [we] might have hope" (Romans 15:4).
- "The holy scriptures . . . are able to make thee wise unto salvation" (2 Timothy 3:15).
- "All scripture is . . . profitable for doctrine, for reproof, for correction, for instruction in righteousness" (2 Timothy 3:16).

- "Whoso would hearken unto the word of God, and would hold fast unto it, . . . would never perish; neither could the temptations and the fiery darts of the adversary overpower them" (1 Nephi 15:24).

- "Feast upon the words of Christ; for behold, the words of Christ will tell you all things what ye should do" (2 Nephi 32:3).

- "The pleasing word of God . . . healeth the wounded soul" (Jacob 2:8).

- "We search the prophets, . . . and having all these witnesses we obtain a hope, and our faith becometh unshaken" (Jacob 4:6).

- "The preaching of the word had a great tendency to lead the people to do that which was just" (Alma 31:5).

- "The word of Christ . . . will point to you a straight course to eternal bliss" (Alma 37:44).

- "The holy scriptures . . . leadeth them to faith on the Lord" (Helaman 15:7).

- "They were . . . nourished by the good word of God, to keep them in the right way, to keep them continually watchful unto prayer" (Moroni 6:4).

- "Treasure up in your minds continually the words of life, and it shall be given you in the very hour that portion that shall be meted unto every man" (D&C 84:85).

- "Whoso treasureth up my word, shall not be deceived" (Joseph Smith–Matthew 1:37).

I'd like to recommend an interesting exercise for you. Take a sheet of paper and make a chart with two columns on it. Label the columns as shown on the following example.

| Blessings for This Life | Blessings for the Next Life |

Now go back through that list of scriptures and place the promises in one column or the other.

What do you learn from that exercise about hope and promises? It was a surprising revelation to me when I first did it.

Earlier we said that when we talk about scripture study we also mean studying the words of modern prophets. Here is what the prophets say about the scriptures:

*Joseph Smith.* We made it a rule wherever there was an opportunity, to read a chapter in the Bible, and pray; and these seasons of worship gave us *great consolation.*[4]

*President Spencer W. Kimball.* I find that when I get casual in my relationships with divinity and when it seems that no divine ear is listening and no divine voice is speaking, that I am far, far away. If I immerse myself in the scriptures *the distance narrows and the spirituality returns.* I find myself *loving more intensely* those whom I must love with all my heart and mind and strength, and loving them more, I find it easier to abide their counsel.[5]

*Elder Marion G. Romney.* I feel certain that if, in our homes, parents will read from the Book of Mormon prayerfully and regularly, both by themselves and with their children, the spirit of that great book will come to permeate our homes and all who dwell therein. The *spirit of reverence will increase; mutual respect and consideration for each other will grow. The spirit of contention will depart.* Parents will *counsel their children in greater love and wisdom. Children will be more* responsive and submissive to that counsel. *Righteousness will increase. Faith, hope, and charity—the pure love of Christ—will abound in our homes* and lives, bringing in their wake peace, joy, and happiness.[6]

***President Ezra Taft Benson.*** It is not just that the Book of Mormon teaches us truth, though it indeed does that. . . . But there is something more. There is a *power* in the book which will begin to *flow into your lives* the moment you begin a serious study of the book. You will find *greater power to resist temptation.* You will find the *power to avoid deception.* You will find the power to stay on the strait and narrow path. The scriptures are called "the words of life" (see D&C 84:85), and nowhere is that more true than it is of the Book of Mormon.[7]

***President Harold B. Lee.*** Do you have a daily habit of reading the scriptures? If we're not reading the scriptures daily, our *testimonies are growing thinner,* our *spirituality isn't increasing* in depth.[8]

***President Gordon B. Hinckley.*** Let me tell you a story about the Book of Mormon. I heard a man who was a banker in California tell this story. He said his secretary smoked, constantly smoked. She was addicted to smoking. She could not set it aside. She said to him one day, "How can I stop smoking?"

He reached down in his desk and took out a copy of the Book of Mormon and handed it to her. He said, "Now, you read this."

She said, "All right, I'll read it."

She came back a couple of days later and said, "I've read

200 pages, and I didn't see the word *smoking* anywhere. I didn't see the word *tobacco* anywhere. I saw nothing that referred to it."

He said, "Keep reading." . . .

She came back three or four days later. She said, "I've read the entire book. I didn't see tobacco anywhere; I didn't see smoking anywhere. But," she said, "there has come into my heart as a result of reading that book some influence, some power, that has taken from me the desire to smoke, and it is wonderful."[9]

*President Henry B. Eyring.* The Holy Ghost will guide what we say if we study and ponder the scriptures every day. The *words of the scriptures invite the Holy Spirit.*[10]

I can't speak for others, but I find that list of promises highly motivational. I want those blessings in my life. I want them for my family. And I have found the promises to be true. I know exactly what Jacob meant when he said the word of God can heal the wounded soul. I have felt the spiritual power that comes into my life when I am studying the scriptures and the words of the prophets of this dispensation.

Remember the first precondition in the process of exercising and learning by faith? It is *hearing the word.* If we are too busy to study the scriptures regularly, we are overlooking a wonderful source of power and some pretty marvelous promises.

With that, let us turn to the second reason people give for not reading and studying the scriptures: "They're too difficult. I don't understand them."

## Finding and Understanding More in the Scriptures

I remember a night many years ago when I was having a particularly difficult time falling asleep. After an hour of tossing and turning, I got up and took out my scriptures. *If I'm going to be awake,* I thought, *I may as well do something productive.* I went to the living room and began to read. In just a few minutes, I found myself nodding off and having to start over again and again. *Well,* I decided, *I didn't get a lot out of that, but at least I'm sleepy now.* I went back to bed. Same thing. I was wide awake, and my mind was still racing.

After another fifteen minutes or so, I got up again. This time I found an espionage novel I was in the middle of reading. I finished it two hours later, unable to stop until the story was finished. As I went back to bed, I thought to myself, *Why can't the scriptures be more like a novel that I just can't put down?*

I think it is safe to say that reading the scriptures is a very different kind of experience than reading a novel, a magazine or newspaper, or even a college textbook. The language and syntax are different, and often more difficult. The people we read about are far removed from us in time and culture. The scriptures contain concepts and principles that are abstract and contain multiple layers of meaning. They are also filled with symbols, parables, allegories, types, shadows, and similitudes—all of which have to be correctly interpreted in order to understand what is being said. It is little wonder that many people find the scriptures hard to understand.

It is a real concern, but not an insurmountable one. In fact, I have come to believe that this unique nature of the scriptures is partly by design. Surely the Lord could have made the scriptures as simple as a child's beginning reader, or as gripping as a novel, had He chosen to do so. Perhaps He did not because, like so many other things in the gospel, we must choose to want something and then work to achieve it. We must act on hope and faith. We must put forth an effort, because the things of greatest value require that a price be paid.

Fortunately, the Lord and the modern prophets have given us much counsel on this aspect of scripture study as well. There are many practical and useful concepts that will help us learn how not to just study the scriptures, but to find more in them and draw out their power.

## Paying the Price

I find it very interesting that the Lord rarely speaks of "reading" the scriptures. He chooses much more powerful verbs. For example:

- *Meditate* on them day and night (see Joshua 1:8).
- *Search* the scriptures *daily* (see Acts 17:11).
- *Study* the word of truth (see 2 Timothy 2:15; D&C 11:22).
- *Hold fast* (see 1 Nephi 15:24).
- Let our hearts *delight* in the scriptures (see 2 Nephi 4:15).
- *Feast* upon the words of Christ (see 2 Nephi 32:3).
- *Ponder* in our *hearts* (see 2 Nephi 32:8, Moroni 10:3).
- *Plant* the word in our hearts (see Alma 33:23).
- *Lay hold* upon the word of God (see Helaman 3:29).
- *Search* diligently (see 3 Nephi 23:1).
- *Treasure up* continually (see D&C 84:85).
- *Ponder* and *reflect* on the word (see D&C 138:1–2; Joseph Smith–History 1:12).

Clearly, if we are going to draw on the deeper power of the scriptures, it will require more than an occasional, casual reading. It will require effort. Patience. Perseverance. When we find ourselves confused or not understanding something in the scriptures, we cannot give up.

I have five simple but practical things that help me get more from my own scripture study. Perhaps they will be helpful for you too.

- *Slow down.* In this hectic, "instant-on, instant-off," "full-speed-ahead" world of ours, sometimes we have a tendency to "speed read" the scriptures. We rush through a chapter or a book because that's the goal we have set for ourselves. When a question comes to our minds, we brush it aside. "I don't have time to worry about that right now," we say to ourselves. Many people are now "reading" the scriptures in an electronic format, or listening to audio versions. There is value in these formats because they are more convenient and portable. (And there are some people who learn better aurally than visually.) But we need to be careful, because these formats, by their very nature, may encourage us to move along without stopping.

- *Pay attention.* This is another way to slow down. Paying attention requires stern mental discipline. How many times do we find our eyes moving down the page, but our minds are far afield? I like to think of paying attention as grabbing my mind by the back of the neck and dragging it back to the task at hand. Sometimes I find I have to read a passage several times, forcing myself to pay closer attention, noting specific words and phrases, or asking myself what it is saying. One thing that helps me stay focused is to always have a marking pencil with me and watch for things that are especially meaningful to me. Another way for me to pay attention is to stop and ponder on what I've just read.

- *Ask questions.* For me, this is one of the most productive things I can do. I'm constantly asking myself questions like "What does that word mean?" "How does this relate to what it says in Alma?" "Why did the Lord inspire the prophet to choose that particular word?" "Is there a pattern forming here?" President Ezra Taft Benson suggested two questions that I have found to be very helpful: "We should constantly ask ourselves, 'Why did the Lord inspire Mormon (or Moroni or Alma) to include that in his record? What lesson can I learn from that to help me live in this day and age?'"[11]

- *Listen.* I find that when I force myself to slow down, to pay attention, and to ask questions, what I am really doing is signaling to the Holy Ghost that I am ready to be taught. Then revelation flows more easily. It has surprised me how often understanding comes almost immediately after the question is asked. There is another thing I have learned to listen for. I call them "nudges from the Spirit." I'll be reading along and come across something that doesn't make sense or may even seem contradictory to other principles. It is easy to shrug these ideas off and move on, but if I do, I may lose an opportunity to be taught.

Here's an example of what I mean. In Doctrine and Covenants 10, I came across this statement in verse 55: "Whosoever belongeth to my church need not fear, for such shall inherit the kingdom of heaven."

I stopped. *Wait a minute,* I thought. *That can't be true. All we have to do to inherit the kingdom of heaven is belong to the Church?* I thought about it for a while, and then finally went on, not sure how to resolve it in my mind.

Twelve verses later I came across this, which I would not have noticed had I not been listening to that nudge from the Spirit: "Behold, this is my doctrine—whosoever repenteth *and cometh unto me,* the same is my church" (D&C 10:67). And there was my answer. I was putting my definition of "church" into that first verse. The Lord's definition is much more narrow. I had an important learning experience that day.

- *Take meaningful side trips.* Sometimes those "nudges" send me looking for an answer in the Topical Guide or the Bible Dictionary. Sometimes I'll check out the cross-references at the bottom of the page, or even stop and look up something I remembered reading in the *Ensign* or another source. Some great teaching moments have come from those unexpected side trips.

We have referred to the scriptures a lot in this chapter, but remember that we include in that general term the words of the prophets, especially as given in general conference. We have cited many scriptures, but we have just as frequently quoted the words of our prophets, seers, and revelators. Aside from the timeliness of their messages—general conference is held every six months—these prophetic words come to us in clear and simple language. There is no archaic language or large cultural gaps between us and them. They focus on our needs under the inspiration of the Almighty.

In the messages of general conference, there is an immediate and specific relevance to our times, our problems, and our circumstances that makes them especially valuable to us as we deal with the everyday challenges of life. The words of our living prophets can lift our heads, cheer our hearts, renew our hopes, and build our faith. They contain the same power to inspire and to change lives today as they did when Alma said that "the preaching of the word had a great tendency to lead the people to do that which was just" (Alma 31:5). When we remember that the first precondition for the process of faith is *hearing the word,* let us also remember that that includes the word as it is preached to us today.

### Suggestions for More Effective Scripture Study

Those who we sustain as prophets, seers, and revelators have also shared many practical suggestions on how we can have more effective scripture study. Here are just a few:

*Elder M. Russell Ballard.* Always have a marking pencil ready as you study. Make notations in the margins. Write cross-references. Make the scriptures yours by marking them. . . .

Study topically as well as chronologically. Both approaches have merit, but we need to go to the Topical Guide or the index from time to time and read all that the Lord has said on repentance, or faith, or some other principle.[12]

*Elder David A. Bednar.* I now want to review with you three basic ways or methods of obtaining living water from the scriptural reservoir: (1) *reading* the scriptures from beginning to end, (2) *studying* the scriptures by topic, and (3) *searching* the scriptures for connections, patterns, and themes. Each of these approaches can help satisfy our spiritual thirst if we invite the companionship and assistance of the Holy Ghost as we read, study, and search.[13]

*President Thomas S. Monson.* Every holder of the priesthood should participate in daily scripture study. *Crash courses are not nearly so effective as the day-to-day reading* and application of the scriptures in our lives. . . . *Study them as though they were speaking to you,* for such is the truth.[14]

*Elder D. Todd Christofferson.* For conversion, you should care more about the amount of time you spend in the scriptures than about the amount you read in that time. I see you [speaking to the young adults] sometimes reading a few verses, stopping to ponder them, carefully reading the verses again, and as you think about what they mean, praying for understanding, asking questions in your mind, waiting for spiritual impressions, and writing down the impressions and insights that come so you can remember and learn more.[15]

*President Henry B. Eyring.* Reading, studying, and pondering are not the same. We read words and we may get ideas. We study and we may discover patterns and connections in scripture. But *when we ponder, we invite revelation by the Spirit.* Pondering, to me, is the thinking and the praying I do after reading and studying in the scriptures carefully.[16]

*President Howard W. Hunter.* To understand [the scriptures] requires more than casual reading or perusal—there must be concentrated study. It is certain that one who studies the scriptures every day accomplishes far more than one who devotes considerable time one day and then lets days go by before continuing. Not only should we study each day, but there should be a regular time set aside when we can concentrate without interference.[17]

In conclusion, let me share what is, in my mind, the best summation of the blessings of studying the scriptures and the words of the living prophets. I don't know who first made this statement, but during my tenure as a General Authority, I heard it quoted by several different brethren.

If you want to speak to the Lord, get down on your knees. If you want the Lord to speak to you, open your scriptures.

When we are facing the dark days of life, this is what we need most in order to maintain hope. We need the Lord to speak to us.

---

## Notes

*Part IV Epigraph.* Joseph B. Wirthlin, "The Time to Prepare," *Ensign,* May 1998, 14.

1. Thomas Jefferson, quoted in *Three Centuries of American Poetry and Prose,* ed. Alphonso G. Newcomer, Alice E. Andrews, and Howard J. Hall (Chicago: Scott, Foresman and Company, 1917), 170.

2. Material in possession of the author. Used by permission.

3. Carlos E. Asay, "'Look to God and Live,'" *Ensign,* November 1978, 53–54.

4. Joseph Smith, *History of The Church of Jesus Christ of Latter-day Saints,* 7 vols., ed. B. H. Roberts (Salt Lake City: The Church of Jesus Christ of Latter-day Saints, 1932–51), 1:189.

5. Spencer W. Kimball, *The Teachings of Spencer W. Kimball,* ed. Edward L. Kimball (Salt Lake City: Bookcraft, 1982), 135.

6. Marion G. Romney, in Conference Report, April 1960, 112–13.

7. Ezra Taft Benson, *The Teachings of Ezra Taft Benson* (Salt Lake City: Bookcraft, 1988), 54.

8. Harold B. Lee, *The Teachings of Harold B. Lee,* ed. Clyde J. Williams (Salt Lake City: Bookcraft, 1996), 152.

9. Gordon B. Hinckley, *Discourses of Gordon B. Hinckley* (Salt Lake City: Deseret Book, 2005), 2:497–98.

10. Henry B. Eyring, "'Feed My Lambs,'" *Ensign,* November 1997, 83.

11. Ezra Taft Benson, "The Book of Mormon—Keystone of Our Religion," *Ensign,* November 1986, 6.

12. M. Russell Ballard, "'Be Strong in the Lord, and in the Power of His Might,'" CES Fireside for Young Adults, 3 March 2002, 4.

13. David A. Bednar, "A Reservoir of Living Water," CES Fireside for Young Adults, 4 February 2007, 2; www.lds.org/library/display/0,4945,538-1-4040-1,00.html.

14. Thomas S. Monson, "Be Your Best Self," *Ensign,* May 2009, 68.

15. D. Todd Christofferson, "When Thou Art Converted," *Ensign,* May 2004, 11.

16. Henry B. Eyring, "Serve with the Spirit," *Ensign,* November 2010, 60.

17. Howard W. Hunter, *The Teachings of Howard W. Hunter,* ed. Clyde J. Williams (Salt Lake City: Bookcraft, 1997), 52.

*Feast upon the words of Christ;
for behold, the words of Christ will tell
you all things what ye should do. . . .*

*. . . Behold, I say unto you that ye must pray
always, and not faint; that ye must not perform any
thing unto the Lord save in the first place ye shall
pray unto the Father in the name of Christ, that he
will consecrate thy performance unto thee, that thy
performance may be for the welfare of thy soul.*

2 NEPHI 32:3, 9

CHAPTER SIXTEEN

# "By Small and Simple Things" —Part Two

—✥—

O UR PURPOSE HERE is not to discuss prayer as a general gospel principle, but to focus on the specific role prayer can play in strengthening and fortifying our hope, especially in difficult times. To do that, I should like to focus on three principles of prayer which seem especially relevant to our study on hope.

## Consistency

When I was a boy, I walked about a mile and half each way between my home and our elementary school. It's odd what memories stick in your mind, but I have a vivid memory of an experience I had over a period of a couple of weeks. My friend and I shortened our walk significantly by taking shortcuts through various farmers' fields. One of those fields was about five acres of alfalfa. It must have been the beginning of the school year because I remember that the alfalfa had been recently cut and the new growth was only four or five inches tall. We angled diagonally across the field, moving from corner to corner.

To my surprise, on our return home that afternoon, we could still see a faint trace of our route. Our feet had pressed down the stalks, and they hadn't fully recovered. Being boys, we decided to retrace our steps as closely as we could. When we looked back again, our trail was clearly visible.

The next morning, the plants had recovered somewhat, but we had no problem following the same trail once again, which we did. And again that evening. And the next day and the next. By the time the alfalfa was knee-high a couple of weeks later, it was no problem to see where we'd been. Our track of faint footprints had turned into an actual pathway.

It was not long thereafter—maybe at a general conference, or possibly at a stake conference—that one of the Brethren gave a talk on prayer.* To my surprise, he likened prayer to crossing a field of grain. The first time we move through it, we barely leave a trace, and we may not be able to see which way we went when we pass through again. But if we follow the same track day after day, soon it becomes a path we can easily follow.

I knew exactly what he was talking about because my buddy and I had experienced that for ourselves. The speaker then likened that journey to our daily prayers. In times of trouble, he concluded, if we have walked that way many times, we won't have trouble finding our way to God, but if we haven't, we may wonder why we can't find our way to Him.

As you consider that analogy, here are three more things to ponder.

The first is a revelation given in the midst of the terrible persecution of the Saints in Jackson County, when they were crying out and pleading for protection and deliverance.

---

* My memory is that it was President David O. McKay, but after careful searching I cannot find it in print, so I cannot give credit for it.

They were slow to hearken unto the voice of the Lord their God; therefore, *the Lord their God is slow to hearken unto their prayers,* to answer them in the day of their trouble.

In the day of their peace they esteemed lightly my counsel; but, in the day of their trouble, of necessity they feel after me. (D&C 101:7–8)

The second is a quote by one of our modern prophets, President Howard W. Hunter:

If prayer is only a spasmodic cry at the time of crisis, then it is utterly selfish, and we come to think of God as a repairman or a service agency to help us only in our emergencies. We should remember the Most High day and night—always—not only at times when all other assistance has failed and we desperately need help. If there is any element in human life on which we have a record of miraculous success and inestimable worth to the human soul, it is prayerful, reverential, devout communication with our Heavenly Father.[1]

The third is a poem from Edwin Markham, and was a favorite of President David O. McKay. It provides a more elegant analogy than two boys walking through a field of alfalfa.

*The builder who first bridged Niagara's gorge,*
*Before he swung his cable, shore to shore,*
*Sent out across the gulf his venturing kite*
*Bearing a slender cord for unseen hands*
*To grasp upon the further cliff and draw*
*A greater cord, and then a greater yet;*
*Till at last across the chasm swung*
*The cable—then the mighty bridge in air!*

*So we may send our little timid thought*
*Across the void, out to God's reaching hands—*
*Send out our love and faith to thread the deep—*
*Thought after thought, until the little cord*
*Has greatened to a chain no chance can break,*
*And we are anchored to the Infinite!*[2]

Consistency in prayer is an important factor in sustaining hope in this life. We're not saying that consistency in prayer is only to prepare us for times of crisis. Earlier we talked about life being "so daily" and how, even in the good times, we need daily inspiration, daily direction, daily comfort, and daily protection. That is one of the wonderful things about prayer. It too is daily. We can pray day or night, standing or kneeling, aloud or in our minds.

What about people who have neglected their prayers, perhaps even for many years? Is there no hope for them? While there are consequences for our slothfulness, it doesn't mean that we are completely cut off from God's help. Even though the Lord sharply rebuked those early Saints for not turning to Him earlier, He immediately added this: "Notwithstanding their sins, my bowels are filled with compassion toward them. I will not utterly cast them off; and in the day of wrath I will remember mercy" (D&C 101:9).

What a marvelous example of God's mercy and His longsuffering. There will be consequences for our neglect. But if we turn back to Him, we can immediately begin to see the Lord's influence in our lives. Of course, it will take time to create that "chain" which anchors us to the Infinite, or to make our prayers a well-trodden path to the Lord, but consistency in prayer can begin today. This very moment. That is one of the blessings of prayer. And whether we are just starting, or our path is a well-beaten one, the promise is there: "Pray *always,* and be believing, and all things shall work together for your good" (D&C 90:24).

## Humility

We have spoken before of the importance of humility, which is often referred to in the scriptures as a soft or softened heart. It means that we open our hearts for instruction, that we willingly submit to God's will and purposes, and that we desire to be in closer alignment with Him and to see things as He sees them. We saw in chapter 2 how a softened heart is a key to starting the process of faith. Here we shall also see that it is requisite to meaningful, effective, power-filled prayer. Note what the Lord says: "Be thou humble; and the Lord thy God shall lead thee by the hand, and give thee answer to thy prayers" (D&C 112:10).

Without humility, prayer loses much of its power in our lives. If our hearts are not humble, not only are we less likely to pray, but also we can end up praying for the wrong things. Or we may find ourselves praying out of habit or because "it's our duty." If we are not careful, our prayers may become shallow and filled with rote phrases that are repeated with no real depth of feeling. We can find ourselves seeking to "counsel God," as we discussed in chapter 9. Our prayers may even take on a selfish aspect, as President Gordon B. Hinckley warned against:

> The trouble with most of our prayers is that we give them as if we were picking up the telephone and ordering groceries—we place our order and hang up. We need to meditate, contemplate, think of what we are praying about and for and then speak to the Lord as one man speaketh to another.[3]

Here are some other teachings about how our heart affects how we pray:

*Jesus.* Two men went up into the temple to pray; the one a Pharisee, and the other a publican.

The Pharisee stood and prayed thus with himself, God, I thank thee, that I am not as other men are, extortioners, unjust, adulterers, or even as this publican.

I fast twice in the week, I give tithes of all that I possess.

And the publican, standing afar off, would not lift up so much as his eyes unto heaven, but smote upon his breast, saying, God be merciful to me a sinner.

I tell you, this man went down to his house justified rather than the other: for every one that exalteth himself shall be abased; and *he that humbleth himself* shall be exalted. (Luke 18:10–14)

*Amulek.* Yea, and when you do not cry unto the Lord [i.e., when you are not formally praying], *let your hearts be full, drawn out in prayer unto him continually* for your welfare, and also for the welfare of those who are around you. (Alma 34:27)

*President Joseph F. Smith.* We are told that we should remember him in our homes, keep his holy name fresh in our minds, and *revere him in our hearts;* we should call upon him from time to time, from day to day; and, in fact, every moment of our lives we should live so that *the desires of our hearts will be a prayer unto God* for righteousness, for truth, and for the salvation of the human family.[4]

*President Brigham Young.* In praying, though a person's words be few and awkwardly expressed, *if the heart is pure* before God, that prayer will avail more than the eloquence of a Cicero. What does the Lord, the Father of us all, care about our mode of expression? The *simple, honest heart* is of more avail with the Lord than all the pomp, pride, splendor, and eloquence produced by men.[5]

In 1832, after visiting the Saints in Jackson County, Missouri, Joseph Smith was on his way back to Kirtland with several other brethren. They stopped and did some missionary work on the way. As they were traveling through Indiana by coach, the horses bolted. Bishop Newell K. Whitney panicked and tried to jump from the carriage. He broke his foot and leg in several places and they had to stop while he recovered. During that time, Joseph was somehow poisoned. He vomited up blood and poisonous matter so violently that it dislocated his jaw. He was given a blessing by Bishop Whitney and was immediately healed.[6] Such difficult times would cause some to lose hope and slip into despair. From a letter Joseph wrote to his wife, Emma, we get an interesting insight into Joseph's heart at that time.

I have visited a grove which is just back of the town almost every day, where I can be secluded from the eyes of any mortal and there *give vent to all the feelings of my heart* in meditation and prayer. I have called to mind all the past moments of my life and am left to mourn and shed tears of sorrow for my folly [not for his current circumstances!] in suffering the adversary of my soul to have so much power over me as he has had in times past. But God is merciful and has forgiven my sins, and I rejoice that he sendeth forth the Comforter unto as many as believe and *humble* themselves before him.[7]

The Lord has said that "the spirit and the body are the soul of man" (D&C 88:15). With that definition in mind, note this prayer by Enos: "*My soul hungered;* and I kneeled down before my Maker, and I cried unto him in mighty prayer and supplication for mine own soul" (Enos 1:4; see also Alma 34:26; 58:10; Mormon 3:12).

When the heart is humble, we become submissive, penitent, patient, trusting, open to instruction, and hungry for the things of the Spirit. When these qualities are present in our prayers, not only do we find greater power and receive more revelation, but our hearts are also *filled with hope.*

## Focus

In an earlier discussion, we saw how "action" is a key step in the process of developing faith and hope and noted how this understanding gives added meaning to James's declaration that "faith without works is dead" (James 2:20). I believe meaningful prayer is one of those works of which James spoke. Here is what the Bible Dictionary says about prayer and works:

> As soon as we learn the true relationship in which we stand toward God (namely, God is our Father, and we are his children), then at once prayer becomes natural and instinctive on our part. . . . Many of the so-called difficulties about prayer arise from forgetting this relationship. Prayer is *the act* by which the will of the Father and the will of the child are brought into correspondence with each other. The object of prayer is not to change the will of God, but to secure for ourselves and for others blessings that God is already willing to grant, but that are made conditional on our asking for them. Blessings *require some work or effort* on our part before we can

obtain them. *Prayer is a form of work,* and is an appointed means for obtaining the highest of all the blessings.[8]

There are so many important concepts for us to remember in that definition. Meaningful prayer is based on an understanding of our relationship with God. Consistent, fervent prayer is for our benefit; it is not how we change God's mind, but how we change our hearts. Prayer is action. It is one of the "works" required if we are to develop faith.

I believe that also means that effective, meaningful prayer takes real effort on our part. We have to work at it to do it properly.

I have come to know from my own experience that the cure for the shallow prayer is focus. Focus takes mental effort. It takes concentration. It takes a conscious act of will to stay focused on what we *should* be praying for, not just what we *want* to pray for. In other words, sometimes we may need to change our perception of prayer. Do we see prayer

- as an emergency exit, or as a place of refuge?
- as a mail-order house, or as an antidote to the infections of life?
- as a way to let people know how righteous we are, or as a confession of how far we fall short?
- as a desperate cry for deliverance, or as a longing cry for forgiveness?
- as a plea for help for ourselves, or as a plea to know who needs our help?

I remember an occasion when the Spirit rebuked me sharply and taught me a great lesson about focus and prayer. I had been frantically preparing for a major presentation for a meeting later that day, and I was late for work. As I stuffed everything into my briefcase and started for the door, I remembered I had forgotten to say my prayers. So I quickly dropped to my knees and hurriedly began to pray. Then came this thought, clearly and with great force.

Remember who you are talking to here! Would you really approach the throne of God as a hasty afterthought before you rush out the door? He is the God of the universe. He has all power, glory, knowledge, and majesty. Do you understand what an incredible privilege it is that you are invited to bring your petitions to Him? Obviously not. You drop to your knees with your briefcase still in hand, half resentful that "doing your duty" is going to make you late for work.

Talk about a lesson in humility and a call to repentance. Even now, years later, as I kneel, I often remind myself who it is I am addressing, and what an incredible blessing it is that I can do so. That self-reminder immediately changes the focus of my prayers.

This is what we mean by focus. There are prayers of faith, prayers of thanks, prayers of submission, prayers of convenience, prayers of anger and frustration and bitterness, prayers for help, prayers for enlightenment and understanding, prayers for direction, prayers for the promises, and prayers of duty. The focus of our prayers will directly influence what kind of prayers we offer and the blessings that come from them.

The invitation to approach the Lord in prayer is found in hundreds of places in the scripture, but the invitation is not without its conditions. For example, in this wonderful promise given by Moroni, there are two conditions included: "Whatsoever thing ye shall ask the Father in my name, which is *good*, in *faith believing* that ye shall receive, behold, it shall be done unto you" (Moroni 7:26). A few verses later, he repeats the promise and adds another caution: "If ye will have faith in me ye shall have power to do whatsoever thing *is expedient* in me" (Moroni 7:33). That same promise is given in the Doctrine and Covenants but with an even more pointed warning: "If ye ask anything that is not expedient for you, it shall turn unto your condemnation" (D&C 88:65).

Elder David A. Bednar once gave a talk entitled "Pray Always." He said he wished to teach us three principles for how to make our prayers more meaningful. These are wonderful and practical suggestions on how to bring greater focus to our prayers. I shall include only a few excerpts from his talk here, but I would recommend studying the entire talk.

> **Principle #1: Prayer becomes more meaningful as we counsel with the Lord in all our doings. . . .**
>
> . . . There may be things in our character, in our behavior, or concerning our spiritual growth about which we need to counsel with Heavenly Father in morning prayer. After expressing appropriate thanks for blessings received, we plead for understanding, direction, and help to do the things we cannot do in our own strength alone. For example, as we pray, we might:
>
> - Reflect on those occasions when we have spoken harshly or inappropriately to those we love the most.
> - Recognize that we know better than this, but we do not always act in accordance with what we know.
> - Express remorse for our weaknesses and for not putting off the natural man more earnestly.
> - Determine to pattern our life after the Savior more completely.

- Plead for greater strength to do and to become better.

Such a prayer is a key part of the spiritual preparation for our day.

During the course of the day, we keep a prayer in our heart for continued assistance and guidance. . . .

We notice during this particular day that there are occasions where normally we would have a tendency to speak harshly, and we do not; or we might be inclined to anger, but we are not. We discern heavenly help and strength and humbly recognize answers to our prayer. Even in that moment of recognition, we offer a silent prayer of gratitude.

At the end of our day, we kneel again and report back to our Father. We review the events of the day and express heartfelt thanks for the blessings and the help we received. We repent and, with the assistance of the Spirit of the Lord, identify ways we can do and become better tomorrow. Thus our evening prayer builds upon and is a continuation of our morning prayer. And our evening prayer also is a preparation for meaningful morning prayer. . . .

**Principle #2. Prayer becomes more meaningful as we express heartfelt gratitude. . . .**

The most meaningful and spiritual prayers I have experienced contained many expressions of thanks and few, if any, requests.[9]

I find it interesting that Elder Bednar uses the word *gratitude* rather than *thanks*. Though closely related, there is a difference between gratitude and thanks. We often find ourselves in our prayers going quickly through a list of things we're thankful for: "I thank

Thee for the gospel. I thank Thee for my family, etc." Far more meaningful is when our hearts are filled with a deep sense of gratitude as we kneel. We try to remember all that the Lord has done for us and our families. As we try to express that gratitude in words, our hearts fill with wonder at His goodness. We consider how different our lives would be had it not been for this blessing or this answer to our prayers. Thus, each expression of thankfulness is surrounded by a richness of emotion and a deep sense of humility for what we have been given. This truly changes the focus of our prayers. To quote again from Elder Bednar:

**Principle #3. Prayer becomes more meaningful as we pray for others with real intent and a sincere heart.**

Petitioning Heavenly Father for the blessings we desire in our personal lives is good and proper. However, praying earnestly for others, both those whom we love and those who despitefully use us, is also an important element of meaningful prayer. Just as expressing gratitude more often in our prayers enlarges the conduit for revelation, so praying for others with all of the energy of our souls increases our capacity to hear and to heed the voice of the Lord.[10]

## Summary

Prayer and scripture study provide another synergistic relationship in the gospel. These two simple and daily practices energize our faith, enliven our hope, broaden our perspective, and bring us into closer alignment with God's will. They help us strengthen the bridges and lift up our heads when they hang down, and they provide two more sources of power for our spiritual navigation systems. It's like having two additional satellites in the sky so that our SPS unit can more accurately tell us where we are, which way we are going, and what paths will lead us to our destination.

Faithful prayer and scripture study come with promises that can add immeasurably to our hope. They are blessings that will help see us through the great challenges of life, as well as through the flat, boring stretches that test our endurance in other ways.

As we more diligently pursue serious scripture study, and then join it with meaningful prayer, our hope shall brighten, our faith shall deepen, and our joy shall be fuller. That is the Lord's promise.

---

## Notes

1. Howard W. Hunter, "'Hallowed Be Thy Name,'" *Ensign,* November 1977, 52.

2. Edwin Markham, as cited in David O. McKay, in Conference Report, April 1946, 116.

3. Gordon B. Hinckley, *Teachings of Gordon B. Hinckley* (Salt Lake City: Deseret Book, 1997), 469.

4. Joseph F. Smith, *Gospel Doctrine* (Salt Lake City: Deseret Book, 1919), 503–4.

5. Brigham Young, *Discourses of Brigham Young,* ed. John A. Widtsoe (Salt Lake City: Deseret Book, 1978), 169.

6. See Joseph Smith, *History of The Church of Jesus Christ of Latter-day Saints,* 7 vols., ed. B. H. Roberts (Salt Lake City: The Church of Jesus Christ of Latter-day Saints, 1932–51), 1:271.

7. Joseph Smith, *Teachings of Presidents of the Church: Joseph Smith* (Salt Lake City: The Church of Jesus Christ of Latter-day Saints, 2007), 243.

8. LDS Bible Dictionary, s.v. "Prayer," 752–53.

9. David A. Bednar, "Pray Always," *Ensign,* November 2008, 41–42; emphasis in original.

10. Bednar, "Pray Always," 43; emphasis in original.

# A Sustaining Hand
# in the Midst of Tragedy

—❦—

T HE FOLLOWING STORY was submitted by a couple with a young family following a serious tragedy that occurred in their lives. Their experience involved a terrible loss and much pain and suffering, yet even as the tragedy unfolded, there was evidence of the Lord's hand. Tender mercies were extended and blessings came to soften the sorrow and sustain their hope.

Though it is a painful thing for them to relate the details of their experience, they feel that by including their story in this book, they might give hope and encouragement to others who have experienced tragedy. They have chosen to use only their first names so that the focus will be on their experience, and not on them.

The family consists of Ben (the father), Tricia (the mother), Julia (not quite five years old), Adria (three years old), and Kara (seven months old).

## Wednesday, August 17, 2011

Ben and Tricia and their three girls were on their way to Utah from a neighboring state to participate in the wedding of Tricia's younger brother, which was scheduled for the next morning. As they neared their destination, they took a short detour out into isolated farm country to see some property Ben had heard about and was curious to explore.

After Ben and Tricia finished looking at the property, the farm-hand showing them the land told Ben that by using the back roads they could save considerable time on their way back to the freeway. Following his directions, they continued their journey.

A few miles later—it was now about 6:30 in the evening—Ben and Tricia reached a well-maintained gravel road and turned east. They were in pretty desolate country, at least twenty miles from any town, or even any paved roads, and about fifty miles from the nearest city. As they were driving, three-year-old Adria complained about being in her car seat. Not waiting for permission, she started to un-buckle herself—behavior typical of this energetic, independent little girl.

What happened next is not completely clear in either Ben's or Tricia's mind. Tricia says she remembers unbuckling herself and turning around to deal with Adria, and thinks that Ben turned his head to watch for a moment.* Whatever the cause, Ben was momentarily distracted. He said he remembers hitting something that jerked the wheel out of his hand.† He lost control of the car and it went off the road and rolled three or four times. Here, in their own words, is what happened next.

**Ben:** When the car stopped, I was dazed and in a state of shock. It took me a moment or two to realize what had

---

* Part of the pain of a tragedy is reliving what happened in your mind and wondering if there was something you could have done differently that would have changed the outcome.

† The road had some bad stretches of washboard at this point, or there may have actually been something in the road.

happened. Julia and Kara were screaming hysterically, but I realized that Adria and Tricia were not in the vehicle. The car was on its side, so I had to climb out through the passenger side window, busting it out with my shoulder because the door was jammed. By then, Julia was really upset. I had to break out another window to get to her and Kara. As I helped Julia out of the car, she immediately calmed down. She looked up at me and said, "Daddy, my best friend is gone."* I started to cry. "But it's all right, Daddy," she added. "Adria's with Jesus now. And she's happy."

Once all three of us were clear of the car, I took Julia and Kara with me and started looking around. I immediately saw Adria's body a few yards away. She was lying facedown in the dirt, and there was a lot of blood. I knew she was very likely dead, but I had to make sure there was nothing I could do for her. I told Julia to stay back, then went to Adria's side. As I knelt beside her and saw the extent of her injuries, I fell apart. I knew we had just lost our precious daughter. I wanted to pick her up, but decided that if there was any chance she wasn't dead, it would be best not to move her until the paramedics came.

Sobbing now, I moved on, looking for Tricia. I believe Tricia was thrown out of the car on the first roll because when I finally found her she was some distance away. She was facedown too and not moving. My heart dropped. I ran to her and knelt beside her. I knew she had been severely injured.† I shook her, but she did not respond. I felt for a pulse,

---

* Julia and Adria always called each other their best friends.

† Later they would learn that Tricia had seven broken ribs, a punctured lung, a broken shoulder, a shattered vertebrae, and a severe break just below the knee in her right leg.

but couldn't find one. I threw back my head and screamed out in anguish, "O God, don't take my wife too!"

**Tricia:** It still astonishes me, but somehow in the depths of my unconsciousness, I heard Ben's cry. I was so far under, so far away, and it was the hardest thing for me to wake up. I didn't want to. I wanted to stay where I was. But I knew I couldn't. I had to respond. I clearly remember choosing to wake up and to come back to him and the girls. I said his name, and then the world slipped away from me again.

**Ben:** After I screamed, I started to cry again. Then I had an impression that Tricia's grandfather was near. That surprised me because Ray had been killed about ten years earlier in a terrible automobile accident. This was before I even knew Tricia. I had seen pictures of him but I never knew him personally. But it was such a strong impression that as I bent over Tricia, I said, "Tricia, your grandpa's here. Ray is here."

Then another thought came to me. This one wasn't as strong, but it was still distinct. I wondered if Tricia had gone with her grandfather to escort Adria to wherever it was she was going. For a moment, I was afraid that once Tricia got there, she would stay with Adria so she could be with her. But immediately I felt that God was going to allow Tricia to come back to us. It was just moments later that Tricia opened her eyes and spoke my name.

When Tricia fell unconscious again, Ben found her cell phone and tried to call 911, but he couldn't get a signal. He knew he had to get help as quickly as possible, but he had no way to do it. He also knew that being so far away from any towns, they might not see another car before morning.

Placing baby Kara near her mother, Ben told Julia that he had to go find help and that she needed to stay there with her mother and Kara. As he started away, Julia said, "Daddy, we need to say a prayer and ask Heavenly Father to help us." Touched, and a little sheepish that he had not thought of that first, he agreed, and they stood together and prayed. Then, reminding Julia to stay close to her mother and to help her if she needed it, he went over to the road and started walking toward where he could see a ridgeline a mile or so away.

When he reached the top of the ridge, he tried to call 911 again, but it still wouldn't go through. In desperation, he cried out, "O Lord, please help me. Help me find a signal." Ben's left shoulder had been injured in the accident and he was in considerable pain himself. He couldn't even hold the phone in his left hand so he could punch in the numbers with his right. Hoping to get any trace of a signal, he held the phone up as high in the air as he could with his right hand. Then, peering at the screen, he again dialed the emergency number. This time, a dispatcher answered.

He explained what had happened and told her to send help as quickly as possible. When she asked where he was, he could only give a general indication. There were no landmarks to describe. And then he lost the call. He tried to call back, but his call was blocked.*

**Ben:** I was frantic. How could I help them find us if I couldn't talk to them? Then I had this thought: "If I can't call out, maybe I can send a text message." Raising the phone again, I texted as best I could with my thumb. To my surprise, when I pressed send, it worked. I sent terse text messages to my mother-in-law, her dad, and my mom and dad,

---

* Cell phones are programmed so that after a 911 call is made, other calls are blocked. This allows communication to be maintained with the 911 dispatcher.

hoping that between them someone would get the message and send help.

Back home, Tricia's grandfather—great-grandfather to the girls—was on the phone with his daughter—Tricia's mother—settling some last-minute details of the wedding plans. Here is his account:

**Grandfather:** As I ended the call with my daughter, I saw that I had a text message from Tricia. That surprised me a little. I talked with her and Ben often, but we never texted. When I opened the message, it read: 911. For a moment, I thought that her girls might be playing with the cell phone, but immediately realized that while they might trigger a speed dial call, they couldn't text a message. I immediately called back my daughter and told her about the message. She told me she had just gotten the same message. Now we were really alarmed. My daughter and her husband decided to call the sheriff's department of the county in which the farm was located and alert them to possible trouble.

Even before they could make the call, Tricia's mother received a second message. It was somewhat garbled, but deeply shocking: "Car. Send help. Adria dead."

Ben's text messages proved to be critical. His first call had alerted the sheriff's department about the accident, but they had no idea where he was. Fortunately, when Tricia's mom and dad called the sheriff's office and told them about the text messages, they could give them a little more information. In a turn of good fortune, Ben had talked to his mother-in-law earlier in the day and had asked her to look up the farm site online and get some directions for him. So while the family didn't know exactly where they were, they at least knew the general area where they had been.

As the sheriff's department launched their search, Tricia's mom and dad immediately began calling other family members and asking them to drive down to the area and join in the search.

**Ben:** The dispatcher finally got back through to me and told me that a search was underway. She told me I had to stay where I was until they found me.

"I can't," I said. "I've got to get back and help my family."

"No!" she exclaimed. "Stay where you are until they locate you."

"I can't," I said. "My little girls are all alone. I have to go." I put the phone in my pocket and started back.

Evidently, law enforcement agencies have the capability of identifying which cell tower a phone call comes through, even though they can't trace the phone itself. Even though that was still a pretty big area, it narrowed the search area down, at least to some degree, and immediately an air-and-ground search was launched.

**Tricia:** I had lapsed into unconsciousness before Ben left, so I didn't know he was gone. I heard Kara crying hysterically. Forcing my eyes open was much harder than I expected. All I could see was dirt and sagebrush. I felt very confused. Where was I? Then I felt Julia's hand on my arm and turned my head.

"Mommy," she said, "Adria's dead. She went to live with Jesus."

I touched her face and nodded. "I know, sweetheart. It will be okay."

Later, I would marvel at my response. I hadn't yet seen Adria's body, but somehow I knew it was true.

The seriousness of our situation began to hit me. Where

was Ben? Kara was screaming, and I realized that it was her crying that had brought me back to consciousness. I looked at the car and saw Julia's quilt. I told her to get it and lay it out beside me. She did, and then she lifted Kara onto it. Miraculously, that calmed Kara and she stopped crying.

With Kara taken care of, I felt a great urgency to find Ben. *What if he's injured worse than me?* I thought. That terrified me. If he couldn't go for help, we might all die. I got to my feet and started to hobble toward the car. The pain was intense, and I nearly fainted again.

"Mommy," Julia cried. "Where are you going?"

"To find Daddy. I have to find Daddy."

Julia shook her head. "He went for help."

I turned back. "Are you sure?"

"Yes, he walked up the road for help."

That was wonderful news, but I had to be sure. "Are you sure you saw him walking?"

"Yes," Julia said.

I sank back to the ground in great relief. If Ben could walk, then he would find help.

It was then I saw Adria's body. I cried out, thinking that if I could just get to her, I could save her. Seeing what I was doing, Julia tried to stop me. "Mommy, Adria's all right. She's with Jesus. She's happy now." Her words barely registered. I had to get to Adria. Something inside me told me not to do it, but I was already moving, trying to stand again. I had to see if I could help her. Then, I distinctly remember someone holding me back. It was a gentle and loving restraint, but it did not let go. Finally I gave up and lay back down again.

I am so grateful now for that restraining hand because I do not have to live with the image of Adria's broken little body in my mind for the rest of my life.

I told Julia one last time that everything would be all right, then collapsed again and passed out.

Ben returned to the accident scene. By now it was nearly 8:00 P.M., about an hour and a half after the accident happened, and it was getting dark rapidly. As he waited with his two girls and his unconscious wife, he finally heard the sound of a helicopter in the distance. When he turned to look, he also saw a cloud of dust and flashing red lights way off in the distance. Help was on its way.

**Ben:** After everyone had arrived and sprung into action, I stood by one of the ambulances getting my shoulder treated. I watched as an attendant spread a white sheet over Adria's body. Suddenly a great sorrow overwhelmed me. My grief was so strong that I remembered King David's lament for his son, Absalom, when he died. That's how I felt. Suddenly I couldn't let a white sheet be the end of it. I started toward the attendants, shouting at them not to do it. I thought that if I could just get to her, maybe I could still revive her. Other attendants grabbed me. I fought to get free, but they dragged me back to the ambulance.

That's when my little angel Julia came to me. She threw her arms around my legs. "It's all right, Daddy," she cried. "You don't have to be sad. Adria's safe now. Adria's happy. She's with Jesus, remember?"

Her faith touched me deeply. I held her close, buried my face in her hair, and started to cry.

**Tricia:** I don't remember much of what happened once the police came. I knew help had arrived and that things would be all right now. I was still moving in and out of consciousness and was barely aware of my surroundings, but oddly enough, as they loaded me into the Air Med chopper, I suddenly had a moment of perfect clarity. "Kara's allergic to milk," I told the nurse. She looked at me in surprise. I grabbed her arm. "Be sure to tell them at the hospital not to give my baby any milk. She will get very sick." And then I passed out again.

As various members of Ben's and Tricia's extended family were headed south to help in the search, Tricia's father got a call from the sheriff's department telling him they had found the family. They confirmed that Adria was dead and that Tricia was critically injured. They said that all four of the other family members were being flown to Salt Lake City by helicopter. They were not allowed to give any additional information on their medical condition.

**Grandfather:** I had left my wife at our daughter's house to help care for the rest of the family while we went out to search. I was alone in the car. Then my daughter called and asked if I could meet her at Primary Children's Hospital to give Julia and Kara a blessing. One of my sons was also out on the search, and he said he would come up to help me. Tricia's father and two brothers (including the groom-to-be) were going to the University of Utah Medical Center (which is next door to the children's hospital) to give a blessing to Tricia and Ben. When I asked my daughter if she had heard anything more about the girls and their parents, she answered in a low voice that she had not.

That was a long drive to the hospital that night. There

were still so many unanswered questions. Would we arrive there only to learn that Julia or Kara—or both—had died en route? Would Tricia survive? How badly was Ben injured? I couldn't close my eyes, and I couldn't stop to find a place to be alone, but the prayers I said that night were as fervent as any I have ever offered. Word was going out to the family members who were waiting at home and to those who were out of state. Their prayers were as fervent and grief-stricken as my own.

Before I reached the hospital, my daughter called again to say that Julia and Kara seemed to be all right and that they were being checked out right then. As I was escorted to the door of the treatment room, I remember slowing my step just long enough to utter one last silent prayer. Then I went in. Julia saw me instantly and with a huge smile, cried, "Grandpa!" As I went to her and gave her a big hug, I asked her if she was all right.

She seemed surprised by the question. "Sure," she said. Then she added, as though she was telling me about her day at the park, "But Adria's not here. She's with Jesus. And she's happy there."

I walked over to Kara, who looked up and smiled at me. One of the nurses was cleaning off what appeared to be grass stains from one arm, but other than that, there wasn't a scratch on her.

This blessing still fills the family with amazement and gratitude. The car rolled so violently that Tricia and Adria were thrown out of the vehicle. The inside of the car must have been filled with flying luggage, toys, and other objects. But these two girls came through it unharmed. Another astonishing thing is Julia's faith. Though not yet five years old, this resilient little girl endured a horribly traumatic experience without either physical or emotional damage. In addition to surviving the accident itself, she stayed with her injured mother, her baby sister, and Adria's body while her father went for help. She was alone for almost an hour and a half, with her mother unconscious during most of that time. And yet through it all, she maintained an amazing spirit of calm and comfort.

Ben refers to her as "our little anchor." She was the one comforting her father, her mother, her grandmother, and her great-grandfather. The family said it was as if she had been cloaked in a protective bubble, both physically and emotionally. This is one of the most tender of the mercies the Lord extended to this family during their tragedy.

**Grandfather:** After my son and I gave Julia and Kara a blessing, it was past 11:00 P.M., and the nurses were preparing to put the girls to bed. My son and I walked over to the Medical Center, where, by that time, several more family members had gathered. There was more good news. The staff reported that Ben's injuries were not serious and that he would probably be released the next day. Tricia was another matter. Her body had taken a terrible battering, and she was undergoing X-rays to see just how critical her injuries were. The report of a shattered vertebrae was especially sobering. But the nurses reported that Tricia had movement in both feet and legs. They also said that her injuries were serious, but not life-threatening. Our relief was enormous and prayers of gratitude were silently given.

There was another tender mercy we learned of that night in the waiting room. Some of the medical crew from the helicopter that brought Ben's family in said that they wanted

us to know how lucky Ben and Tricia were. They reported
that one of the pilots of the search helicopters had a feeling
they were looking in the wrong place, and he told the other
chopper to look seven miles to the north. That chopper went
right to the accident. Had they been fifteen or twenty minutes later, they would have had to call off the air search until
morning.

With things finally settling down, there were other things to
consider. It was after midnight, and there was still a wedding scheduled to happen in less than nine hours. There in the waiting room,
the family held a hurried conference with the prospective bride and
groom. After some discussion, the decision was made to postpone the
wedding for two days.

**Grandfather:** I was privileged to be the one to perform
the sealing that Saturday morning. Never had the meaning
of eternal families been quite so precious. And never had the
promise of an endowment of heavenly power been so clearly
confirmed. So in the midst of the tears and the loss, there was
also rejoicing and celebration and a reminder of the promises
God has extended to His children.

Adria's funeral was postponed until Tricia was released from the
hospital. Her body was finally laid to rest on Saturday, September 3,
2011. Tricia gave the eulogy for Adria from her wheelchair. The children—mostly Adria's cousins—and others put flowers on the grave.
Many of the flowers were purple—Adria's favorite color. There were a
lot of tears. But they were tears of temporary separation, not tears of
permanent loss. It had to be so, for as Julia kept reminding everyone:
"Adria's not dead. She's with Jesus. And she's happy."

Here, in her own words, is Tricia's account of the weeks following the accident.

## "Our Adria"

I remember very little from my first week after the accident. What I remember most clearly is a peace in my heart. As I was in and out of consciousness and fighting the haze of all the medication, I knew in my heart that my daughter was safe and that the Lord was watching over my whole family. I think this peace also played a large role in how quickly my body healed. My testimony of life after death had been strong ever since my grandpa had been killed in an automobile accident when I was sixteen. Now, that testimony became the most important thing I had. I clung to it and felt peace.

The peace, however, was followed closely with a longing to hold Adria's body one last time to say good-bye. When it became clear that this wasn't going to be a possibility, I wept and couldn't stop. Adria was a cuddle bug through and through; her cuddling is one of the things I miss the most.

One of the many tender mercies that the Lord gave our family was the peace we felt in our hearts in spite of our loss. Ben believes that the peace came to me because I knew that Adria was in a new and better home. I can't remember anything about that except hearing Ben's cry of anguish, and then fighting to come back to him. I didn't want to, but I knew I had to. What could give a mother more peace than seeing her child safely to the arms of people who would love her until they could be reunited forever? Perhaps that is why my first response to Julia when she told me that Adria was dead was not one of surprise, but rather one of peace. Even though at that point I didn't even know Adria had been killed, I was still able to say, "I know. It will be okay." That memory alone is a tender mercy, because I remember so little else of the accident.

I know the Lord strengthened me as I began to recover. But it's important for me to say that it wasn't always easy. Often as I lay in bed, I would feel the grief and sorrow overcome me. My heart ached so badly at times that it felt like it was going to stop beating. One of the hardest moments was when I saw a portrait of all three of my girls that my mom put in my room. I started crying hysterically. I realized I could never again take a family picture with all of us, and that was devastating. The Lord strengthened us and blessed us, but He in no way took away the pain of losing our child.

The day Adria was born is a story all on its own. It was one of the hardest days of my life. I had an extremely difficult labor, and afterward the doctors couldn't stop the bleeding. The situation was very serious. I felt like my grandpa was near during that time. I didn't feel that when the other girls were born, but I did with Adria. After Ben felt that Ray might have been there for Adria's death, too, I can't help but wonder if there is a special bond that exists between them.

And here's another thing. Not long after Adria was born, I had the strongest impression that she would not stay with us long. The impression came several times during her first year of life. I would go in her room and watch her sleep at night and would plead with God not to take her yet. As time passed, those memories faded, but when my sweet daughter died, all the memories of when she was a baby came back to me and I remembered those promptings. It was a great comfort to us. It helped Ben and me know that our daughter was meant to return to heaven, even though she was so young.

Ben and I cried together as we watched a slide show of Adria's life that had been prepared for her funeral. In the past, we had often worried about mistakes we had made as parents. But as we watched those pictures, we realized we had done a lot of things right too. We had given Adria the chance, not just to experience life, but to enjoy it. She truly lived life to its fullest. I consider that to be a direct blessing from our Heavenly Father.

Another blessing we enjoyed actually began a month before the accident. Most nights Adria would wake up around 2:00 or 3:00 A.M. and wander into our room to sneak into our bed. For a long time, Ben and I fought that sharing of our bed. However, in July something changed. Ben stopped me in the early hours one morning and said, "Let her stay." The next day, he explained to me that he felt we needed to let her sleep in our bed for as long as she wanted. He assured me that I wouldn't regret it. I'm so glad I trusted his spiritual wisdom. My fondest memories of Adria will be of those mornings we spent cuddled together. Once the sun finally poked its head over the horizon, Adria would touch my cheek and say with the biggest smile, "Good morning, Mommy." Then she would jump out of bed and run off to start the day. That was the way Adria took on life. Everything was worth running to and smiling about. She loved life.

These memories and blessings bring us such hope and comfort now, because even though we weren't perfect parents, and we've made mistakes in our lives, we provided Adria with the home that she needed, and I really do believe she has forgiven us for our parenting mistakes. Instead of focusing on my mistakes, I remind myself that I cannot regret a single day I spent with her because I know that we loved her every minute of her life. What greater comfort can a parent have than that?

The final thing I want to share is one of my first memories of being in the hospital. I was constantly in and out of sleep because of the pain medication I was receiving. One time I was half awake and heard a conversation between Ben and my mom. When I heard them start talking about Adria, I woke up completely, but I don't think they knew I was awake. My mom told Ben that it was okay for him to grieve, to feel sorry, and to even be a little angry. She said, "Even if you feel angry at God for awhile, that's natural."

Ben replied, "How could I be angry with God? He gave me my family. He kept my other daughters safe. And He has given us the gift of eternal families. If I walk away from God, I have nothing left because He has given me all that I have."

I ask myself that same question. How can I be angry with God when He has given me so much? Yes, He took my daughter from me in this life before I was ready to let her go and there are times when I ache inside and can't understand how I'm supposed to go on. But I know without a doubt that Adria is in a better place. I know that she is surrounded by people who love her. I have decided to hold on to that rather than focus on the questions, the doubt, or the loss.[1]

---

## Note

1. Written September 8, 2011. Material in possession of the author. Used by permission.

*P*ress forward with a steadfastness in Christ, having a perfect brightness of hope, and a love of God and of all men. Wherefore, if ye shall press forward, feasting upon the word of Christ, and endure to the end, behold, thus saith the Father: Ye shall have eternal life.

2 NEPHI 31:20

# CHAPTER SEVENTEEN

# IN CLOSING

WE HAVE COME to the end of our examination and exploration of the concept of hope. I should like to end by sharing some of the insights and conclusions that have come to have the greatest meaning for me personally. I would invite you to make your own list.

## The Pivotal Role of Hope

Before I started writing this book, I didn't fully understand the critical role that hope plays in how we cope with life. There was even a time when I wondered why hope was linked with faith and charity as one of the three fundamental Christian virtues. I don't wonder that anymore. Now, I find myself filled with a sense of wonder at how absolutely central the gift of hope is to our spiritual well-being and to our spiritual progression.

Hope changes our perception and focus. It influences how we interpret, process, and respond to adversity. In many cases, it is the pivotal point which determines whether we will hunker down and endure our trials with patience, or throw up our hands in disgust and turn away from God completely.

We have referred to President Dieter F. Uchtdorf's definition of hope several times because it is a grand key to understanding hope: "Hope is not knowledge, but rather *the abiding trust that the Lord will fulfill His promises to us. It is confidence that if we live according to God's laws and the words of His prophets now, we will receive desired blessings in the future."[1]

As a child during World War II, President Uchtdorf became personally acquainted with great suffering and adversity. He is someone who personally knows the importance of hope. He has said:

> Each time a hope is fulfilled, it creates confidence and leads to greater hope. I can think of many instances in my life where I learned firsthand the power of hope. I well remember the days in my childhood encompassed by the horrors and despair of a world war, the lack of educational opportunities, life-threatening health issues during youth, and the challenging and discouraging economic experiences as a refugee. The example of our mother, even in the worst of times, to move forward and put faith and hope into action, . . . sustained our family and me and gave confidence that present circumstances would give way to future blessings. . . .
>
> . . . To all who suffer—to all who feel discouraged, worried, or lonely—I say with love and deep concern for you, *never give in.*
>
> *Never surrender.*
>
> *Never allow despair to overcome your spirit.*
>
> Embrace and rely upon the Hope of Israel, for the love of the Son of God pierces all darkness, softens all sorrow, and gladdens every heart.[2]

## Life Is Tough—and That Is Good

This mortal journey can be difficult. It is filled with spiritual, intellectual, moral, emotional, and physical dangers. From our birth until death, mortality is filled with challenge and opposition. The very learning process of how to walk and talk and live requires long years of development and effort.

For many people throughout the world, life is a daily, never-ending struggle for survival. Most of you reading this book will be blessed with security, safety, and a comfortable level of affluence. You and your families have numerous opportunities for education, travel, growth, recreation, as well as the freedom to pursue them. But sickness, death, disability, injury, deprivation, loneliness, financial loss, depression, oppression, violence, and upheaval are hovering just over our heads. Virtually no one escapes this life unscathed. President Harold B. Lee spoke of the "'*inevitable* tragedies of life.'"[3] That is not a comforting statement, but it certainly describes reality.

Yet, we have also tried to show why a loving Heavenly Father, who is all-powerful and all-knowing, would allow such things to be. Indeed, we have shown that He actually designed our experience to include such things. He sent us to live in a fallen world where challenges abound because there are lessons we have to learn, choices we have to make, and things we need to experience, and they can only happen in a world such as this. Remember how Father Lehi put it—these things "must needs be" (2 Nephi 2:11).

When we acquire knowledge and skills—both physical and spiritual—we have to do it ourselves. No one can get a testimony for us any more than they can learn to play the piano for us. Only we can live our lives, and only we can learn what we must know to return to live with God and become like Him. We strengthen our muscles and our bodies by subjecting them to opposition—lifting weights, walking, running, and endless practices. So it is with developing spiritual strength—stamina and endurance are required. They too come through opposition. *It must needs be!*

Elder Neal A. Maxwell summed it up so well in these words:

> A superficial view of this life . . . will not do, lest we mistakenly speak of this mortal experience only as coming here to get a body, as if we were merely picking up a suit at the cleaners. Or, lest we casually recite how we have come here to be proved, as if a few brisk push-ups and deep knee bends would do. . . .
>
> One's life . . . is brevity compared to eternity—like being dropped off by a parent for a day at school. But what a day! . . .
>
> I believe with all my heart that because God loves us there are some particularized challenges that he will deliver to each of us. He will customize the curriculum for each of us in order to teach us the things we most need to know. He will set before us in life what we need; not always what we like. And this will require us to accept with all our hearts the truth that there is divine design in each of our lives and that we have rendezvous to keep, individually and collectively. . . .
>
> God gives to us the lessons we need most, not always the ones we think we need.[4]

## Enduring Well

We are living in a particularly challenging time in history, in what Paul called "perilous times" (2 Timothy 3:1), and we are moving toward the great millennial day. Before that day can come and Christ can usher in a thousand years of peace, though, wickedness will increase, warfare will be everywhere, men of violence will grow ever more terrible, and natural disasters will become more numerous. *This too must needs be!*

Couple that fact with the normal tragedies and sufferings of life, and we better understand why the Lord tells us over and over in the scriptures that we must "endure to the end." However, we are not just asked to endure, but to endure well, to endure with faith and hope and courage. Elder Jeffrey R. Holland has reminded us that discouragement is not an inherent part of adversity, that while it often is a natural reaction to trouble, it does not have to be. He also warned that if we give in to the "germ" of discouragement, "it takes an increasingly severe toll on our spirit, for it erodes the deepest religious commitments we can make—those of faith, hope, and charity."[5]

No matter what our circumstances are, we can choose hope— that wonderful gift of the Spirit which can bring us up, steady our feet, enrich our understanding, and stiffen our courage. This is why we are told to earnestly seek those gifts (see D&C 46:8). I love this thought by George Q. Cannon, who served in the First Presidency under Brigham Young, John Taylor, Wilford Woodruff, and Lorenzo Snow: "Whenever darkness fills our minds, we may know that we are not possessed with the Spirit of God, and we must get rid of it. *When we are filled with the Spirit of God, we are filled with joy, with peace and with happiness no matter what our circumstances may be;* for it is a spirit of cheerfulness and of happiness."[6]

President Henry B. Eyring reminded us of the challenges that come in our lives, and gave us a key for coping with them:

> I wish to bear witness of God's power of deliverance. At some point in our lives we will all need that power. Every person living is in the midst of a test. We have been granted by God the precious gift of life in a world created as a *proving ground* and a *preparatory school. The tests we will face, their*

*severity, their timing, and their duration will be unique for each of us.* But two things will be the same for all of us. . . .

First, the tests at times will stretch us enough for us to feel the need for help beyond our own. And, second, God in His kindness and wisdom has made the power of deliverance available to all of us. . . .

. . . The power of deliverance is *available—not to escape the test but to endure it well.*[7]

May we come to the point where we can sing in our hearts the words of one of our hymns:

> *Come, let us anew our journey pursue,*
> *Roll round with the year,*
> *And never stand still till the Master appear.*
> *His adorable will let us gladly fulfill,*
> *And our talents improve*
> *By the patience of hope and the labor of love. . . .*
>
> *Our life as a dream, our time as a stream*
> *Glide swiftly away,*
> *And the fugitive moment refuses to stay;*
> *For the arrow is flown and the moments are gone.*
> *The millennial year*
> *Presses on to our view, and eternity's here. . . .*
>
> *Oh, that each in the day of His coming may say,*
> *"I have fought my way thru;*
> *I have finished the work thou didst give me to do."*
> *Oh, that each from his Lord may receive the glad word:*
> *"Well and faithfully done;*
> *Enter into my joy and sit down on my throne."*[8]

## All Hope Centers in the Father, the Son, and the Holy Spirit

If hope is to trust in God's promises, then all hope centers in, depends on, flows from, and operates through a deep and abiding faith in God and Jesus Christ.

It was the Father's plan for our eternal happiness that started us on this journey. He clothed our intelligences in spirit bodies and allowed us to become individuals with unique personalities, characters, and attributes. With His perfect foreknowledge, He knew that without a physical body we could not have a fulness of joy. With His perfect knowledge, He understood that without this physical body living in a world of opposites and opposition, we could never learn to walk by faith. Because of His perfect knowledge, He understood that we would make mistakes. We would commit sins. We would make foolish choices. And yet, "God so loved the world, that he gave his only begotten Son, that whosoever believeth in him should not perish, but have everlasting life" (John 3:16). Because of the life Jesus lived, and the sacrifice He made in our behalf, He has taken upon Himself our sins, our frailties, our sufferings, our infirmities, our sicknesses, our pain, and our sorrow.

The Father and the Son together are the source of all the promises, and therefore, all hope centers in and flows from Them. The Holy Ghost is the primary means for teaching us about the promises and confirming those promises to us. God is our Father. He knows us intimately, and He loves us infinitely. Jesus is our Savior. In Him is all power to save. Their greatest desire for us is that we find "peace in this world, and eternal life in the world to come" (D&C 59:23). The Holy Ghost is the Communicator of Their will to us, and the Comforter to us in difficult times. That is why we worship the Father in the name of the Son through the influence of the Holy Spirit.

Is it any wonder that John saw in vision all the hosts of heaven and heard them join in a great hymn of praise and adoration, saying, "Blessing, and honour, and glory, and power, be unto him that sitteth upon the throne, and unto the Lamb for ever and ever" (Revelation 5:13).

## Alignment and Perspective

Aligning our lives with God and changing our perception so that we see God's hand in all things are both essential to our development of faith and hope. When anyone asks, "How can I find hope in times of despair?" or "How do I fortify my hope when all seems hopeless?" the answer is always the same. Hope comes from Jesus Christ—His life, His teachings, His Atonement. It also comes from living the gospel. Hope comes from committing ourselves to keeping our covenants. Hope comes from true conversion, which involves a change of heart and not just mentally embracing a set of principles. Hope comes from aligning our lives with His will. But it is only through the gifts of grace that we can do so. As we have said several times, our efforts, our actions, and our choices are critical to acquiring this alignment, but it is only in and through the permeating power of Jesus Christ and the Atonement that these empowering gifts are extended to us. Our actions are essential, but His grace is what makes it all work to our benefit.

Remember, God will never force our hearts. He will never pull us onto the right path against our will. Agency is too sacred, and too much a part of the proving process. The scriptures are very clear on the subject. While the Lord did say that He took upon Himself all of our sicknesses and infirmities, in addition to our sins, so that He could "*succor* his people according to their infirmities" (Alma 7:12), in another place, He warned, "I *will not succor my people in the day of their transgression;* but I will hedge up their ways that they prosper

not; and their doings shall be as a stumbling block before them"
(Mosiah 7:29).

## On the Other Hand . . .

The counsel to put our lives in harmony with God, to commit
to live the gospel, and to repent when necessary is clear, sobering,
and critical to our spiritual progression. On the other hand, it is not
uncommon for those who are living good and faithful lives, and who
are striving to keep themselves aligned with God's will, to feel like
they are forever falling short of what God expects of them. We tend
to "beat ourselves up" by focusing on those areas in which we clearly
fall short of perfection.

As President Boyd K. Packer said: "Some worry endlessly over
missions that were missed, or marriages that did not turn out, or babies that did not arrive, or children that seem lost, or dreams unful-
filled, or because age limits what they can do. *I do not think it pleases
the Lord when we worry because we think we never do enough or that
what we do is never good enough.*" [9]

I believe strongly that these thoughts and feelings are whisperings of Satan, and are his way of trying to counteract the hope that is
within us.

I love this reminder from President Howard W. Hunter:

> Many Latter-day Saints are happy and enjoying the op-
> portunities life offers. Yet I am concerned that some among
> us are unhappy. Some of us feel that we are falling short
> of our expected ideals. I have particular concern for those
> who have lived righteously but think, because they haven't
> achieved in the world or in the Church what others have
> achieved, that they have failed. Each of us desires to achieve
> a measure of greatness in this life. And why shouldn't we? As

someone once noted, there is within each of us a giant struggling with celestial homesickness.[10]

## In Conclusion

These are truly sobering times. All around us, people of faith are facing tremendous challenges or terrible tragedies. Some are faltering. Some have lost their way. Some have deliberately turned away. We may think that we have—like people preparing for a hurricane—battened down the hatches, covered the windows with plywood, and secured anything that might blow away. But life has a way of catching us by surprise, of sneaking in under the corners or through the cracks and tearing at things we thought were safe.

So, with all our preparations, let us not forget hope. Let us not forget that it is our trust in the promises of God that gives us the strength to endure. The promises are sure. There is life after this life. We shall see loved ones again. There is deliverance and sustenance from Him who descended below all things. Things will be made right in the next life. There will be perfect justice. Lost opportunities will be restored.

There are things we need for our experience, and some of them will stretch our souls until it feels as though we can bear no more without breaking. But the Lord is there. When Christ faced the greatest personal test of His entire existence, He pled with the Father to remove the cup if it was possible. But it was not possible. He had to drink it all in order to save us all. Yet there is something that we often overlook when we speak of that terrible time in the Garden of Gethsemane. Luke records that at the very time when blood came from every pore, "There appeared an angel unto him from heaven, *strengthening* him" (Luke 22:43). President Henry B. Eyring said of that experience: "The Savior prayed for deliverance. What He was given was not an escape from the trial but comfort enough *to pass through it gloriously.*"[11]

If we are to pass through our trials gloriously, we too can turn to the Lord for help and ask for His sustaining power, His great gifts, and His wisdom and enlightenment so that we may endure our trials well, and learn from them. President Eyring went on to note what followed after this angelic help in Luke's account: "When he rose up from prayer, and was come to his disciples, he found them sleeping for sorrow, and said unto them, Why sleep ye? rise and pray, lest ye enter into temptation" (Luke 22:45–46). Then President Eyring says this:

> [This] command to His disciples, who were themselves being tested, is a guide for us. . . . We can determine to rise up and pray in great faith and humility. And we can follow the command added in the book of Mark: "Rise up, let us go." (Mark 14:42.)
>
> From this you have counsel for passing the physical and spiritual tests of life. You will need God's help after you have done all you can for yourself. So rise up and go, but get His help as early as you can, not waiting for the crisis to ask for deliverance.[12]

I close with two promises that have been particularly meaningful to me and that have sustained my family in many circumstances. They are two promises that we not only cling to, but that we have seen fulfilled again and again. From them, we have gained the hope that sustains us as we await whatever great adventure lies around the next bend in the road.

Come unto me, all ye that labour and are heavy laden, and I will give you rest.

Take my yoke upon you, and learn of me; for I am meek and lowly in heart: and ye shall find rest unto your souls.

For my yoke is easy, and my burden is light. (Matthew 11:28–30)

I can do all things through Christ which strengtheneth me. (Philippians 4:13)

---

## Notes

1. Dieter F. Uchtdorf, "The Infinite Power of Hope," *Ensign,* November 2008, 22.

2. Ibid., 24.

3. Harold B. Lee, *Decisions for Successful Living* (Salt Lake City: Deseret Book, 1973), 220.

4. *The Neal A. Maxwell Quote Book,* ed. Cory H. Maxwell (Salt Lake City: Bookcraft, 1997), 196.

5. Jeffrey R. Holland, "For Times of Trouble," in *1980 Devotional Speeches of the Year* (Provo, Utah: Brigham Young University Press, 1980), 39.

6. George Q. Cannon, *Gospel Truth,* ed. Jerreld L. Newquist (Salt Lake City: Deseret Book, 1974), 17.

7. Henry B. Eyring, "The Power of Deliverance," *Brigham Young University 2007–2008 Speeches* (Provo, Utah: Brigham Young University Press, 2008), 1.

8. "Come, Let Us Anew," in *Hymns of The Church of Jesus Christ of Latter-day Saints* (Salt Lake City: The Church of Jesus Christ of Latter-day Saints, 1985), no. 217.

9. Boyd K. Packer, "The Least of These," *Ensign,* November 2004, 87.

10. Howard W. Hunter, *That We Might Have Joy* (Salt Lake City: Deseret Book, 1994), 103.

11. Eyring, "The Power of Deliverance," 4.

12. Ibid., 4–5.

# INDEX

Abilities, judgment according to, 218–19

Abuse, 87–91

Action(s): faith and, 35–36; showing conversion through, 134–39, 142–45; desire and, 208–9, 210; learning through, 277–82; prayer and, 334–35. *See also* Works

Adam and Eve, 60–61

Adria (car accident victim), 341–57

Afflictions. *See* Trials

Agency, 32, 59, 65, 101–2, 213–15, 366

Alfalfa field, path through, 327–28

Alignment with Lord, 129–30, 366–67. *See also* Conversion; Will of God

Alma the Elder, 244

Alma the Younger, 191–92, 212–13

Amulek, 191–92

Angels, 212–13

Anger, 50–51

Apostasy, 257

Asay, Carlos E., 158–59, 310–11

Ashton, Marvin J., 40

Atonement: faith, hope, and charity bound by, 29; David A. Bednar on,

72, 83, 289; remembering, 73–74; hope in, 74–77, 83–86; enabling and redeeming powers of, 77–79, 274–75, 289–90; scope of, 79–83; healing through, 87–91; Christ strengthened during, 368–69

Ballard, M. Russell: on conversion, 133–34, 137; on self-control, 279; on scripture study, 323

Bednar, David A.: on learning by faith, 39; on Atonement, 72, 83, 289; on grace, 77–79; on scripture study, 323; on prayer, 337–38, 339

Beelzebub, 118. *See also* Satan

"Before Thee, Lord, I Bow My Head," xiv–xv

Behavior, 61–62, 64–65

Belliston, Rebecca, 179–184

Belliston, Troy, 179–184

Benson, Ezra Taft: on temple ordinances, 159; on becoming Christlike, 190; on scripture study, 316, 321

Bitterness, 9–10

Blessings, 233–40

Boasting, 50

Laman and Lemuel, 209

Larsen, Dean L., 288–89

Latter days: trials of, 11–14, 93–96, 362–63; prophecies on, 96–98; natural disasters in, 98–100; misuse of agency in, 101–2; and nature of mortality, 102–4; hope in, 104–5

Learning, temple as house of, 154–56. *See also* Experiential learning

Lee, Harold B.: on temple ordinances, 147–48, 153; on scripture study, 316; on trials, 361

Leukemia, 107–11

Lewis, C. S., 272–73

Life. *See* Mortality

Looking up, xi

Lucifer, 117. *See also* Satan

Lund, Cynthia (Cyndie), 269–70; 308–9

Lund, Julie, 254–56

MacDonald, George, 273

Marathon, 283–84

Marriage, 28, 159–65

Marsh, Thomas B., 257

Martin Handcart Company, 3–6, 234–35

Mastery, 283–88, 290–92

Maxwell, Neal A.: on faith, hope, and charity, 27; on faith and hope, 32–33; on doctrine, 62; on real hope, 65–66; on Atonement, 82–83; on feeling overwhelmed, 186; on patience in spiritual progress, 190, 300–301; on trials, 194, 362; on enduring, 201; on judgment, 218; on desires, 219; on premortal existence, 229; on God's plan, 258–59; on feeling inadequate, 260, 263; on changed values, 270–71

McConkie, Bruce R., 272, 278–79

McGuire, Diana Harman, 154–56

McKay, David O., 329–30

*Mecapal*, 16–17

Media company, 221–27

Melissa (abuse victim), 87–91

Mellor, Louisa, 234–35

Misery, of Satan, 116

Missionary work, 212–13, 216–17

Monson, Thomas S., xi, 323

Mortality: purpose of, 59; nature of, 102–4, 361–62; blessings of temple in, 147–48; difficulty of, 170; patience and courage to face, 195–96; day-to-day nature of, 198–99; perfection in, 262–63, 271–73; learning in, 277–79

Motivation, 311–12

Mount Olympus, 295–97

Movies, 221–27

Moyle, John Rowe, 142–43

Natural disasters, 98–100

Neilson, Peter, 138–39

Nelson, Russell M.: on faith, hope, and charity, 27; on covenants, 152

Nephi, 209

Nielson, Christian, 21

Nielson, Stephanie, 20–24

Nietzsche, Friedrich, 215

Novel writing, 241

Nudge, gentle, 240–43

Oaks, Dallin H.: on plan of salvation, 128; on childrearing, 196; on desires, 206, 214

Obedience, 140, 159, 168

Onion patch, Henry Eyring works in, 144

Opposition, 59–60, 102, 169

Order, 156–57, 288

Ordinances, 151–53, 157, 159

Organist, 238–40